"In *Between Certain Death and a Possible Future*, a groundbreaking anthology of essays edited by Mattilda Bernstein Sycamore, the contributing authors, in prose that is urgent, lyrical, and at times astonishing, describe coming of age in the United States and abroad in the years and decades after HIV/AIDS had already gained a vise grip on the marginalized. Unlike AIDS literature's dominant narratives, these stories are not primarily about being sick from a deadly virus or the mass loss of friends, lovers, or family. Rather, they cover the far-reaching trauma on individuals of subsequent generations that, despite revolutionary HIV treatments, find themselves unable to escape the conflation of queerness with death, desire with danger, or the racism and transphobia of the dominant HIV response that cleaved the momentum of progress away from trans, immigrant, and BIPOC communities. The authors' stories also embody a generation that inherited the insidious legacy of HIV stigma born from anti-queer hatred, sensationalized media, and fear-based and sex-phobic HIV prevention campaigns, and the destructive effects this stigma has had on feelings of self-worth, on intimate relationships, and on their understanding of community.

Between Certain Death and a Possible Future is an essential contribution to AIDS literature because it invites the reader to wrestle with the unceasing impact of HIV beyond the 'crisis years,' beyond heroic activism, into under-explored narrative terrain where effective medical treatments redefined the ongoing epidemic from certain death to something else we're still figuring out, damaged but resilient, in search of a possible future."

—TONY VALENZUELA,
writer and former executive director of the Foundation for the
AIDS Monument and Lambda Literary

BETWEEN CERTAIN DEATH AND A POSSIBLE FUTURE

Queer Writing on Growing Up with the AIDS Crisis

Edited by

MATTILDA BERNSTEIN SYCAMORE

ARSENAL PULP PRESS
VANCOUVER

ARSENAL PULP PRESS
Suite 202 – 211 East Georgia St.
Vancouver, BC V6A 1Z6
Canada
arsenalpulp.com

Arsenal Pulp Press acknowledges the xʷməθkʷəy̓əm (Musqueam), Sḵwx̱wú7mesh (Squamish), and səl̓ilwətaʔɬ (Tsleil-Waututh) Nations, custodians of the traditional, ancestral, and unceded territories where our office is located. We pay respect to their histories, traditions, and continuous living cultures and commit to accountability, respectful relations, and friendship.

Cover and text design by Jazmin Welch
Cover art by Kirk Maxson, *Blue Boy*, 2017, hand-cut aluminum
Copy edited by Shirarose Wilensky
Proofread by Alison Strobel

Printed and bound in Canada

Library and Archives Canada Cataloguing in Publication:
Title: Between certain death and a possible future : queer writing on growing up with the AIDS crisis / edited by Mattilda Bernstein Sycamore.
Names: Sycamore, Mattilda Bernstein, editor.
Identifiers: Canadiana (print) 20210212136 | Canadiana (ebook) 20210212527 | ISBN 9781551528502 (softcover) | ISBN 9781551528519 (HTML)
Subjects: LCSH: AIDS (Disease)—Social aspects. | LCSH: AIDS (Disease)—Psychological aspects. | LCSH: Sexual minorities. | LCSH: Gays.
Classification: LCC RA643.8 .B48 2021 | DDC 362.19697/9200866—dc23

For JoAnne, 1974–1995
For Chrissie Contagious, 1974–2010
For David Wojnarowicz, 1954–1992
For Colin Blakeney, 1948–1993

CONTENTS

BETWEEN CERTAIN DEATH
AND A POSSIBLE FUTURE:
AN INTRODUCTION

MATTILDA BERNSTEIN SYCAMORE

One time in 1985, when I was twelve, I remember standing in the checkout line at the supermarket with my mother when I glanced at the cover of the *National Enquirer*, and the headline screamed, "ROCK HUDSON IS GAY."

Kids at school had always called me gay, it was an insult hurled at me as much as any other greeting. But I didn't know exactly what this meant beyond not being sufficiently masculine until my first sex ed class, when the teacher described homosexual behavior. I remember holding my breath because I realized then that all the kids who taunted me were actually right. But how did they know before I knew?

So when I saw "ROCK HUDSON IS GAY" on the cover of the *National Enquirer*, I held my breath too. "Who's Rock Hudson," I asked my mother, as casually as possible, when she wasn't facing the magazines anymore. "A famous actor," my mother told me.

But actually, looking for that cover now, I realize it doesn't say Rock Hudson is gay. It says he's dying of AIDS. Were these the same thing? Kids had always called me gay and sissy and faggot—the best I could do to get away from them was befriend the girls, hide in books, excel in school, and try to be perfect so that everyone wouldn't know I deserved to die. But then there was Rock Hudson dying on the cover of the *National Enquirer*, as if to prove it.

When I first started jerking off, I worried I might get AIDS from tasting my own come—I would study the texture, smell it on my hands, bring it almost up to my lips but not too close. I started having sex with men in public bathrooms when I was fourteen, almost every day after school, but I was trying not to feel it, what was happening between my legs. Maybe if I didn't feel it, then I would win.

When I finally escaped to college, everyone knew I was queer, just like everywhere else, but suddenly this was okay. And the outsider image I'd cultivated in high school, now it worked. It drew people to me. But after spending a year mostly protesting against racist and classist admissions policies, I knew I needed to get further away from childhood and everything I was supposed to be. So I drove cross-country to move to San Francisco.

What I remember most from that drive was stopping at a rest area somewhere in the middle of the country where I'd never been and getting out of the car to throw out my trash—while I was stretching, the rest stop attendant came out wearing orange rubber gloves that went up to his elbows, pulled my trash out of the garbage can, and put it in a giant blue plastic bag that he immediately tied to dispose of elsewhere. "You need to leave," he said, "or I'm going to call the cops."

To be a nineteen-year-old faggot at a rest area in so-called middle America in 1992 meant you were a threat. What if someone got AIDS from your trash?

In San Francisco, I found dancing, drugs, and activism, in that order. I needed all three, but I especially needed activism. I knew that being queer meant everyone was dying, and ACT UP taught me to politicize my rage. ACT UP showed me that fighting AIDS meant fighting racism, classism, misogyny, and homophobia, all of them together, all of them at once, or else what was the point.

In San Francisco, I found the dykes and fags and gender-bending weirdos and other outsider queers like myself, vegans and drop-outs and incest survivors, druggies and anarchists and freaks, sluts and whores and direct action activists. We needed one another to survive the world that told us we deserved to die—we broke down every day, in every way, but we believed we were creating something else. We needed to believe, in order to live.

This was a generational story, but I didn't think of it this way, not yet. Because it was the only story I'd known. The idea for this anthology came about when I was on tour for my most recent novel, *Sketchtasy*, which follows a group of queens in Boston gay club culture in 1995, with all its pageantry and hypocrisy. Boston was where I lived after I fled San Francisco (and before I returned). When I started to write about 1995, I didn't know this would be a novel about AIDS, but how could it not be, once I really went back to that time.

In 1995, more people in the United States died of AIDS than in any other year. From our current vantage point, we can see that something was about to change, that soon there would be medications that would make HIV into a manageable condition for many, but there was no way for me—or the characters in *Sketchtasy*—to imagine that then. So I realized that *Sketchtasy* was a generational novel about growing up knowing that desire meant AIDS meant death, that there was no other option. This generation that came of age in the midst of the crisis. The crisis was our lives.

Usually we hear about two generations—the first coming of age in the era of gay liberation, and then watching entire circles of friends die of a mysterious illness as the government did nothing to intervene. And now we hear about younger people growing up in an era offering effective treatment and prevention, and unable to comprehend the magnitude of the loss. We are told that these two generations cannot possibly understand one another and thus remain alienated from both the past and the future. But there is another generation between these two—one that came of age in the midst of the epidemic with the belief that desire intrinsically led to death, internalizing this trauma as part of becoming queer.

By telling this specific generational story in all its complications, how do we explore the trauma the AIDS crisis continues to enact, and imagine a way out? Could this offer a bridge between the other two generations?

When I first started to mention the idea for this anthology on social media, I didn't know what to expect. But the response was electric. I was flooded by messages from people who told me they couldn't wait for this book and people who told me they couldn't wait to submit.

This is my sixth anthology, and I always start with an open call for submissions that I circulate as widely as possible. When I was writing the call for submissions this time, I was careful not to impose specific dates on the generational frame. Because I knew that this would vary depending on a wide variety of factors, including race, class, gender, religion, ethnicity, rural/urban experience, regional/national origin, HIV status, and access to treatment and prevention (over time and in shifting contexts). I knew that any generational frame only offers a partial truth, so I didn't want to impose artificial boundaries. I wanted to put out the idea and see who responded.

I originally thought of this generational frame as including anyone who came of age sexually in the midst of the AIDS crisis and before the advent of effective treatment. But as soon as I started reading submissions the scope of the anthology expanded to include people who grew up well after the emergence of protease inhibitors but still felt like they were living between certain death and a possible future. So I decided that anyone who described a sex life before AIDS didn't quite fit into this project, but I didn't impose an end point.

Like any conditions for inclusion, this generational frame, however fluid, may be a fraught one. My goal is not to create a definitive text but to inspire even more stories, from even more angles. To facilitate more conversations. To deepen the analysis. To complicate the narratives.

As I was reading the submissions, I was flooded by my own memories, so many stories that I'd almost forgotten, hovering at the edge of my awareness. Especially memories about coming of age in San Francisco in the early '90s—how AIDS was everywhere and how this was a given.

Now I think about how much shutting off was required, just to exist in day-to-day experience. You couldn't express shock at everyone dying right in front of your eyes, because shock felt like a form of cruelty. So you would act like everything might be okay, even when nothing was okay.

You met some queen on the street, and she was showing off her lesions in a campy way, and then she was dead. You went to the beach with a group of people and some boy was flirting with you, and then you were asking around about him because there was that look in his eyes and you wanted to see that look again. But he was dead. Someone came over to look at a room in your apartment, this queen who wanted to do touch healing on everyone, and you were like, girl, get the fuck out. Then you would see her around on the street, and she was so friendly that you actually started to like her. And then she was dead. You slept with some boy who you knew was positive and he wanted to make it romantic, so he lit candles around the bathtub before you got in together, and a few weeks or months went by and you wondered what happened to him, but he was dead.

I didn't go to memorials because I felt like I didn't have a right to be there. I felt like I would be stealing other people's grief. And this is a generational story too, I think, now, as I'm sobbing. We were coming of age in the midst of all this death. But we felt like it was not ours to mourn.

Now I wish I had gone to all those memorials. If there's one thing I want this anthology to do, it's to open up the possibilities for feeling, for feeling everything. Grief is not something you can steal. You can silence it, yes, and I think that's what our culture has done— dominant culture, gay culture, queer and trans cultures. The grief has been internalized, and the consequences have been devastating— intimately, interpersonally, culturally, and communally.

I've included thirty-six essays in this anthology. I could have included many more. In this introduction, I could attempt to summarize each of the essays, but I'd rather allow them to exist in all their complications. I will say this—every time I read through these pieces, I find myself overwhelmed by emotion in surprising places, even after the work has become familiar, from reading it over and over. I can't predict what you will feel, but I can predict that you will feel. Maybe it will be grief, or rage, or loss, or laughter, or longing, or curiosity, or inspiration, or empathy, or craving—expansion or contraction, devastation or catharsis, connection or confusion, revelation or confirmation. Or all of these at once.

Let's talk about everything, so we can feel everything. Let's feel it all, so our future remains possible.

What Survival Means

KEIKO LANE

FEBRUARY 1991

It's already dark when I drive into West Hollywood. I circle around until I find parking on a residential side street. Walking toward Santa Monica Boulevard, I hear the chanting before I turn the corner.

"We're here! We're queer! And we're FABULOUS!"

I can hear counter-yelling but not the words. As I round the corner onto Santa Monica, I see where the noise was coming from: Wayne, Cory, Judy, Kate, and about a dozen other queers covered in bright crack-and-peel stickers form a human wall protecting the front of A Different Light bookstore from about a half dozen protestors carrying signs that say, "Sinner Repent," "God Hates Fags," and, in unintentionally ironic tonal juxtaposition, "Jesus Loves You."

I stand on the corner, watching, until Cory looks up and sees me. He waves and reaches his hand out toward me. I run over and hug him hello, then hug Kate and Judy.

"Welcome to Friday Night Fundies," Cory says.

"Fundies?"

"Fundamentalists. They're from Calvary Chapel in Orange County."

"Yeah, I know Calvary Chapel." My friends and I had come across this same fundamentalist Christian congregation on many Saturday mornings, as they worked with Operation Rescue to try to sabotage and close abortion-providing women's health clinics, and we tried to keep them open.

Cory tells me that Calvary Chapel has been sending members of its congregation to harass queers as they walk along the sidewalks between Micky's and Rage, two of the main clubs in the heart of West Hollywood, and A Different Light, the gay and lesbian bookstore.

For a few hours we walk parallel to the fundies as they move along the sidewalk between the bookstore and the bars. There are enough of us to form a tight line toward the street side of the sidewalk, keeping space clear between the sidewalk and the storefronts. Wayne passes out condoms to the queers walking in and out of the clubs.

A broad-shouldered Chicano queer with bright pink hair wearing a shirt so covered with stickers that I can't tell what color the fabric is introduces himself as Pete. "Cory told me about you."

I raise my eyebrows at Pete. "What did he tell you?"

"That a new ass-kicking teenage dyke had just joined Queer Nation."

I turn my back to the fundies to face Pete, looking at him as he smiles at me. I'm trying to think of a smart response, but I can't distinguish sweet teasing from what feels like strange, unnameable pressure. Before I can respond, Pete's eyes cloud over.

One of the fundies, an older man, is coming up behind me, waving a Bible right at me, coming closer, fast. I turn around to face the man as Pete pivots to stand between me and the fundie, who continues waving his Bible. I realize that he is yelling at me. "It's not too late! Save yourself! Come join us!"

I'm stunned. He's still yelling. "Repent! Sinner, repent!" I have faced off with these people before but defending clinics, protecting a space, ensuring access for other women. They have never targeted me as an individual. I'm frightened. He's so loud.

Something in me, some bit of calmness or distance breaks off, and I feel my anger. Taking a deep breath, I step out from behind Pete and stand next to him, planting my feet firmly on the sidewalk. "I am saving myself!" I yell back.

"Sinner!" he starts yelling at me, even more outraged. He lifts his Bible up over his head, yelling louder as he takes a step closer to me.

Pete moves back in front of me, straightening his spine, raising himself up on the full height of his boots, his arms stretched out, the neon-red light from the club behind us making his pink hair glow, taking up as much space as he can, making himself twice as big as the fundie, and keeping me safe behind the reach of his arms. "You can't have our young people!" Pete yells as loudly as he can. People driving past slow down to watch. "You're already destroying your young people!" Pete continues. "Stay the fuck away from ours!"

The fundie takes a step back and is enfolded by his circle of people. Pete turns back to me. Kate, Wayne, and Cory appear next to me. "I'm fine," I tell them, but I'm trembling.

"Yeah?" Kate puts her fingers under my chin, tilts my head up under the streetlamp and the glare of the neon bar sign, and looks me in the eye. "Really?"

"Really. Fine." And I am. Trembling from adrenaline, but the rush of fear has shifted into something brighter, hopeful. I am standing up for myself.

Twenty minutes after the protest ends, I pull the car up to the curb in front of Millie's Cafe on Sunset Boulevard in Silver Lake. The waitress, arms tattooed, nose and eyebrows pierced, waves toward the open tables in the small room, then smiles and nods slightly as her eyes scan the neon stickers on Cory's shirt. We find a table against the wall. Over salads, we're telling stories about where we came from and how we got to Queer Nation and ACT UP. Cory tells me that he's been sick for a few years. "ARC, though, not AIDS," he says. He's playing with his fork, twisting a piece of a spinach stem from his salad. He looks far away. "I haven't been that sick," he continues. "Not yet. Maybe I won't be. Maybe there will be a cure." He looks up at me. I don't yet know how to read the expression in his eyes. Hope. Irony. A dare.

There are so many things I want to say. That of course there will be a cure. That he'll be fine. That we'll ... That we'll what? Make it through this together? Everyone? I want to have something useful to say, but I don't. He's sitting across the little table from me, my new friend whom I am so quickly starting to adore. Maybe there will be a cure.

"Do you really think so?" I ask him.

"No." He puts his fork down and sighs. "They don't care about us enough to find a cure. The faggots and the whores and the drug users. Yeah, I know, not only us. But visibly only us. We're expendable."

I want to argue with him. I don't want to believe him. Except that I do believe him. I just don't want it to be true. I'm looking out the window at Sunset Boulevard. We're just down the street from the women's clinic where we gather some Saturday mornings to wait for notice of where Operation Rescue has sent people to shut down other health clinics. We jump into cars and race to the far corners of LA County to keep the clinics open. I know that ACT UP has organized similar kinds of actions to keep open the AIDS ward at County Hospital and to open the Chris Brownlie Hospice in the hills a few miles away. But those demonstrations weren't about the fundies. That would have been easier. They were about the LA County government. And the federal government. I look back across the table at my friend.

"I don't regret any of it," Cory says to me, sitting taller, straightening his spine.

"Any of what?"

"Sex. Living. Love. Survival."

I wonder what it would feel like not to have regrets. I can only imagine it by keeping still, by not taking risks. But I have already broken the silence, my silence, yelling back at the fundies. I can still feel the vibration in my throat. I don't think I've ever yelled that loud.

"What are you thinking?" he asks me.

I stare at him. I can't figure out how to tell him what I'm feeling, the gut sensation that I am betraying something my family has worked for, just by sitting with him in the little Silver Lake diner where I have spent so much time with student organizer friends, planning demonstrations against the Gulf War, or US military involvement in El Salvador, passing mostly unnoticed. He has a bright green Queer Liberation Not Assimilation sticker on his chest.

"It's the sticker." I put my fork down, giving up on my salad, and push my plate away.

"What about it?"

"The Okinawan dance, at least in my family, has been about how to maintain cultural values about right and wrong but also go unnoticed, assimilate. To draw attention to difference is to be at risk."

"At risk for what?" He pushes his plate away. We're delighted by the challenge of each other, energized, eyes shining, smiling as we work it out, out loud.

"At risk for everything." I think back to the stories of Internment, families rounded up and imprisoned for months in the holding pens in converted stalls at the racetrack before being shipped to Manzanar. I flash back to choreographer Mehmet Sander's quarantine enactment at Highways Performance Space on World AIDS Day and tell Cory about that night. Sander rounded up the whole room of us there for the overnight vigil, wordlessly herding us from room to room so that we felt the panic and helplessness that comes with loss of autonomy.

Cory listens to me, his eyes tearing up when I tell him about the push-pull I feel between rebelling and freezing. He takes a deep breath before speaking. "Do you really think that they don't hate us if we don't stick out? They just don't notice. So we live in fear and they get to be in charge through their obliviousness and we don't know who might stand up for us. With us. When they notice they hate us, or they don't hate us, but we know it, know where we stand. And we don't spend our energy hiding. And when we hide, we have a harder time finding each other. What if it's the Okinawan in you that connected you to queer rebellion?"

I'm silenced by this idea. "Keep talking," I say, my breath catching a little, excited and scared of what might come next.

Cory continues more emphatically. "Any form of survival is an act of rebellion when they don't want us to survive. It doesn't matter if it is silence or screaming. That's the thing; our survival is the rebellion. Our bodies are always on the line. Always at risk, whether it's infection or quarantine."

"And so," I say, picking up where he left off, trying it out, "we put our bodies on the line for each other, for ourselves. It could always be any of us. It isn't just an idea. It's our experience as bodies in the world."

Both of us are teary. At some point in the conversation we had reached for each other's hands, and now our fingers are interlocked on top of the table. We keep them there as the waitress clears the remains of our salads. We're quiet for a few minutes, taking each other in. I feel the heat of his palm, the cooler, soft tips of his fingers.

AUGUST 1991

A summer night, warm, even with the breeze coming through the open window on top of the hill. There's a sheet pulled halfway up our naked, post-sex bodies. We were rough with each other in ways that usually work, the muscularity of struggle and strain. Erotic as a reminder of aliveness. Arms pinned. Knees bruising the inside of a thigh. Hard teeth against the back of a neck. Languageless precision of bodily attunement. When it doesn't work, we pull away, annoyed. Without words.

We're both irritable, trying to settle into sweetness. Cory is unbraiding and rebraiding my hair. He tugs the loose strands down, tucking them into the braid, and I flip the braid back up, away from my neck in the heat. We had stopped at the hospital earlier. Robert has been admitted again. Wade was there, hanging out with Gabe, keeping him company, but when we walked in Wade didn't look much better than Robert. Robert stayed asleep the whole time we were there. None of us said much. Gabe and I held hands. Cory sat on the side of Robert's bed with Wade. Wade looked like he was fading, so I rubbed the knots that I could from the tight sinew of his neck. "Save your energy for him," Wade murmured, though it didn't occur to me until later that I didn't know which of the other hims Wade meant. Gabe eventually shooed us away, saying that he was going to spend the night and we should go home to rest. Cory and

I walked out with Wade and kissed him good night before heading home.

Now here we are. In bed, talking about Wade and Robert.

"Will he get better?" I ask Cory.

"Who, Robert? Or Wade?"

"Well." I consider the question. "Either. Both."

"Yeah, they'll get better. A little, for a while. But you do know it will get worse."

"How much worse?" I can't imagine it.

"We're nowhere near the end."

I'm quiet, thinking about Robert, already in pain, already getting a little confused, Wade looking too thin and pale, his brown hair falling limply around his eyes. And Cory isn't feeling well. He won't talk about it, not really, but he's a little out of breath, a little tired, and he's had a headache for a few days. He skipped an ACT UP committee meeting that he'd said he was coming to and snapped at me that he had gotten busy when I asked about it.

In our restlessness, Cory gets up and fusses with the stereo. He plays a Diamanda Galás cassette loud and gets back into bed. She's too much for my nervous system, and I'm having a hard time settling. After a few minutes I get out of bed and turn her off. I fiddle around with the radio until I find the jazz station, with Ella Fitzgerald singing "I've Got You under My Skin." We both hum along with her a little.

"Hey," Cory says, softly, tracing the side of my face with his fingers.

"You want me to switch the music?" I ask and start to get up.

"No, stay. I like her."

"Okay. What?"

"I want to show you something. I mean, I want to tell you about something. But I don't know if you"—he takes a slow breath, lets it out—"if you want to know."

I look at him. I have no idea what he's talking about.

"The pills. I want to show you where they are."

"Pills? Your meds? I know where your meds are. Do you need me to get something for you?"

"Not those pills. The other pills." He looks at me, waiting for me to catch on.

I feel a glimmer of recognition, and then it slips away. I shake my head.

"You know, the pills. The ones. Enough of them."

"Oh." I stare at him, trying to find words.

"You don't know how bad it gets. Can get. Will get. You haven't seen it," he says, sitting up in bed. "I don't want that. I don't want to be stuck in the hospital. I don't want to not have control over what happens. I want to make my own decisions."

"And one of those decisions ..."

"Yes."

I nod, slowly. "And you want me to ...?"

"Help me." Cory took my hand.

"How will I know?"

"You won't have to. I'll know."

"Then what will you need me for?"

"Not to be alone."

"You're not alone."

"What?"

"You're not alone." I take a breath. I can feel my heart start to race, the edge of panic. Of wanting to convince him of something.

"What do I have? Who do I have?" He looks at me warily, like he's tired and disappointed.

"What about the story you told me? That you all borrow each other's T cells whenever someone has something important to do and needs a little extra boost? Just that checking in on each other. Doesn't that account for something? Everyone loves you. And you have me." I'm talking faster in my panic. From a distance, I feel my body pulling farther back from his body.

"That's what I'm asking. If I have you." He looks at me steadily. We're both quiet for a minute.

I try to slow myself down. "How will I know that you'll be right? How will you know?"

Cory looks away from me. "I'll just know."

"But how?" I insist. I can feel myself starting to panic again, starting to argue.

"I just will. You won't have to. I will."

I let go of his hand and cross my arms so he won't feel me shaking. We argue about it a little more.

"You want me to decide," I say flatly.

"No." He's frustrated.

"How is it anything else?"

"I want you to help me. I don't want to be alone."

I close my eyes. "Not yet," I whisper.

He takes my hand back. "Not yet." He repeats my words back, as though they should soothe me. "When it's time. It isn't time yet."

I exhale shakily. I can't imagine it being time. I can't imagine it feeling clear.

"You want to love me? This is what it means to love me."

I hear him say it, and I don't know how to reconcile it. I think I understand how it is love, but I can't imagine that it will feel like love. I feel my love for him as the desire to always hold him close, safe. To never let go.

I let go of his hand. Then I get up and start pacing.

"Come sit," he says. I sit on the bed, then pick up my clothes from the floor and stand up to put them back on. He sighs and gets up, pulls on his jeans and an Infected Faggot T-shirt. "Come on."

"Where are we going?"

"Walking."

I follow him down the long stairway and out onto Echo Park Avenue. As we approach the park, I hear the sound of water moving though the filtration system of the artificial lake. We walk around the lake, silent, listening to the sounds of the urban park at night. I see the silhouettes of ducks and geese in sleep poses on the steep banks.

I've never been in this park after dark. As a little kid, my parents used to take me here. We'd bring any leftover bread and feed the ducks at the lake's edge. I'd laugh as they swarmed around us, trying to steal the bits of bread from my little hands. The paddleboats are tied to the docks of the boathouse. Sometimes we'd come and pedal around the lake. I close my eyes and remember the first time I was old enough to reach the pedals.

We walk toward the northern edge of the lake. Toward the lotus in the moonlight. But moonlight is strange in Los Angeles. We want to think it's moonlight. That's the story we tell ourselves. But it isn't the moon. It's houses. The streetlamps glaring down on us, catching us in the cross fire as they mean to illuminate the junkies and the sex workers, to discourage nighttime cruising and sex in the bushes.

We sit in silence by the path at the edge of the lake. Behind us is a large patch of bushes and, beyond that, the bridge onto the small island at the northeastern side of the lake, lined with tall reeds and trees. As we sit in our silence, I begin to tune in to the sounds around us. To really listen to them. For them. In urban Echo Park, when we hear rustling in bushes near us, we don't think of bears, or of cougars, or even of the coyotes that come down from the dry hills late at night searching for food, for water. We think of sex, we think of cruising, we think of not having other places to go, or of wanting the internal feeling of risk amplified or matched by the external risk of violence.

"If you don't want to, then say no," Cory says. "Say it out loud. Don't just nod and hope it doesn't come to it. It will come to it."

I turn my attention away from the tall reeds and back to him. "What if it doesn't?"

"Don't do that."

"What?"

"Make me take care of you."

"How am I making you take care of me?"

"By making me pretend that it will be all right."

There's nothing left for me to say. There is everything left to say, but no words come. I reach for Cory's hand and we sit together, quietly. Gradually, our stiff bodies soften toward each other again and we lean shoulder to shoulder. Finally, the breeze is starting to cool the air.

We listen to the sounds of intimacies around us and feel closer in their wake. And in our closeness, I feel the impossible distance between his story and mine. It's the strangest of queer intimacies, this blurring of desire and death and negotiation of risk. Not the cruising around us but the risk of having to let go.

Under the gritty yellowed light, the lotus blossoms glow. There's a moan and a quick hush from the darkness behind us. We listen to the kinds of joy that remain possible. Even in what we grow up thinking are the darkest places.

Surviving My Cousin

BRYAN M. HOLDMAN

"She got a man living in the basement."

That's how my cousin Demetrius—Dee, we called him—greeted me one summer, in the mid-'80s, as I fetched my luggage from under the Greyhound bus in Colorado Springs. My sister and I were there for a week to visit Mamaw, our grandmother. Dee had been living there the entire summer; his warm brown eyes and wide, toothy smile told me he was eager for our company.

Back home, I spent my playtime with my sister and our girl cousins. But at Mamaw's, Dee and I were a pair. Sent outdoors to play all day. Plopped in a soapy tub to wash off the outside. Getting our Afros cornrowed and our scalps Afro-Sheened. Through it all, Dee always had an objective—like drinking the entire pitcher of Kool-Aid in Mamaw's refrigerator, though we'd been told not to. I was good for remembering the details that kept us out of trouble— like where Mamaw kept the sugar and drink mix, and to remake the replacement batch in the same metal pitcher so that no one would notice. But I could never figure out how to camouflage our telltale bright red tongues that gave us away. Yes, indeed, Dee and I could get into some mess. And this summer, Dee made it known that I'd arrived just in time to back him up in a new scheme.

An air force officer was renting the basement from our grandmother for the summer. He had shared use of the house kitchen, but otherwise, he stuck to the basement. That was usually *our* domain—home to a pool table, a radio, couches for lounging, a closet full of vintage board games and toys, and an old typewriter we'd use to play school, office, or newspaper. With Ol' Petty Officer in the basement, there'd be nowhere for us to occupy ourselves when summer heat, rainy afternoons, or tornado warnings forced us indoors. Worse than the incursion into our space was the fact that this buzz-cut, clean-shaven, tucked-in, white gentleman lodger had also assumed too much authority in our Black grandmother's house.

It wasn't long before I saw exactly why Dee wanted him gone. This man took it upon himself to order us around like we were cadets at the air force academy up the road. Lounging in chairs sideways, lingering at the breakfast table, leaving the house barefoot, leaning on kitchen counters—all things we'd done for years at Mamaw's house—caused him to mutter and bark commands. First we tried things my way. According to my middle school logic, relentlessly exploiting the lodger's obvious pet peeves would be most effective. I'd cop a seat on the countertop—right next to where the lodger was making himself a sandwich. Dee would melt across the recliner in the TV room, limbs sprawled every which way. I figured the lodger would slip up and chastise us too gruffly in front of our sweet, doting Mamaw, who made up silly songs in her Alabama drawl as she put collards in the pressure cooker and let us eat from a bag of grapes while we did the weekly shopping. She wouldn't appreciate his taking a tone with us, and that would be that. Ol' Petty Officer's starched shirts and creased slacks would be *out of there*. But he left for work in the afternoons, shortly before Mamaw returned from her job. There was no opportunity to goad him in front of her. So Dee came up with another plan.

My sister played lookout at the top of the stairs as I hovered over Dee's shoulder, watching him pick the simple lock on the lodger's basement bedroom door. Before long, we were in the lodger's room—which I found surprisingly musty and messy for someone who was supposed to be tightly tucked and barracks-level spotless. I wasn't sure what to look for, but I knew Dee and I would have to look fast. There wasn't much time before the dog would start barking out back at the sound of Mamaw's sedan pulling up the driveway. Dee, however, moved with methodical assurance through the room. Bottom dresser drawer. Nightstands. Under the mattress. Bingo!

We found the lodger's porn stash.

Dee was ecstatic in his moment of victory, already on to his next objective: coming up with a good enough lie to minimize our breaking and entering so that Mamaw would stay focused on Ol' Petty Officer's stack of smut falling into the hands of her innocent grandbabies. My sister wanted to know what we'd found that was eliciting such a gleeful reaction from Dee. All my thoughts of how we were going to explain breaking and entering dissolved; I could only focus on getting that stack of glossy skin mags all to myself so that I could peek beyond the covers and get a real look at what was inside.

Did I mention that the lodger's stash was gay porn?

As a kid, I was always ogling the male figure. The skin-on-skin contact and colorful Speedos of the '70s World Wide Wrestling Federation. The broad shoulders on all those Olympic divers and gymnasts in '76 and '84. I'd even suffer through trips to see the Denver Nuggets play, because the NBA shorts were *much* shorter and tighter back then. But those viewing experiences were always such fleeting glances. Anyone could be in the room with you when you were watching wrestling on TV. And our Nuggets seats were often up in the nosebleeds, paid for by my mom's teacher's salary.

To really get my eyes on the male form, my guilty pleasure was the Spiegel catalog. Back to school, Christmas, and my birthday gave me the right to go through the catalog and dog-ear pages of things I liked or needed so that my mother could share my wish list with relatives. I'd spend hours pretending to decide between certain items, claiming I was unsure which sweater I liked more, or whether I truly did need new winter boots. Really, I was lasciviously perusing the underwear section, wondering what was filling out the front and back of all those dazzling white cotton briefs.

Now I had in my hands page after page of the real deal. Muscular thighs, hairy chests, and full biceps were now connected to erect junk and perky asses ... with tan lines! Not only did I finally have a complete map of the male anatomy, but I also had a pathway to the pleasure I'd been trying to find my way toward, through the fabric of scantily clothed athletes and underwear models. I finally had an idea of what I could do when given the opportunity not only to look but also to touch.

This revelation was both joy and nightmare. A few years prior— just as the idea of sex and sexuality was beginning to dawn in my brain—I sat rapt as Ted Koppel explained on *Nightline* that there was a disease killing gay men that was spread through sexual contact. And in this moment, holding a stack of porn magazines stolen from an air force officer ... I understood that "gay" meant "me."

I still sometimes wonder if Dee's plot was more elaborate than I realized at the time. The ease with which he picked the lock. How swiftly he found the magazines. Dee had been there for weeks before us; was the whole thing an exercise to get to those magazines ... for himself? To tell me and my sister about himself? To tell me something about myself? I know that we never talked about how immediately mesmerized I was by the images I saw as I flipped through the porn rags, arguing that I needed to see what was in them because they may not be appropriate for my little sister's eyes. I know that the entire operation only served to get us in trouble with Mamaw, who was livid that we had disrespected that man's privacy.

Within a couple of years, I was struggling through my freshman year at an all-boys Jesuit high school in Denver. Dee was struggling too—as he told us when he showed up unexpectedly on our door-step on a school night, agitated, informing my mother that he'd walked the almost seven miles from his home in a nearby suburb. He'd fought with his mother and had to get out of the house—even though he had walked all that way in the dark and cold, I could still feel the heat of the argument rising off his spirit. I tried to get him to tell me what the fight was about. The most he would divulge—the most he probably *could* divulge at the time—was "My mom won't let me be who I want to be."

Once again, my cousin was reflecting my own struggle right back to me, whether he knew it or not. While he was fighting hard to claim his identity, I was fighting just as hard to deny and repress mine. I had already absorbed the "death sentence" messaging that the mainstream media had attached to the act of gay sex. I certainly wasn't going to sign up for that. Added to that pressure was the environment I was in. Catholic dogma and toxic male culture con-spired to penalize even the slightest whiff of difference that came off me. Every day at school was a battle to keep the murmurs and slurs to a quiet din in the background. Why would Dee be fighting to subject himself to violence even more direct than the minefield of persecution I was gingerly picking my way through? I stayed camouflaged, counterbalancing my burgeoning interest in theater and art with a gig managing the wrestling team. That gig didn't last because … well … it was very difficult for me to disguise my interest in muscles and singlets.

As Dee and I continued to mature, a million little differences began to separate our paths toward growing up and coming out.

The private Catholic school I attended included summer jobs and work-study programs. My crafty, creative mind was getting molded by Jesuits with a God-ordained mission to educate young leaders. Dee, in the public school system, could only find an outlet for his goal-oriented, big-picture, somewhat mischief-bent brain within the confines of ROTC. I was a child of a single mother but had an enormous extended family on my mother's side to fill in the gaps. Clothes got paid for, field trips had spending money, books were bought, tuition stayed current, and cash rewards for good grades were regularly posted. Dee, living with his mom and maternal grandmother, could barely call his conflict-filled house a home. And our shared relatives in Colorado Springs were often denied access to him as part of an ongoing rift between his mother and father.

Looking back, I can also perceive that Dee and his mom shared a different dynamic from my mother and me. Where I can now understand that Dee's mom was restricting his self-expression, I look back in gratitude that my mom's parenting style recognized that kids need and deserve space. A philosophy of earned freedom, plus my schedule of responsibilities and extracurricular activities, led to a lot of autonomy for me. In addition, my mother offered the same sanctuary to Dee that she offered to my friends over the years. Despite my efforts to fly under the radar at school, I had some complicated relationships with boys who were themselves complicated. My mom let them sleep over, and let me sleep over at their houses, no questions asked. She stayed informed about my comings and goings, and whom I was coming and going with ... but never judged. I had freedom to come and go as I wished. Dee had a different set of rules and expectations, and his only option for freedom was to flee.

Freedom and safety at home, and the incredible blessing of private school, should theoretically have afforded me some level of confidence and self-possession. But moving through the world with these privileges also meant walking a path that never left the confines of my personal closet. On some subconscious level I wondered: Would sharing my sublimated identity cut away the economic and emotional support net of my extended family? Would I end up as untethered as my cousin if I were to declare my own truth? Through school, I was also navigating a lot of white and wealthy spaces; the gaps in experience and economics between my schoolmates and me further served to keep me from feeling safe enough to disclose my sexuality to anyone. Dee seemed to be cutting a path through his mother's resistance toward coming out. I ought to have been able to follow his example ... but there was no way I could follow his lead. We were moving differently through the world, at a time when we needed one another to survive.

Gang violence could have killed us. Police brutality could have killed us. The school-to-prison pipeline could have killed us. And to top it off, our childhood years were scented with the panic of a serial killer in Atlanta who was targeting Black boys our age. The streets we walked were not safe. Loving men was not safe. We hadn't even been able to put our most important point of commonality into words yet ... and the monstrous existence of a virus was already adding bricks to a growing wall between us, in an already sharp, bullet-riddled, hard-edged world that was hunting us. In addition to all the things that could obliterate Dee and me because we were Black, AIDS could obliterate us because we were gay. The media chronicling Rock Hudson's coming out, decline, and death in 1985 sent a perilous message to my young brain. There would be no private planes to Paris for experimental treatments, no Doris Day to speak lovingly of our memories—not for someone regular and of color like me, or my cousin. Who were we supposed to turn to for guidance in figuring out how to be gay? Rock Hudson did not survive, despite wealth, access, and fame. I expected that were I to come out, I wouldn't survive either.

In the spring of 1990, our senior year of high school, I was in the middle of creating a photography project for my AP English class with a cast of classmates. A neoclassical pavilion in a park was the backdrop. The park was in one of Denver's wealthier neighborhoods—and was also central to the city's gay community. Dee just sort of ... appeared out of the bushes this time—a grinning, mahogany-skinned jack-in-the-box. It took me a moment to recognize him through the lens of my borrowed camera, clowning in the background of a carefully composed shot. When I finally saw him, we both struggled not to laugh at how weird this was.

We'd had enough of these run-ins by now that I knew, from his stuffed-to-the-seams backpack, that my cousin was at least periodically homeless. He confirmed this fact after letting me prattle on about how I'd thrown away my applications to Stanford and Dartmouth, simply to avoid classmates I didn't want to spend four more years with. He feigned interest as I explained my project for class, a retelling of *Medea*, inspired by an image of silent movie actress Theda Bara. As I tried to turn the conversation to my senior directing project for drama class, he quipped: "You sound good. Just be glad you're not out here in these bushes."

Dee was just months into his eighteenth year, and this was what adulthood looked like for him: Black, queer, and without consistent housing or family ties—placing him among the most vulnerable in the gay community. The shelter that community offered him was a public park. But whatever he was enduring and overcoming, it hadn't changed the light in his dark brown eyes, or how naturally he opened his mouth to release a booming cackle of hearty laughter.

I was getting closer to coming out; I had switched to a public high school, where I thrived, leaving behind the homophobia of Catholic school. This had allowed me to get more comfortable in my own skin. But I wasn't really in honest contact with any other gay men—for sex, friendship, or anything in between. My privilege allowed me to mull over my identity in a protected bubble, peeking out at a world I was still hesitant to join.

In the same park, two years later, I saw my cousin Dee while I was waiting for the bus. I had been over in the gayborhood, checking out a new coffee shop and bookstore. I was out of the closet now, and fumbling with identity, and maybe hoping to cruise a cutie and be a ho-ho-ho while I was home from college for Christmas break. I had learned a lot in Chicago—and yet, at my university on Lake Michigan's north shore, socializing in campus peer organizations and partying in the bars and clubs of Boystown meant that I was still looking for my Black gay self in largely white spaces. Black and brown queer spaces were located much farther south, sometimes beyond where public transportation could reasonably carry me for a night of drinking and dancing to the city's unmistakable house music. And even if my friends and I could make it out to a club or two ... my prescription glasses, sweaters, and khakis often stood out among my skinfolks as much as my skin tone differentiated me from other gays on campus.

Majoring in film and getting heavily involved in campus theater exposed me to a lot of art that was created in response to AIDS and the devastation it wrought in a gay community that fought to survive the '80s. Much of it gave me an understanding that the generation before me was nearly decimated by a decade of death that the government seemed uninterested in preventing. In the much-lauded plays of Larry Kramer, Tony Kushner, and Craig Lucas, the playwrights were fictionalizing their own lived experiences, and I couldn't see myself reflected in their largely white and well-to-do worlds. Films such as *Looking for Langston*, *Tongues Untied*, and *Paris Is Burning* were beautiful celebrations of queer people of color, many of them thriving emphatically and artistically while battling AIDS personally and culturally. From that part I could gain some sense of pride, but on the whole these films offered versions of Black gay lives that, in my youth and inexperience, I was unable to correlate to my own life. On campus, I wasn't connected to many out Black gay men. Finding friendship with Black men at all meant tucking in my gay enough to hang with straight brothas. The effort was minimizing and exhausting at times. Just as taxing were relationships with white peers, some of which only served to add more layers of isolation to my world. Those relationships, with their inappropriate jokes and outright slurs, were littered with emotional landmines. There was no building of trust, goodwill, or emotional intimacy. Often I resorted to connecting only over known points of commonality—safe topics—excluding whole chunks of my being from the conversation.

Sex positivity wasn't something I was exposed to yet. The message was still one of caution, driven home with buzzwords like "prevention" and "barrier" and "safe." I was horny and college-aged, and getting off with someone else meant outwitting a viral plague. Added to that was the ignorance I encountered from peers, who often leaked misinformation and casual racism all over me. White boys and men had no problem telling me that the only valuable part of my body, mind, and soul was my dick. They thought they were wooing me with compliments while repeating tired Mandingo stereotypes. Their fantasies relied on reinforcing my oppression. Simultaneously, in attempting to keep myself informed and safe, I read both gay and straight media on HIV and AIDS. Every headline I consumed seemed to be problematizing the virus on Black bodies. Rates of infection among men of color, drug use, questionable sexual practices, and careless infection of Black female partners seemed to resonate most loudly. As I was making sense of it at the time, the message I heard was this: Black gays were dying of—and killing each other with—HIV.

My lived experience was not centered in mostly Black spaces; nor was I completely at home in the rarefied and majority-white world of private academia. I felt somewhere in between and mostly alone. I was so confused as to whom I could let touch my body and who would want to. I was out but not fully seen.

As much as my cousin was out of house, home, and family, I was out of bounds no matter where I turned, it seemed. But my philosophical conundrum wasn't too far from my cousin's visceral experience of the same issues. When he sat down next to me on the bus stop bench in the park, I noticed the way in which he was colder. Harder. Different from the person who had sheepishly couched his precarious living situation as a joke. Now he said he was living nearby, with a friend. Some older white guy. Doing "this and that" to pay the bills.

"You still out there in Chicago?" he asked.

I was surprised that he knew where I'd ended up at college. The last time we spoke, I hadn't decided yet. I rushed to tell Dee that I'd come out, and he regarded me with the kind of look one gives a cute but annoying puppy.

"Child, I *been* out," he said, echoing our Mamaw's particular drawl.

Just then, a rather sporty car slowed to a crawl as it passed the two of us at the bus stop. Dee peered in the windows as it went by, and then looked over his shoulder at it, while the driver idled at the curb several feet past us.

"Is that your friend?" I asked.

"It's a friend, I guess you could say." He got up and we hugged before he crossed to the idling car. After a moment of conversation with the driver, he opened the door and looked back at me, a little bit of the old mischief and light playing across his face. "Don't wait for that bus too long. Somebody gonna snatch you off that bus stop if you're not careful." Dee climbed into the car and rode off with his "friend."

Five minutes later, a silver-haired man pulled up next to me and rolled down the window of his BMW. "You look cold out there. Need a ride?"

This would not be the last time I was approached and misidentified as a sex worker. But it was the last time I saw my cousin Dee.

I was surprised, one evening in 1996, when my roommate told me that a social worker from San Francisco was trying to reach me, as next of kin, on behalf of "D. Holdman." For privacy reasons, the social worker would only leave a return phone number and the name. Donald Holdman was my former stepfather—over a decade after my mother had divorced him, I figured I was still receiving unwanted calls that were fueled by his substance abuse and narcissistic personality.

I slept on it. Knowing a social worker was involved, I woke thinking this might actually be some sort of real emergency that needed attention. The next day my mother and sister, still in contact with my former stepfather, verified that he was fine, and ... living in Atlanta. Perhaps I wasn't actually related to this social worker's client and this was all a misunderstanding ... unless ... *Could she have meant my cousin Dee?* Thrown by the term "next of kin" and the call from San Francisco, I hadn't even thought it might be him.

This momentary lapse in consideration sits like a hot cast-iron pan in my chest when I think about it. How had I not thought of him? Why had he thought of me as the person to call on in crisis, whatever that crisis may have been? Had there been no one else? Was it something he thought only I would have understood? Two years out of college and struggling to make a living in Los Angeles at the time, I don't know what help I would have been able to offer ... but it would have been nice to be able to speak with him and check in. By the time I reached the social worker, the case was no longer on her desk. As a result, she couldn't share any forwarding or contact information; nor could she confirm where my cousin was, or if he still needed me.

The next call came in 1998. "He's dead," my sister told me. Not tearful but tense and irate. "This is some bullshit."

Then my mother took the phone. Calmer but just as tense they were being asked to accept pneumonia as the cause of Dee's sudden, dire hospitalization ... but my mother had thought to ask a relative about some inconsistencies between what Dee's father was telling them and what she was hearing the nurses say. A nurse herself, our relative deduced that the pneumonia was AIDS-related. It was early October. It hadn't even snowed yet, much less been cold enough for someone just shy of their twenty-seventh birthday to catch pneumonia, unless they had a compromised immune system.

I had just finished spending most of my extra money on grad school application fees, so I couldn't afford a plane ticket to attend the rather rushed memorial service. Sitting alone in my studio apartment, I felt like someone took my heart out that day and replaced it with an empty soda bottle. A cold wind kept blowing across the open bottle neck, making that distinct, low kind of fog-horn sound.

It's likely that my cousin's death was as much a function of his Blackness as it was a function of HIV and its insidious attack on the human immune system. Black people statistically suffer more negative outcomes with regard to health care, both because of medical institutions' refusal to provide equity in care and the pharmaceutical industry's prohibitive pricing of antiretroviral drugs. Had Dee been wealthy, white, and gay, he may have had access to better treatment ... but gay is not gay is not gay. Twenty years after Dee's departure from this world, homos everywhere were up in arms over the symbolic gesture of adding more colors to the rainbow flag in an attempt to create space for more inclusivity.

This is symptomatic of how our queer community has continued to exclude people of color from resources and has continued to fail us.

Of course, my cousin weren't no fool. Always bright, and with mother wit beyond his years from an early age, Dee was obviously a survivor, despite his basic needs such as resources, community, and shelter not being consistently met. I want to believe that he should have known more, been more cautious, taken better care. But I don't know if any of my belief is based in fact. I've only heard second- and thirdhand accounts of his seroconversion. And I can only guess whether his death was hastened by not seeking treatment, by not having access to enough of the right kind of treatment, or by not having support in finding the resources he needed. At the same time, these questions make clear my own privilege in having access to experiences, places, and people that contributed to my own survival.

I also remain HIV-negative out of an abundance of caution and a fear I hate to admit. The wall of experiences and perceptions that separated me from my cousin extends in either direction for miles. As a person who works to examine his own life, I am constantly amazed at the ways in which solid borders exist in places where I was certain I had broken through. My brash younger self saw HIV as a rabid dog on a long chain. In trying to test its power over me, I got close enough to feel it snapping at my heels, more than once. I let the constant, external messaging about my worth—as a Black American and as a gay man of color—convince me to gamble with how valuable my life was.

White men were conquests; if I could get one to sleep with me, it meant I wasn't the potentially toxic vector of transmission that the statistics and headlines would have me believe. Condoms were sometimes forgotten; I didn't want to make other partners of color feel accused of those same statistics and headlines. I was stumbling through a self-created obstacle course where the objective was to emerge at the finish line HIV-negative and in a committed, monogamous relationship. But I had built this course on the edge of a chasm; and I had unleashed that rabid dog to chase me while I tried to navigate it blindfolded, hopping on one foot. I faced the dog, taunted it, haphazardly protected myself from it—and survived. Had my cousin played a similar game   and lost? Had he done everything right ... and just been unlucky?

And now, in this age of PrEP and antiretroviral therapies, I can't quite get comfortable in the new reality that these medications could ever allow me to live. See ... surviving HIV doesn't mean I will necessarily survive Blackness. That has never been guaranteed.

My cousin Dee and I could get into some mess. He had the big ideas, but I always had the detailed exit plan. We were meant, I think, to function as some sort of team. We were placed in one another's paths to be allies. A normalizing force. Mirrors of one another's experiences. A source of support. Company. Backup. Validation. Community. Friends. Family. But no matter how I review our shared history, I can't see the version where I could have kept him out of *this* trouble, against all those odds.

For all the answers I want to have, I'll always be asking myself the same questions:

Why am I here?

Why isn't he?

Class of '88

RIGOBERTO GONZÁLEZ

The first time I spoke of AIDS was with a girl in my journalism club during our senior year in high school. Lisa and I were laying out the latest issue of *Sandscripts* before it got sent out to be typeset and printed. She was the master of photograph dimensions and knew how to adjust the size of a picture on the page to accommodate the text. I was the word counter, turning each article from paragraphs to column inches. As newshounds, we had to keep up with the goings-on in the school, and then reduce them to digestible snippets for our readers. My beat was academics, so I got to interview the latest student of the month, the new vice principal, and the competitors of the Debate Club. The outside world didn't enter the halls through the newspaper but through the chatter between classes, or during lunchtime club activities, which is when Lisa casually mentioned the subject of AIDS.

"I wouldn't be afraid of a person who had it," she said. "Unless I had a cut or a sore on my finger. Then I wouldn't feel safe shaking hands."

I didn't want to point out how contradictory her statement sounded because at the time I wasn't confident about pushing back. I didn't want to ask her where she had gotten her information from because clearly this was common knowledge. Once again, I felt embarrassed that I lived in a Mexican household where the news came to us in Spanish, where the elegant anchors mentioned SIDA by name once in a while but didn't say much else. It was all a big mystery.

"How can you tell if someone has AIDS?" I asked.

Lisa looked at me in disbelief. "Well, if a person is gay or a drug addict, they're likely to have AIDS," she said with certainty.

I nodded my head, though I didn't see the connection between the two. Except that in our community these were the outcasts and undesirables who lurked in the neighborhood after dark. "Don't go out at night," warned Abuelo. "Nothing but junkies and faggots out at this hour." This was California in the '80s, but I had grown up hearing the same warnings from my grandparents in Michoacán.

There was no asking about these matters at home. Or rather, I didn't dare ask, afraid that opening this topic of conversation would lead to questions and, upon further inquiry, the eventual discovery that I was a homosexual, that I might have this deadly touch that threatened them all.

I understood, however, that as a gay man I wasn't born with AIDS. But somehow it would blossom in my body, a type of puberty that occurred when a person came out of the closet. To keep AIDS at bay, I remained safely hidden. By my twisted logic, I could have sex with men, but I wasn't gay; therefore, I would not contract the disease.

The other relief I had was that when those late-night news programs like *20/20* featured people succumbing to AIDS, they were all white men in cities I'd never been to—New York, San Francisco, Chicago, LA. I was Mexican and not yet gay, so I was free to sneak into the beds of other men and orgasm quietly beneath the sheets. The sticky fluid wiped clean with my underwear, which I would push to the bottom of the hamper when I got home.

There was no discussion of safe sex. In fact, there was no discussion of anything. The entire courtship took place with a look and a smile, a gesture and a caress. If neither of us said anything, then no one would really know what kind of pleasure had taken place. Exiting the neighbor's house was like waking up from a dream. Any evidence of intimacy evaporated, except for the excited heartbeat, which was neither visible nor audible.

The white gays of the city met in public places—bars and bathhouses, bus depot bathrooms, park benches and park bushes—their hunger on full display. Our Mexican housing project had none of these things. The only words of caution delivered to us high schoolers were "Don't get pregnant" and "Don't get a girl pregnant." No one ever said, "Don't get AIDS." It must be, I deduced, because that was not an actual danger here.

Public figures who died of AIDS were also white gays. First there was Rock Hudson in 1985. And then Liberace in 1987. Both outed only after their deaths. I was living in the town of Indio at the time, not far from Palm Springs, where Liberace took his final breath. I couldn't stop thinking of the teacher in health class who had remarked, "If you diet, do it responsibly. Don't do like Liberace and his watermelon-only meals. Watermelon is ninety-two percent water. He's going to starve to death." No one had to be convinced that Liberace was gay. But Rock Hudson?

"You would never know, watching all those Doris Day movies," said one of my female friends.

I was about to say that I too felt the loss of this beautiful man but stopped myself in time. I kept my crush on Rock Hudson a secret, like I did everything else. My adolescent desire was burning a hole in my pants and I was afraid to give myself away.

Still, AIDS seemed so far from my everyday reality. It was not perceived as a hazard but as a joke, even long after I graduated from high school. There was that banda song "La ruca no era ruca"

(The chick wasn't a chick), whose catchy tune became so popular on the radio in the '90s. The story: a Chicano gives a ride to a pretty blonde but realizes his mistake when she starts to seduce him. The chick is not a chick; she turns out to be a dude. "Squeeze me, homeboy," she says. And the homeboy replies, "No, because my wrist will go limp." And then she says, "Give me a kiss, homeboy," to which the homeboy replies, "No, because you'll give me AIDS." And finally, that atrocious pun:

Hombre con mujer? No da. (Man with a woman? No infection.)

Hombre con hombre? Sí da. (Man with a man? AIDS.)

The pun would make its way into those silly movies with drunk losers stumbling down the street on their way to the brothels. As long as the whores were not transvestites, there was nothing to fear.

What saved me from becoming HIV-positive as a teenager, except sheer luck? The ignorance and misinformation about AIDS was rampant in my community. The first people I met who were HIV-positive were a white woman who visited my biology class in college and a young white man who spoke at a rally on campus. Both pale, blue-eyed, and dirty blond. I couldn't see myself in either of them. When the biology professor embraced the young woman, I confirmed that my community's belief that AIDS could be transmitted through touch was stupid and wrong.

But that eye-opening moment was still years away when I was in high school. Until then, I had to walk among my peers who shouted insults at the guys who dressed like the members of Duran Duran—feathery hair beneath hats, eyeliner, jackets over T-shirts, and ankle boots.

"They're gays," high schoolers said with the same disinterested tone they used when they pointed to a group of students in the distance and said, "They're sophomores."

They were gays, but no one was afraid of them. Meaning they didn't have AIDS, or rather that AIDS didn't exist where we lived. It was a plague that thrived in places too remote to concern us. And so we moved about carefree and careless, side-eyeing the girls who got pregnant and had to drop out of school.

I wasn't exactly curious about the disease either because I was rarely reminded of it, except by those after-hours reports that were too dull and too educational to attract a young audience. I watched them because I wanted to see what gays looked like. The only one I was familiar with was the one in the mirror. The Duran Duran groupies, I deduced, were not gay; they were just different. The real gays were on TV, dying before our eyes.

Their startling thinness, their sunken eyes, and their aggrieved expressions moved me to tears. I felt sorry for the certainty of their deaths, but I was saddened even more that their bodies were being punished for their unavoidable desires. The damage was exacerbated by the fact that they became exiled from the rest of society, and disowned by their loved ones.

I came across one notable exception. The parents of a man suffering from AIDS were interviewed. The household had gone bankrupt trying to meet the expense of the treatments, which were still experimental then. The father and mother sat in two chairs, their hands on their laps, while the son was prone on the top mattress of a bunk bed. Only his head resting on his arm. He wasn't hiding. He was simply weak, defeated.

"Will you stand by your son to the very end?" the reporter asked.

The father took a deep breath and said, "We don't have quitters in this family. Right, Jackie?"

From the recesses of this scene, a solemn voice responded like an object dropping to the floor in the other room. "Right," Jackie said.

The mother stared blankly at the camera. She had nothing left to say.

I was relieved for Jackie. His blessing was having parents who didn't abandon him. I didn't trust my community, or my family, to respond the same way, so I simply let that part of me dissolve into the everyday heterosexuality I already lived in. That meant tolerating the teasing of the aunties who were always matchmaking whenever the neighbors walked past, arm in arm with their pubescent daughters.

"Rigo should marry Doña Domitila's youngest," one said.

"Oh no, that's a terrible choice," the other said. "Doña Domitila would make a horrible mother-in-law."

"You're right," the first agreed. "Too involved with her children. How about Doña Rosita's girl? She's already a teenager by now."

"But she walks funny. Pigeon-toed, I think."

Straightness was out in the open, so uncomplicated and natural. What I had was secretive and shameful. I wasn't sure I even had a word for it. All the ones tossed out by my cousins and friends were charged with derision and hatred. Only on one occasion was the topic of homosexuality not shot down with contempt.

"They say guys turn gay if women don't give them the time of day," a young man said once. The guys had gathered in the evening around a small fire to tell stories and make jokes. That statement made everyone go so quiet that suddenly the crackling of the wood became loud. They stared intently into the flames until someone finally broke the uncomfortable silence with a laugh-inducing fart.

That moment stayed with me because I sensed that young man was trying to reveal something about himself. But such an admission was not going to find a sympathetic ear in this gathering of male adolescents who liked to talk dirty and shove their stinky socks under each other's noses. If anyone was willing to listen, it was me. I, too, didn't understand the origin of my desire. But I was too afraid to disclose my doubts and insecurities about sexuality because this crowd, most of them my cousins, would not admit to not knowing something. As males, they had to move through the world with confidence and authority.

I never saw that young man again. Maybe he was never invited to join the group again. Maybe he made that decision on his own. And maybe, I said to myself to ease my own guilt, he was no longer adrift but had found the shore he was looking for.

On another occasion, I was working on the layout of *Sandscripts* by myself. The young man who sat at the same table I did in English class must have seen me as he walked by the open door.

"What are you doing?" he asked as he stepped into the classroom. He was not particularly attractive. In fact, of the guys who sat with me at the table, he was the one I glanced at the least. He was too skinny and pale, and he was the rudest of the bunch, tossing balls of paper at the table of overachievers, who ignored him and never dared complain to the teacher.

"I'm working on the next issue of the newspaper," I answered and kept to my task.

"That's nice," he said.

There was something chilling about the way he said that. A strange combination of condescension and ridicule. He had pitched his voice a bit higher, which I knew was a mocking imitation of my own voice. I swallowed hard and stayed focused. One thing I had learned about bullies was that they didn't let something go if they knew it was inflicting discomfort or pain.

A strange silence filled the room, except for the sound of my pencil drawing lines along the side of the metal ruler. I shifted my body to see what he was doing. I didn't want to be surprised by a flying object. My body froze and immediately I began to sweat. He was arousing himself, the outline of his erection quite visible beneath his pants.

I wasn't sure if this was an invitation or a trap, something he would use to torment me for the rest of the school year.

"You can do what you want with it," he said. This time his voice struck a different timbre altogether. It was more of a seductive whisper.

I was no stranger to men's penises. But I had only slept with Mexican men, no white ones. That's when those images came flooding into my brain. The anxious mouths, the skeletal frames, the sunken eyes, the dark bruises on colorless flesh. *This is how I get AIDS,* I thought to myself. *This is how I die.* The sweat came pouring off me and down on the paper layout, blurring the perfect pencil lines. I turned my head, nauseated and dizzy. I began to shake, rattling the ruler on the table.

He must have seen how close to having a seizure I was that he did something I had not thought him capable of: he took pity on me.

"Hey," he said. "It's all right. I'm not going to hurt you."

He rose from his seat and placed his arm on my back, tapping lightly, the way my mother used to do when she had me bend over a pan of hot water and VapoRub with a towel over my head so that the fumes could clear my sinuses. Her touch was reassuring and gave me the strength to hold my pose.

I began to cry. I had done wrong to this young man, despite his initial mocking act. I had just demonstrated the most homophobic reaction. And in the end, he didn't want to hurt me, not really. He wanted me to see in him something he saw in himself, or something he saw in me. And what did I see in myself but a clandestine lover who surrendered to the closeted men in the neighborhood because only in the dark, and only for a moment, could we experience our true selves?

His tenderness consumed me. I wanted to tell him I didn't deserve it. I wanted to let him know what a coward and complete asshole I was to project on him what I feared most—a sickness that I knew I was susceptible to, especially in my Catholic community because none of us used condoms, but that was okay because only the white gays and junkies got AIDS.

But I didn't tell him anything. I stopped the sobbing and the shaking. And he appeared relieved. Neither of us wanted this moment to move past the lunch hour. The bell was about to ring and everyone would come rushing in.

"You okay?" he asked.

"I'm okay," I said.

Those were the last words we ever said to each other. During English class he returned to being that troublemaker in the back of the room. Though I noticed that he never picked on me again. I avoided eye contact as much as I could. But once in a while I glanced over. And if he caught me looking, I turned my gaze immediately. Graduation was in a few months. Senioritis was widespread because we were anxious to grow up and take our first taste of independence. I, too, was itching to leave the school, the town, the neighborhood, my house. I was going away to college like many others. But I was off to discover all those things never discussed by either my high school teachers or my family.

Less than a year later I would have my first sexual experience in college. When my date pulled out a condom from his backpack I stared at it with amazement. We were still calling them rubbers at the time, just like the horny teenagers in the slasher flicks.

"We don't want to make any babies," he joked.

I must have chuckled, but it was tinged with disappointment that, in 1989, we still were not acknowledging the real purpose for protection.

Hockey Night in Canada

BEREND MCKENZIE

EDMONTON, 1984

I am underage and working in the gay bars. Randy is a waiter. I am a busboy. Randy is bearded and into leather. I am small and effeminate. I am told I look like a girl. He has a laugh that fills the room and his eyes dance with mischief as he chases men around the bar. Randy is always having sex and I am jealous because it isn't ever with me.

Randy gives me a key to his apartment so I always have a place to go. He sleeps in and I clean up while watching soap operas and *The Oprah Winfrey Show*. One day I hear Oprah talking about "the gay cancer." Her guest is a man with purple marks on his face.

You are going to die of that.

I push the thought out of my head and take the dirty dishes to the kitchen.

One day Randy asks me to meet him at his favorite restaurant at four in the afternoon. He has to tell me something. He is drunk and has been crying.

I have it, the cancer, the gay fucking cancer.

As he speaks, I can see the same purple blemish on his temple that the guy on *Oprah* had. I reach across the table and grab his hands. He cries and drinks until he is falling out of his chair. I ask for the check and take him home.

The next day he is up early. He is cheerful and resolute, like nothing is wrong.

I need you to take care of the cats. I'm going to travel: New York, San Fran, and Boston. I'm calling it my Screw You Tour. I'm going to fuck my way across America and give it to everyone that gave it to me!

I am left alone in his apartment for a month. I am lonely and depressed. It all starts to sink in. He is going to die soon. I can hear it in his voice. Every time he calls me, he sounds weaker. I can feel the walls closing in on me. Everyone I know and care about is now getting sick.

Randy phones me late one night, wasted.

I'm coming home. I'm ready.

I light candles in the bedroom and change the sheets on his bed. Randy looks so different from the man who left a month ago. He has lost most of his body fat and his face looks like a wooden puppet. The purple splotches are everywhere. I sit him on the edge of the bed and take his hand in mine.

Sleep with me. Have sex with me so I can die with you.

His eyes flash with rage. Spit flies out of his mouth as he screams inches from my face.

You selfish fuck! You have everything going for you. Look at me! Look at my face! I am covered with fucking lesions! You are pristine and young and smart and beautiful. Where do you get off asking me to kill you? Get out! Get out of my fucking house!

He kicks me out of his apartment and refuses to see me again. I am busing tables at the bar when one of Randy's fuck buddies tells me that he is dead.

I am sixteen years old.

VANCOUVER, 1994

The lesions on my legs keep moving up. The sores cover my feet from the tips of my toes to just above my ankles and show no signs of stopping. I have nerve damage and my feet are hypersensitive to the touch. Even a bedsheet brushing against them makes me scream out in agony.

The specialist says this is because the AIDS virus has nowhere to go, so it is settling in my extremities. Feet first. Hands later. His main concern is to control the pain and stop the spread of the lesions. If he can't, they may have to consider amputation.

I have been placed on a number of pain pills but have built up a resistance to them. Now I am on liquid morphine, which I can administer myself every four hours through a shunt in my arm.

The doctors don't know about my addictions:

Cocaine ...

Alcohol ...

Sleeping pills ...

Antianxiety medications ...

Valium ...

Morphine ...

Dilaudid ...

NeoCitran ...

My trips to the doctor are exhausting and I get in bed as soon as I arrive home. The ringing phone jolts me out of my sleep. I hear a tired voice on the other end.

It's time.

Tom is whispering. He doesn't want to wake up Billy-Boy's mom, dad, and brother, who arrived yesterday. Billy-Boy's family disowned him after he came out of the closet. They just showed up out of the blue when they heard he didn't have much time left.

Tom is an angel who stepped in to help when Billy-Boy needed care. They met in Edmonton and moved out to Vancouver together when they were teenagers in the early '80s. Tom and I dated the same man at separate times. We became fast friends.

If you want to say good-bye, now is the time. The doctor says he won't make it through the night. The guys will pick you up in about an hour.

I hear noises in the background that sound like an animal moaning. Tom says he has to go and hangs up the phone.

My pain right now is really bad and I have to get it under control before Sandy and the other guys pick me up. I hate taking this drug with me everywhere I go, so I load up my syringe with extra cc's of morphine and push it through the shunt. I pack a flap of leftover cocaine in case I need to take the edge off, and I wait.

I examine my bloodshot eyes in Billy-Boy's bathroom mirror. I wipe the last remnants of cocaine off the tip of my nose. I look like shit.

The familiar feeling of numbness mixed with stinging in my feet is starting to return, which means the last hit of morphine is wearing off. I should have brought some with me. Hopefully, I won't be here too much longer.

I open the bathroom door and I see the three factions. In one corner of the living room, Billy-Boy's family sits watching the hockey game. At the opposite end, and squished into the dining room, are fifteen of his closest friends, ranging from my age to the respected old guard of our community, the Gaggle of Gays. In the middle of the living room, separating good and evil, lies Billy-Boy, moaning on the Hide-A-Bed.

We've been here for hours. The doctor said he would be dead soon, but Billy-Boy is being stubborn, as usual.

When Greasy Dad, Scraggy Mom, and Stinky Son arrived, they insisted on taking over the bedroom. This meant that Billy-Boy and Tom had to set up camp in the living room.

The Gaggle of Gays talk in hushed voices. We have all lived this death scene before, especially the elders: disrespectful relatives swoop in and infect everything with their religious dogma and hatred.

The New York Rangers are up 3–2 in the last quarter of the final period. The Canucks need to score once more to force the game into overtime. The family's stress is palpable.

I hate hockey, but this is the first time in years that the Vancouver Canucks have gotten into the Stanley Cup Finals. If we win, the police are expecting Vancouverites to flood the streets in celebration. I wish Billy-Boy weren't sick because then we would be getting into drag and joining the party. We're gay, not stupid.

Tom waves me over to the kitchen.

You okay? You're sweating like a pig.

Pigs don't sweat, I say. *And besides, that's a cliché.*

Tom ignores the joke and presses on.

I need to change his diaper and I need some help. Can you grab Sandy, Richard, and David?

I wade through the cramped dining room as the haze of cigarettes and pot hits my throat. Some people are talking quietly while taking quick glances at the game. Others stand alone, lost in thought, or stare helplessly at Billy-Boy. We've learned through the years to give each other space to grieve the way we need to.

The zombie noises coming from Billy-Boy are only muffled by the volume of the television and his family screaming at the game.

I see Sandy and Richard sharing a quiet chuckle. Sandy is a six-foot-four ex-football player. He is a dreamboat with a handlebar moustache and cowboy boots. He grins widely when he sees me.

Hey. What's up, bud?

I like it when he calls me that. I ask Sandy and Richard if they would mind helping Tom. They clink beer bottles and chug down the rest of their liquid courage. Sandy winks at me as they turn and walk toward Billy-Boy.

David is leaning against the wall in the corner. I don't like him, but shit like this puts things into perspective. He looks scared when I ask him to help us. I put my arm through his for support and meet the others near the Hide-A-Bed.

Tom is wearing rubber gloves and a face mask; he carries a basin, some towels, and a fresh diaper. I am nervous as I stand across from David, near Billy-Boy's shoulders, while Sandy and Richard take their places across from each other at Billy's waist. My stomach begins to turn as the morphine withdrawal kicks in.

I can't stop looking at Billy-Boy's emaciated body. I see my future. A shiver rushes through me and I think I am going to be sick.

The hockey commentator's voice fills the room:

And welcome back to Hockey Night in Canada, *where the New York Rangers lead the Vancouver Canucks at the bottom of the third. The players have headed to their respective boxes as Vancouver calls for a time-out. What an action-packed event ...*

We huddle around Billy-Boy to get instructions from Tom. He is going to change Billy's diaper, and then we are to lift him off the bed so he can change the sheet. I am not the best at following instructions, so I try to listen intently.

Tom unlatches the sticky tape on the front of the diaper and pulls it down. I close my eyes and fight back the pangs of nausea that overtake my stomach.

What's that smell?

Greasy Dad is holding his nose. Tom keeps his head down and completes the task.

Okay, Billy-Boy. We are going to roll you onto your side and get you all cleaned up for the big drag ball, dear.

Billy-Boy responds to this with his zombie noise.

Greasy Dad makes a comment about not being able to hear the game and Scraggy Mom rises to turn up the TV.

I close my eyes as we roll Billy-Boy's atrophied body out of his shit-soaked diaper, and pain wrenches through my stomach. The morphine withdrawal is taking over as Tom tells us it is now time to lift Billy up and change the sheet. Tom looks at me and I hear him say ...

I've got his head.

Tom counts us down.

One ...

Two ...

Three ...

Lift!

The referee blows his whistle for the final face-off. The puck hits the ice and hockey sticks clash against each another. Everyone in the family leaps to their feet, screaming at their team.

Something isn't right. Billy-Boy is trying to sit up on his own. His head is stretched forward until his chin touches his chest.

Tom's voice pierces the chaos.

His head! I told you to grab his fucking head!

I go to move my hand as I hear the commentator shriek ...

And the New York Rangers score!

But I am too late.

Billy-Boy's body suddenly relaxes like a popped balloon and his head snaps backwards with a loud crack.

We all freeze.

The sound of the stadium full of people celebrating erupts as the five of us hold Billy midair.

We gently lower his body onto the bed.

Greasy Dad gets up from the La-Z-Boy and shuts off the television. He turns and faces the sobbing boys in the dining room and proclaims:

The Canucks were always a bunch of wimpy faggots.

I run to the washroom and throw up in the toilet.

I sit in the passenger seat of Sandy's car and stare out the window as he drives us all home. David and Richard are in the back seat. We are all silent as we watch the crowds gather on the sidewalks. Sandy breaks the silence.

Fucking breeders.

He goes back to humming softly to the Garth Brooks song playing on the radio. My head rests against the coolness of the window. My stomach is twisted in pain from the morphine withdrawal. I can't stop sweating. A shudder of guilt rips through my body. Sandy notices and places his large hand on my leg.

It's okay, little buddy. It was an accident. We aren't doctors and I hate how this shit always falls on us. The dude hated hockey anyway. You did him a favor.

Laughter shoots out of me with sudden violence, and it feels good.

There are now thousands of angry hockey fans flooding Robson Street. The farther we get, the slower we go. The mass of people has turned into an enraged mob. A group of men push over a telephone booth. A little ways farther a car has been set on fire. Store windows are smashed and people run in front of the car, loaded down with clothing they snatched from Gap.

We need to get off this street.

As the car passes a back alley, Sandy jerks the steering wheel to the left as a car goes up in flames. He breathes out deeply.

I fucking hate hockey.

VANCOUVER, 2020

I close my computer and put it in my bag. I grab my bottle of hand sanitizer and rub a ton of it in past my wrists. This is the sixth time I've done this since I arrived at the airport. My fingers are beginning to crack because of dryness, so I grab my hand cream. My phone rings and I see it's Tom.

After Billy-Boy passed away, Tom and I went our separate ways, but we always kept in touch. I moved into a recovery house to get sober. I just celebrated twenty-one years clean and sober. Tom works with the homeless on Vancouver's Downtown Eastside.

It's great to hear his voice. He sounds jovial and happy-go-lucky, like always. He says he's been working hard. Busy with friends. Writing a lot. Then he says he called to remind me that it has been just over twenty-six years since Billy-Boy passed.

"Weren't we supposed to be dead by now?"

We laugh a bit at that and throw out the names of other people we've lost.

"What about David and Richard? Didn't they die around a year or so after Billy?"

His voice changes as the list grows. My throat starts getting tight. I decide to lighten the mood.

"You know, Sandy and I made a pact that if we lived through this and were both still single ten years later, we would get married. He knew it would be hell living with me, so, well, you know ... he's gone now."

Tom says he has to get back to work but wanted to say hi, and he asks me to keep in touch.

"I'm glad you called, Tom. Take care." I hang up the phone and dab at my eye. Tears. Even now.

A man in a suit paces back and forth in front of me while talking on his phone. Terms like "stock market," "unprecedented," and "401(k)" come out of his mouth at rapid speed.

A family walks by. They are very tan and look exhausted. The kids lag behind their parents as the dad prattles on. His booming voice and thick Australian accent are loud enough for everyone to hear. His wife looks embarrassed as he shouts into the phone that he doesn't have to wash his hands if he doesn't want to.

I grab my hand sanitizer.

An announcement comes over the intercom, apologizing for the delay, but "Due to current health concerns, the airline is taking extra precautions to ensure your safety on this flight."

The plane is full, but eerily silent, as I board.

There is a woman wearing sunglasses and a surgical mask sitting in the window seat in my row. I am relieved that the middle seat is empty. I put my bags away and take out my sanitizing wipes. I wipe down the television screen, armrests, and tray before settling down.

I pull out my hand sanitizer once more. Before I put it away, I turn to the woman next to me. She is reading the *National Post*. COVID-19 CASES SPIKE IN 24 HOURS is splashed across the front page.

I offer her the bottle of sanitizer and she says no thank you, she just applied some. I lean back in my chair and breathe out, grateful to be going back to the safety of my own home in Edmonton.

A voice clear as a bell rings in my ears ...

You will survive this.

The woman next to me puts down the paper and says how disappointed she is that the NHL has canceled the hockey season because of the virus. She asks if I'm a fan.

"No. I hate hockey."

Billy-Boy would be so proud.

OPEN 24 HOURS

NELS P. HIGHBERG

Adult bookstores made me the gay man I am today. Perhaps that sounds hyperbolic, but my experiences in these spaces had the greatest influence on the attitudes about sexuality and identity that I currently hold. After growing up in a small town of about 5,000 people in south Texas, I moved into the University of Houston dorms in August 1988. Over the next five years, I read a lot of books and sucked a lot of dick. I regularly patronized several adult bookstores throughout Houston and the neighboring suburbs, sometimes several times a week. The back rooms drew me in, hallways lined with booths, each containing a small television set built into the wall, constantly flickering pornographic films of all stripes as men would lock themselves in these booths or slowly cruise the halls. Oh, there were glory holes between most of the rooms, too.

All those years, and all those men, and there is probably one fact that is the most unbelievable: I never swallowed. I don't use "never" to mean "rarely." I mean that I never did it. I turned nineteen and approached college life in the city knowing what AIDS was. I was even able to understand the difference between that syndrome and HIV, the virus itself. And I was terrified. AIDS equaled death. I would see it with my own eyes. The thing was, everyone else felt pretty much the same way. Safe sex (and this was before "safe" became "safer") was the only option, and in these back rooms, ejaculation was almost always instigated by our own hands while standing, in various states of undress, come aimed into the corners or onto crumpled tissues for those who had planned ahead. I became a top because my mind kept my own ass clamped: HIV could not enter if the door was always locked tight. My mouth, however, was open.

I have always wondered why I went back so easily, why I was not afraid enough to avoid sex, or at least try. I would later meet men who survived by doing just that. Is it dismissive to regard my constant visits amid fear as the hormones of a horny teenager, or overreaching to treat this as something more? Maybe I was pissed at having just spent an adolescence watching a whole lot of straight people make out, even if there was no way I would have articulated it as such at the time. If anything, I spent high school thankful I was never really pushed into dating. Comments were made, rumors were circulated, but I was largely left alone. No one saw the three novels I bought in Austin senior year: Edmund White's *A Boy's Own Story*, John Fox's *The Boys on the Rock*, and Larry Kramer's *Faggots*. Those books taught me a lot of different things, but they also turned me on. I arrived in Houston as a skinny white guy, nineteen, with what I would later call a daddy fetish. Adult bookstores made it so damn easy.

I won't say shame was not a factor in why I had to go into the back, into the dark, to touch men. For a while, sure, I would have been terrified if anyone had recognized me, even though they would have likely been doing the same things. Later, I would stop caring. Had my shame transformed into pride? Or is it too simple to ask that, too? Two things drew me to adult bookstores: the movies and the men. The first film I saw on the night I entered an adult bookstore for the first time (September 21, 1988) featured two young white men, one blond and one brunet, shirtless and washing a '70s van to a disco soundtrack. By contemporary standards, the film was banal. There was a water fight that led to the removal of their cutoffs; sex followed. There was oral sex and anal sex, but the image I can still recall with precision is when they first kissed. It was the first time I had ever seen two men kiss. To see men kiss for the first time, I could not rely on the thirteen television channels in the house where I grew up, or the six-screen movie theater thirty miles away in the next county over. I had to drive two hours to Houston, pay a three-dollar admission, walk down a hallway with only one flickering, unshaded lightbulb above the main door, and step into a booth with balled-up tissues likely containing the semen of at least one man nestled in the corners. I journaled about the kiss, but there was more I could not articulate then. The entire time these two guys fucked, they smiled and laughed. They said nice things to each other. They made happy noises. They showed no signs of fear or embarrassment.

After watching the guys in the van, I stepped into the hallway. A bearded man in a cowboy hat smiled at me. I followed him into another booth, and I kissed a man for the very first time. He invited me to his apartment about a mile away. The first night I saw two men kiss was the first night I kissed a man, which turned out also to be the first night I would ever roll a condom down my own incredibly excited penis and engage in anal sex, whereupon I experienced the biggest orgasm of my life and the first not caused by my own hand (or the mouth of that guy a year earlier from Free Enterprise and Christianity Week at Dallas Baptist University). It was a big night. All thanks to an adult bookstore.

My entire sex life was not located in the bookstores, but these were places where I met men who played both minor and major roles in my development as a gay man. Like one guy who took me to my first gay bar on the other side of town, where I saw men two-stepping and line dancing just like at my high school prom, but with nary a woman in sight. With another man I experienced the birth of what would be called New Queer Cinema when he took me to see Gregg Araki's *The Living End*, a film that depicts the murder of a homophobic cop followed by a road trip taken by two gay men, one a hustler and one a film critic, both HIV-positive; it was one of the first overtly gay films I ever saw in a multiscreen Cineplex and something I would write about in grad school just a handful of years later.

I experienced humiliations, too, whatever romanticizations I have presented so far. I liked scruffy, pot-bellied married guys long before I became one, but lust could alchemize into disgust instantaneously after a comment, say, post-blow job: "You'd be cute if you went to the gym." There were guys who wanted to fuck me, always with condoms but not with my consent. It would take more than one "No" or "Stop," usually loud enough for anyone in the hall to hear, for these guys to back off. I'm sure others were not so lucky.

I was a college student living the life I was supposed to be living, or at least my particularly queer version of one. I had stories to share with my slowly expanding group of gay friends, to get everyone laughing at a party in the dorms or generate sympathy at three a.m., when we were squeezed into a booth together at House of Pies. Only one other guy admitted to having been to adult bookstores, in his neighborhood on the other side of town. We ran into each other between classes one spring semester and came up with a game while sitting on the benches outside the library. How long would it take before you'd go into a booth with a particular man walking by? Like that guy in the camouflage cap, or the Spanish professor who walked out with all the books? At least twenty minutes for the guy with the work-study job at the circulation desk but under five for the beautiful new history professor with the sleeve-busting arms.

OCTOBER 1991

I swung by a bookstore on the edge of downtown on a Wednesday night, turned a corner in the hallway, and saw a man at the end standing with the booth door fully open, the light from the TV illuminating his face. He smiled at me. He didn't reach for his crotch, tweak his nipples, or wave me inside. He just smiled, bulbous cheeks up against his glasses and a little shine off his balding head. I stepped in and shut the door. We kissed, turning our heads in different directions, and never thought of unbuttoning or unzipping anything, even with moans and slaps of skin against skin emanating from the porn around us.

We exchanged numbers in the parking lot, but it took a few weeks before either of us called the other. I'm not sure who called whom first, but we developed a pattern of eating cheap Chinese food and watching used videotapes from Blockbuster. One Sunday, on my couch watching *Backdraft* for the sweaty, heroic men, Blane asked if I'd ever thought of moving the furniture around. I had everything shoved up against the walls. So we turned the couch perpendicular to one wall, and Blane grabbed a little table from the bedroom and told me to get a couple of the posters that were rolled up in the closet. I keep wanting to write that he turned the house into a home, so why balk at that? I felt one way residing within those four walls before Blane arrived in my life, and quite a different way after.

One night on that couch, he told me he was HIV-positive. His lover of three years had died of AIDS a year earlier, but Blane waited to get tested until after the funeral. I asked about his doctor, and he told me things were good with his health. It didn't occur to me to stop seeing him. If anything, it finally made sense why he wasn't interested in pursuing anal sex and was happy with hours of making out in bed or on the couch or in the car.

I had always said I would go to graduate school after college, somewhere out of state since everyone said it would be good for me to stretch and learn in a new environment. The thought of choosing career over a man was not something I had ever expected to encounter. I never even knew two men could have a relationship. Meals and movies, maybe, and orgasms for sure, but a life? Finally, one night I broke down and told him how afraid I was, not that he would die but that I would have to leave him behind in Texas while I went to Ohio or New York or Illinois. He said there was no reason for him to stay without me. Having grown up in Pennsylvania, he really liked the idea of Ohio and told me I'd love Ohio State. I sent letters all around asking for applications.

On May 15, 1992, we stood with a few dozen friends for what the African American woman from the city's gay church who was officiating called "A Rite of Blessing." We had grocery store sheet cake and a CD player playing "The Nightingale," by Julee Cruise, written by David Lynch and Angelo Badalamenti and performed by Cruise in the premiere episode of *Twin Peaks*. A coworker from the photography gallery I worked at took so many photos of everyone and everything. Friends gave us wineglasses and soup bowls and butter dishes.

Blane and I went to bed in his condo that night, both exhausted, but his exhaustion didn't improve with rest. He stayed in bed for days. Whenever I was home, he wanted the room kept dark except for the lamp by my side of the bed, and the radio by his side turned to an R&B/soul station, Anita Baker and Sade being his favorite singers. I'd help him into the bathroom every few hours when I was home, though he barely ate or drank anything. Every couple of days, he asked me to lower him into the empty tub so he could fill it only after I'd left, his spine growing more prominent as the days passed. I called the number on his jury duty notice to say he wouldn't make it. The woman kept telling me he had no choice until I finally blurted out, "He has AIDS!" She hung up.

I think Blane had put all of his energy into making it through the ceremony, and I was too wrapped up in our preparations and finishing the semester to notice any changes, too self-absorbed or naïve or young to ask questions. Yeah, there was the emergency room visit in April when his coughs turned out to be thrush, but a couple of prescriptions later, he was fine. I never understood what all of the pills in the bathroom were really for, but I made sure he followed each label's directions.

In June, Blane called his mother and brother when I was at the gallery. They showed up to take him back to Pennsylvania. Blane told me, "I made a promise to myself that you would not stop your life to take care of me." My mother and stepfather drove up from my hometown the day before Blane flew out to Pennsylvania. I said good-bye as fast as I could. He was still in bed.

On Sunday, July 12, 1992, I called Blane after my mother and I had gotten home from church. His brother's wife answered. "Oh, no one's here. Blane died this morning, and everyone's still at the hospital." His mother never said not to come to the funeral, but she did tell me it was going to be a Catholic funeral, in a Catholic church, several times. The obituary his brother mailed to me said Blane died from pancreatic cancer. The funeral itself was on July 15, two months to the day after our Rite of Blessing. I asked that he be buried with his ring. His mother sent it back to me.

I had another year left of college. The art gallery where I worked kept my job for me when the school year began, and I took over the apartment of a friend leaving for grad school. My car died, but I had my first credit card and bought a red Suzuki moped and rode it on the side streets between my apartment and my job in the museum district and campus just a few miles away. Getting to the adult bookstores was not a problem, though I never returned to the one where I met Blane. I could be at the Gaslight on Bissonnet Street outside Bellaire in twenty minutes (the largest bookstores always sat just beyond the more conservative, fully incorporated towns in and around Houston). My friend Richard would sometimes drive by and know I was inside because even in a city that large, few guys owned mopeds, and no one else was parking theirs outside an adult bookstore. Richard couldn't criticize, though, since we had met right there in the Gaslight's hallways by booth thirteen a couple of months before graduation.

That summer, we even went to the Gaslight together, usually after a Saturday night at Heaven or JR's near Montrose and Westheimer, Houston's unofficially official gay district. We would sometimes end up in an orgy together in the larger main room that always switched from straight to gay porn after midnight. Sometimes, one of us would wait while the other finished up in a booth with someone else. After we returned to his car, he would often say, "You really do have the worst taste in men." I'd remind him I found him attractive. "Exactly," he'd respond.

But dating was the last thing on my mind, especially with graduate school around the corner. I was going to find out if Blane was right that I would love Ohio State. The night before my departure for Columbus, after Richard and I had a huge Tex-Mex dinner at Cafe Adobe, I hopped on the moped and went to the Gaslight. It was about midnight. There was a goateed guy in Wranglers and a blue-and-white chambray shirt. I always thought Wranglers framed a man's ass and crotch perfectly. In a booth, I got on my knees and stayed there, feeling his wedding ring against the back of my head.

Relationship to Fear

EJ COLEN

1988

In the unoccupied girls' locker room between lunch periods a boy named Asher licks the side of your face and runs his fingers over the back strap of your bra. You can smell peanut butter on his breath and a light scent of body odor, which you hold on to as something to remember and think about later.

"Show me your bra," he says. If it had been a question. Part of you still wants to. You are one of only three girls in the sixth grade who wear one.

"No," you say.

"You're fat," he says.

You shrug.

"You're a fat whore."

"I don't think you know what that means."

In health class you play a kind of bingo about all the ways one could catch AIDS. You make a list of images drawn in boxes and a "Yes can catch AIDS"/"No can't catch AIDS" to circle next to each.

Answer key:

Share a razor?	**Yes** / No
Share a toothbrush?	**Yes** / No
Share utensils?	**Yes** / No
Deep kissing?	**Yes** / No
A kiss on the cheek?	Yes / **No**

You note, even then, you and Cass, there is no question about sex. "Isn't sex how most people get it?" you ask. Cass is sexually active already, though you try not to think about that. Or about how the boys seem way too much older than her. You try not to think about whether she uses a condom.

In class Asher stares at the side of your head from two rows away. You can feel it.

Later, he will tell you he's glad he never kissed you, glad he didn't let you suck his dick. He tells you that you are "a fat whore with AIDS."

Your interest in boys is strong, and you will kiss them every chance you get. You decide mouths are fine—the information you are taught is constantly evolving—but penises are not worth the risk. And so you never do more than touch them.

"Please," all three boyfriends you have in high school ask.

But even if they go down on you, you refuse to reciprocate.

1994

Mel was getting fucked by a self-proclaimed slut when the condom broke in his ass. This was months ago. Mel has sex with a lot of people. But he hasn't done anything since.

"You have to go," you say. You say you'll go with him.

"I don't want to know," he says.

"Why?"

"False positives."

You know the latest test avoids most of that. "Bullshit," you say.

"Okay, I just don't want to know. I always said I wouldn't want to know. I'm worried someone will find out I got tested at all; that I was worried about it. They're looking for any reason to fire me at work." But, finally, he says he'll go, go to the clinic, give up some blood, take a number, wait for the call.

"I don't think I want to do this," he says when he meets you at the clinic.

"What if I do it too? You know I hate needles."

You go inside.

You have a doctor at the time who says you don't need Pap smears if you aren't having sex with men. Won't perform them.

"My mother had cervical cancer," you tell her.

"It doesn't matter." The doctor doesn't say she's uncomfortable treating lesbians, but you get that impression and you never go back. You will go years without going to a doctor at all.

Mel gets his paperwork, starts to fill it out.

"I want to get tested too," you tell the man behind the desk. He looks skeptical before you even open your mouth.

"Are you sexually active?" Your haircut, your baggy clothes, the BUSH HATES ME BECAUSE I LOVE BUSH pin on your lapel.

"Quite," you say.

"With men?"

"No."

"You don't need this test."

No questions about your sexual history, your drug history.

"I want the test."

He shrugs and pushes the clipboard at you.

Two weeks later, the results. You're both negative. Mel waits three years to get tested again. You think being told he was negative once was enough for him to convince himself he would be safe. Three years later, Mel will test positive, but you're still not ready to talk about that.

1994

Sam comes home from the bookstore with a pocket full of dental dams, puts them on the kitchen table in front of you, and says, "We're trying these tonight."

You laugh. You've been exclusive almost four months.

"I'm not kidding," she says. "We're having safe sex tonight. I want to see what it's like."

"For when you finally decide to have sex with that girl you work with? So you don't bring something home?"

"Exactly, I want to know how it works."

That night, you open the plastic packaging, carefully unfold the tiny square of latex, and take turns spreading it over each other's parts and licking.

"This isn't fun," she says. "I can't taste anything but plastic."

"It's certainly different," you say, laughing.

You pull a condom out of her bedside table and cut the tip off the way the instructions she'd found somewhere had said to do, cut a slit up the side, and open it up. You try all the ways the pamphlet suggested. Knowing this is likely to be the only time either of you try this experiment.

Later that night, before drifting off to sleep, you tell her, "Just don't go down on her without talking to me first, okay? And I can decide if I want to stick around."

1997

You and Peter go out dancing every weekend and every weekend he stays at your house because it's walkable from Backstreet and he's usually too fucked up and that way he won't go home with some random guy. The first time he stays on the couch, but your room mate says it's unacceptable to have to tiptoe around a stranger until two in the afternoon. So he stays in your bed and it's nice and you giggle and talk about the boys he has seen and the girls you have seen and you say how happy you are you're both single so you can curl around each other telling stories and laughing until you fall asleep at six a.m. every Saturday night/Sunday morning. Then one night he kisses your mouth to say good night and you open your mouth a little and the next thing you know you're making out and after that that's how you go to bed every Saturday night, Sunday morning, talking a little and then making out for a long, long time. "You're a really good kisser," Peter says. "You too," you say. And you are usually out of your mind on MDMA or coming down and in any case it feels especially good to have a mouth on you and a few times he kisses your tits because they fascinate him and they don't really feel like they belong to you, so it doesn't matter to you, but it never goes any further than that.

Then Peter moves to New York with some guy he dated the year before and you don't hear from him for a long time. Your feelings aren't too hurt, though, because you have his number and you haven't called him either.

You run into a mutual friend at a party one night maybe six, maybe eight, months later, who tells you Peter got sick and has been in the hospital a few weeks.

"I guess he had a regular cold that turned into the flu or something and then a respiratory infection that landed him in the hospital and he's been there ever since."

"Is his mother there?"

"She is, yes," he tells you.

"Do you have his number?" you ask. And he shakes his head no but says he can find it and get back to you and he never does and when you run into him again another month later in Publix he tells you that Peter died the week after he saw you and he was sorry not to have let you know. And that the understanding is it was AIDS related, that Peter hadn't known he was positive and he was fine until he wasn't and then it was over.

"But the obituary only said flu," he says. "Can you fucking believe that?"

"Had he never gotten tested?"

"I think not," he said. "But I don't really know."

And suddenly you're standing in the chip aisle in Publix thinking about Peter pulling your hair and how you'd bite his lip sometimes because of that. Sometimes a bit too hard, but all in good fun. Once or twice to the point of blood. "You fucker," he would say. And you would tell him he was the fucker and to stop pulling your hair so hard and at least one time there was blood on his shirt in the morning. "Did I do that?" you had said. "Who the fuck else?" he had said. You're standing in the chip aisle and your mind is racing, but everything around you is still and the guy who has just given you this information is standing there silently watching it all sink in and the low static that has been present the whole time, the humming from the fluorescent lights, seems to fill the space and then the music that had somehow paused starts up again and Madonna's "La Isla Bonita" comes on.

1997

You feel like an asshole for not sleeping with her. You find out on the second date she did sex work all through the early '90s, until late last year, and though you keep going on dates with her, because you really like her, the conversation is good, goes deep immediately, and the chemistry between the two of you is strong, you never get past making out, grinding around on her couch some, sometimes getting her off manually, before you head home. After date five, you realize you're being shitty to the both of you and you call it off. You recognize that she's probably a lot safer than many of the girls you've been with, some of whom you knew let guys fuck them unprotected all the time. Girls who slept with guys and never got tested. And this girl was open about her history, all of it, what it looked like, the times she had been scared, the way she handled those things. Things you didn't even ask. Said that it was always as safe as possible. And that she's been tested so many times.

You tell a friend and she says, "That's a hard pass for me."

This doesn't make you feel better.

From the Inside

One Prisoner's Perspective

TIMOTHY JONES

From ages six to eighteen, I lived in various institutions run by the state of Colorado. The continuous forms of abuse I suffered while in those institutions is a story all its own, but one aspect of being raised in this manner was that I was secluded from the outside world. After my release at age eighteen, in 1986, I only lasted two years in society before coming to prison on my current sentence. I've spent the past thirty-two years as a guest of the Florida Department of Corrections.

During my time on the street between 1986 and 1988, I was a transient, moving around a lot and surviving through prostitution and by occasionally breaking into stores at night. The gay clubs where I hung out had a regular crowd that showed up every weekend, and we all knew there was this disease called AIDS running wild, but no one wanted to talk about it.

The few times that AIDS was discussed, it was always in somber tones and tinged with fear. Conversations about AIDS were kept short, as if discussing it for too long would bring the silent killer into our midst. HIV was never mentioned; it was always AIDS. Everybody had their own theories, most of them centering on the government. The government created the AIDS virus to kill (depending on who you were talking to) gays, Blacks, drug users, lower-class people, prostitutes, or all of the above.

The year that I was in the county jail, I completely forgot about AIDS. Jail was a world within itself, and if there were AIDS patients in the jail, they were kept on the medical wing separate from the rest of us.

Upon entering prison in 1989, my HIV/AIDS orientation consisted of a redneck corrections officer telling us, "AIDS will kill you. If you don't want to catch it, then keep your dick out of other men's asses and keep dicks out of your own butts. Don't get involved in any of that faggot shit, and you won't die."

In Florida prisons back in the early '90s, if you were diagnosed with HIV, then you were given AZT or Videx. If you were diagnosed with AIDS, you were sent to a medical unit; your numbers leveled out, or you died. It was rare to see anyone return from an AIDS unit.

Those who were HIV-positive hid the fact. Being HIV-positive in prison made you an outcast; nobody wanted anything to do with you. HIV awareness was nonexistent in Florida prisons back then. So many people believed that you could catch AIDS through physical contact, sharing a drink or smoke with an infected person, or even having an HIV-positive person sneeze on you.

Homosexuality in prisons is very intricate; it is completely different from the streets. To simplify things without going into too much detail, you had "men"—those who were top only—and "girls"—anyone who sucked a dick or got fucked, no matter how butch they were. Many "men" did not feel that they were gay, since they were not bottoms in any way.

Prison was also an environment where "girls" were secondary citizens—a bitch was expected to stay in a bitch's place and not disrespect a "man." Many times, the "girl" had no choice about when they had sex; the "man" was in control.

Some "girls" survived by tricking for canteen, others were pressured into it, some did it for protection, and some did it because it was the only way they could feel accepted, loved, and wanted. No matter the reason, if it was revealed that they "had that shit" or "had the ninja" (terms used for HIV), then they were treated like lepers.

In some cases, if it became known that someone was HIV-positive, they were forced to seek protective custody. It was always assumed that it was the "girls" who infected the "man," and the reaction was usually "that punk tried to kill me by giving me that shit."

In prison, HIV and AIDS were always blamed on those who were getting fucked, while the "men" were always portrayed as the victims. Knowing that you had HIV meant that your whole world changed, and in the early to mid-'90s, it was seen as a death sentence. Most of us did not get tested because if we did have it, we did not want to know.

It was common for people to say they'd tested negative when they'd never been tested, and those who tested positive often lied about it so no one would know. Prison offered no HIV awareness classes; there were no support groups. Many of us did not even know where to order literature from to learn about HIV, and most of those who did know would not order literature for fear of being labeled HIV-positive.

We had a warped way of thinking back then. We had our preconceived notions about HIV, and that's what we went by. If you looked healthy, then you were not positive. Anyone who got sick for a long period of time, who lost a lot of weight, who went to medical a lot, or who had any type of sores that would not heal was infected.

When it became known that someone was infected, word spread quickly—nothing travels faster than bad news about someone else in prison. Those who'd had sex with that person did not speak up, because guilt by association would have labeled them positive as well.

No one wanted to live with that stigma—we did not want people avoiding our touch or refusing to shake our hands. Most of all, we did not want to face what we believed was a death sentence.

HIV was not even part of our thinking; AIDS was all that any of us knew about. If you were positive, then, no matter what your CD4 and viral load were, you were considered to have AIDS. To make things worse, Department of Corrections medical did not do much to help. Instead, they used scare tactics to try to dissuade inmates from engaging in homosexual activity, so condoms were never provided and the medical staff did not give out much information on HIV or AIDS.

The officers and the medical staff held the attitude that if an inmate became HIV-positive, then they deserved it. I actually once heard a nurse tell an inmate that he had known the risks, and if he did not want to get infected, then he should never have indulged in "that disgusting behavior."

The end result of all of these things—misinformation, lack of information, hostility toward gay inmates by staff, hostility toward HIV-positive inmates by everyone, the stigma of being "sick"—was that many of us pretended that HIV did not exist, even though it was spreading at a rapid pace.

I was one of the "girls," and a "flip-flop artist" (a term used for a homosexual who goes both ways, also known as a "bulldyker"), so my risk was even greater. But I believed that I would not catch "the ninja" because I took care of myself. I always cleaned myself out before and right after sex, and I never allowed anyone to come inside me.

I rarely thought much about HIV or AIDS unless someone I knew got sick or was sent to a medical institution, and even then my reaction wasn't too deep. But when that person was someone

I'd had sex with, it was a completely different reaction. The fear started to creep in, and I would worry. I would reassure myself that I'd done everything right: he didn't come inside me, and I'd cleaned up right away—I'm not feeling sick, no open sores. Yet that fear would remain; it was a constant companion until I received my test results.

Even getting a test was uncomfortable. The nurse would look at me with that judgmental eye and tell me that most men who'd had sex with an infected person would become infected themselves. "Abstinence is the only way not to be infected." It took three to five weeks for test results to come back, and it was three to five weeks of worry and fear. You try not to think about it, but you have no choice.

When the rest results came back, they placed you on the call-out to see medical the next day—that meant a sleepless night, as I would think of all the possible outcomes. Lying awake in bed, I would tell myself that I didn't want to die of AIDS, that I couldn't be positive.

In medical, you sit and wait for your name to be called. Then comes the long walk to the nurse's office. You go into the office, and the nurse looks at your test results. Your heart pounds in your chest, your hands are clenched, you are scared to even take a breath. Then the nurse says, "You're clean, nonreactive." You are so relieved that you don't even hear the rest of the lecture about abstinence and how the percentage of infected inmates is increasing weekly.

In 1993, I was stabbed eighteen times by a man after I refused to have sex with him. After my wounds healed up, I was transferred to an institution with an AIDS ward, where I became an orderly for six months. While most of those in prison lived in a bubble and pretended that HIV and AIDS were not that bad, I had my eyes opened during those six months.

The men housed there were on their last leg. Meds had not worked; their immune systems were so battered that they could not fight off anything. They were sent to this unit as a last-ditch effort and given experimental drugs.

It was there that I learned the difference between HIV and AIDS, where I learned the truth of the disease, and where I saw firsthand how devastating it was. Men reduced to skin and bones, unable to move around or even bathe themselves. Covered in sores that wouldn't heal, constantly sick with one illness or another.

And death, lots of death. I can't count the number of times that I cried for men that I hardly even knew. Those men had lost their ability to be self-sufficient. I felt their embarrassment and shame every time I would clean them up when they soiled themselves, or had to help them get out of bed, or pushed them around in a wheelchair.

They had an aura of defeat. Most of those men never made it out of that unit—a rare few would have a positive reaction to whatever cocktail they had been a guinea pig for and would recover enough to return to a regular institution.

In 1994, I met a man who swore his eternal love to me. I told him that the inmate who had stabbed me was HIV-positive, plus I'd just spent six months as an orderly at the AIDS unit, so I wanted to wait for my test results to come back before we had sex.

He was so understanding and sweet. We waited a couple of weeks, and my test came back nonreactive. Life was good, and we were together for two years before we ended up being transferred to different institutions.

During an annual physical, the doctor recommended that I take another test, so I did. I walked into the nurse's office just knowing I was nonreactive, and then she told me that I had tested positive for HIV. I froze.

I had her repeat it, twice. I explained how I couldn't be positive. Since my last test, I'd been in a monogamous relationship with a nonreactive man.

That night, I sat in my cell and thought about those men I used to assist. I thought of how many had died, how desolate their situation was. I had no idea what I was going to do, and I cried most of the night.

I wrote my "husband" through a friend of his on the street, who forwarded my letter to him. He was so understanding. He told me that he had gotten tested and came up positive, too. He told me he was not mad at me, that the doctor explained that HIV could remain undetected in a person for years and that was probably why my first test had come up nonreactive.

I should have had a follow-up test six months later, but I didn't. Now I was living with a death sentence, and I had infected the man I loved. I was severely depressed for a couple of weeks. I even contemplated suicide.

The doctor started me on a cocktail of Norvir and Combivir. He told me that we had caught it early, my CD4 was in the low 700s, and my viral load was around 60,000. Three months later, my CD4 was above 900 and my viral load was undetectable. My numbers would remain like this until 2009.

In 1998, I received a packet of legal papers from my "husband" because I was helping him with a medical lawsuit he wanted to file. I was unprepared for what those records revealed to me.

The man I loved—my understanding, accepting husband who loved me—had lied to me. When I had met him in 1994, he had not only been HIV-positive, but he had been on HIV meds for more than three years.

I was crushed. My emotions ran the spectrum—I was furious that he had lied to me and infected me; I was depressed, heartbroken, even a little confused. I wrote him a letter expressing my feelings. He wrote back trying to justify his actions by claiming that I was already HIV-positive when we met—contrary to what my test results stated. I've had a rough life, and I did a lot of self-therapy to work through my childhood traumas. I decided that I was not going to lie down and die; I was not going to go quietly.

I started writing to various organizations to get information on HIV and AIDS. I even subscribed to *POZ* magazine. I learned all I could about HIV, and I started to teach other people who would listen.

It took a decade for the Florida Department of Corrections to make a few improvements in HIV education. By 2004, whenever new inmates came into the system, they had to watch an informational video on HIV and AIDS. Institutions started having mandatory HIV awareness classes for inmates getting ready to be released from prison, and some institutions even formed HIV support groups through the mental health department.

Medications had improved. HIV was no longer a death sentence, and inmates' views had progressed to a point where an HIV-positive inmate was not an outcast, even though inmates were still uncomfortable playing sports with someone who was positive and used bleach on toilet seats.

In 2009, the doctor recommended that I take a "medication vacation," since I'd been on meds for thirteen years. He explained that, because I was doing so well, I could take a few years off to give my body time to recover from the toxins that the meds may have accumulated in my body.

For two years, I went off my meds, and I was fine. I never got sick, my sores healed normally, and, since I did not go to the pill window, nobody knew that I was HIV-positive.

In 2011, I went back on meds when my CD4 dropped to the low 600s, and my viral load was close to 200,000. Three months later, my viral load was undetectable and my CD4 was in the high 800s, and I've been steady ever since.

As I write this, I can't help but think about how much the opinions about HIV have changed. Inmates today look at HIV as "nothing serious." The question is not "Are you HIV-positive?" anymore; the new question is, "Are you undetectable?" There is no longer as much fear of HIV; it no longer carries the same stigma. There are even commercials on TV advertising HIV medications that allow you to "only have to take one pill a day."

In the early '90s, people kept quiet about being positive, resulting in the virus spreading throughout the prison system. In 2020, the lack of fear of the virus, the length of time positive people are living, the idea that "a cure is right around the corner," and the "undetectable = untransmittable" mentality have resulted in the virus spreading to a more accepting inmate population; more people are testing positive because they are less afraid of the virus.

Some of the younger inmates coming into the prison never had to deal with a virus that meant a death sentence. Many of them have not seen the men who got sick, who shriveled up and died. In prison, we only hear about all of the progress that is being made. We hear about the two men who were cured of HIV. We hear about one-a-day meds, people living thirty, forty, or more years with the virus and leading productive lives.

The news doesn't show us stories of millions of people who still don't have access to treatment, both in the United States and around the world. It doesn't report on how people in prison often still don't even have access to basic HIV prevention tools, comprehensive sex education, or a caring medical system. While I'm glad that we now have effective treatment for HIV, I worry about the consequences of a lack of fear for those who lack access to adequate care.

To Make a Whore Of

EMILY STERN

HIGHLAND, INDIANA, 1991

"Mom?"

"What is it, Emily?"

The last part of my name became thinned, crackled netting as her voice lost its shape and sent her coughing again. I waited until I heard her spit.

"Mom?"

She didn't answer but opened her door and walked past me into the kitchen. I followed and stood by the table, waiting as she poured a glass of water and put a cup of that morning's coffee into the microwave.

Her collarbone created a crease in her gauzy leopard-print button-down shirt. Her short black skirt, usually classy-slutty and risqué, was limp at her waist with no "cornbread booty"—as her boyfriends used to call it—to speak of. The seams that were once bursting now hung, slightly bent and confused.

I wasn't confused, though. I was increasingly sure my worst fear had manifested. It was just like the research papers I'd written in my English classes and the speeches I'd given in Mrs Petrin's public speaking course. First came an unexplainable weight loss, and then a weird flu that didn't go away. What happened next depended on the person. It could be purple splotchy lesions all over the body, Kaposi's sarcoma, but that seemed to happen more with men. Women often got pneumonia. They had a shorter incubation period and almost always died faster. Aside from that, in 1991 there wasn't much information about women who contracted HIV.

Abstinence education—the government's and, in turn, the media's answer to HIV infection—seemed more dangerous and destructive than all STDs combined. More shame. More secrecy. More puritanical bullshit, and so, more stigma. If you'd secretly polled most of the teenagers I knew about whether the threat of hell, or "gay cancer," was keeping them pious on a Saturday night, their answer would be no.

Where we lived in Northwest Indiana, no one talked about safe sex. At Highland High, the nurse's office refused to offer condoms, so I got free condoms at Planned Parenthood and strategically left them in bathrooms around school and around town. Sometimes I'd leave them in our bathroom at home, tucked inside a *Star* or a *Mademoiselle*, along with pamphlets about safe sex, HIV, and hepatitis. I figured that if she wanted to be loved so much that she'd date men who hurt her kids and stole her car, she probably wasn't enforcing a "No glove, no love" rule. My mother never mentioned finding the condoms, and I didn't mention leaving them. I never saw any pamphlets at Planned Parenthood about using clean needles, or I would have left those too.

I watched my mom drink her coffee over the sink. Steam floated from the mug; it looked like it was coming out of the top of her head. She made a loud slurpy sound, and for the billionth time I wondered why she didn't just wait for her coffee to cool. I started to say that, to make her laugh, but shut my mouth, held my breath, and chewed on the inside of my lip.

Staring at her diminished figure, I tried again. "Mom?"

Silence.

"Mom ... um ... Have, have ..."

She was facing me and leaning against the sink. She looked irritated and suspicious and ready to fight with me. She also looked tired and sad. I decided now was as good a time as any.

Deep breath. "Have you ever had an AIDS test?"

"What?"

I stumbled backwards, feeling indignant. And then angry. And then genuinely surprised.

Had she really not considered HIV? Or that her string of horrible boyfriends and her ongoing drug addiction might scare or upset her kids? Though maybe she hadn't. I was almost certain that Jessica hadn't ever called her out on anything. Jess was a drug-addled mother's wet dream who instinctively followed the rule that children should be seen and not heard, an expectation seeping from our maternal, old-world mix of Catholic/Sicilian DNA. And, most likely, David had also never said anything, which was probably more of an adherence to rule number one of the Sicilian first-born-male bylaws: loyalty no matter what.

My loyalty was to the truth, and the truth seemed as obvious as the ever-growing lines of exhaustion on her face, and the windy echoes of a skirt searching for fifty lost pounds.

"Emily! What are you talking about?" she snapped.

"Well, it's ... it's just that, well, you've lost so much weight. And you keep saying you have the flu, and you keep coughing. I ... I was just wondering."

I forced myself to look her in the eye, but she didn't meet my gaze. Instead, she looked out the window, at the remains of a quickly fading sunset.

"Mom."

Silence.

"You know what, Emily? Fuck you!"

She stormed into her room and slammed the door.

Fifteen minutes later, my mom emerged from her bedroom and stood behind the couch where I was sitting, punishing myself by watching the TV show *Small Wonder*. I didn't look up.

"Yes, I have," she said. "It was negative."

I turned around, and we really looked at each other. I was surprised she'd come out of her room, and I was also surprised the test had come back negative—if she'd really gotten one. I just didn't think I could be wrong, not that I wanted to be right about her having HIV.

"You went back for the results?" I asked her.

"No, Emily. They called me."

I thought that was strange. One time I'd asked Planned Parenthood how it worked to get tested, and they'd made a big deal about how I'd have to come in to get the results no matter what.

"Where did you go? They don't usually give those results over the phone, Mom."

"I went to the Board of Health. In the city, okay?"

She waved both hands in front of her like a Sicilian member of the Supremes and said, "Now, stop! Enough! I'm going to lie down."

She disappeared into her room and I thought it over. I knew from my studies that there was a three-to-six-month window between being exposed to the virus and the antibodies actually showing up on a test. My intuition was that she hadn't lied to me about taking the test, or even testing negative, but, based on her symptoms, I thought she was actually now HIV-positive.

I'd asked my mom about the AIDS test in February 1991. In May, I was still worried. Her health was deteriorating or staying the same, depending on the day. Now she also had night sweats and chills. She seemed even more exhausted than before, but it was hard to tell whether it was from working. She had a new job with Baroni, a new company at Bloomingdale's, where she made various shades of lipstick and eye shadow on-site, right at the makeup counter. I was so happy when she got that job.

Her best friend Barbara had once told me that mom had wanted to go to the Art Institute of Chicago before I was born, and that she'd been a painter—mostly oils. Only two of her paintings were in our house, and they were both buried in the basement somewhere. One was a still life of roses; the other was a Dracula-looking clown with a blank expression. I wanted my mother to experience colors and creativity and success, and her new job gave her that. The customers loved her, and she was brilliant at it.

I'd still been studying AIDS every chance I could. I'd just finished my final research paper for my AP Biology class, and it was on the opportunistic infection cytomegalovirus.

Cytomegalovirus (CMV) is a member of the herpes virus family. Around 80 percent of people have it, but it doesn't show up as more than occasional swollen lymph nodes or a fever, unless you have a compromised immune system. If you have an autoimmune condition, CMV can escalate quickly, leaving the patient blind and in pain, and his or her nervous system crippled.

I can't remember why I'd picked that particular disease, but I'd written ten pages about it, and I got a grade of ninety-eight percent. Well, no, actually, I didn't get the ninety-eight percent. The friend I gave my paper to got the ninety-eight percent, but had I been able to turn it in, that would have been my grade.

I didn't get to graduate from high school. Three weeks before graduation, I was kicked out. I wasn't failing any classes; I just didn't go as often as I should have. It was extra awful because I'd been awarded a scholarship to go to college for musical theater. My beloved guidance counselor, Mr Hedges, said, "Em, just go anyway. It'll take them at least six months to figure it out, and by then they probably won't care!"

I replied, "Um ... yeah. No, thanks. I'm not into that kind of humiliation."

By late spring, my fears permeated my thoughts every day, including a random Friday afternoon hanging out with my best friend Jason at my mother's house. I stared into the insipid yellow-with-stock-clip-art-pictures-of-flowers wallpaper, thinking about how ridiculous it was that someone who'd gotten a ninety-eight percent on a paper had just been kicked out of high school, which then made me think about HIV ... and then my mom.

I turned my brain off, lit a cigarette, and realized I'd been waiting for what seemed like forever for Jason to finish fixing his makeup and Boy George hairdo. Finally, he sashayed his gloriousness out of the bathroom, fanning himself with a stack of pamphlets (my campaign of infiltrating my mother's magazines had continued), and sat down next to me at the kitchen table.

"What's up with these?" he asked as he spread the pamphlets for services offered by Planned Parenthood—including the proper way to put a condom on a banana and how to do an at-home breast examination. He pulled out the pale blue one—free HIV screenings every Wednesday between three and six p.m.—and held it up.

I ignored the brochure and gave him my most defeated, forlorn face.

"I can't believe it, Jason. I'm a goddamn statistic. I can't believe I'm not going to graduate from high school!"

"Um ... really? No offense, but you weren't exactly winning any awards for attendance." He crossed his eyes and stuck out his tongue.

I laughed. "Fuck. You."

"Ha! Whatever. Fuck you, too. Anyway ... So, what's up with these?" He waved the HIV information in front of my face.

"I'm just worried about her," I said.

Led by his shoulders, Jason's torso began to involuntarily move back and forth, while his neck became an unwavering frozen steak; he nodded and looked down at the papers again, silent. He was tough in a lot of ways, but anything involving sex, nudity, or blood easily pushed him over the edge.

"Yeah. Me too. I'm worried, too. Do you really think she might have AIDS? Really?"

"Yeah. I do. God ... She's so annoying. Why couldn't she just marry for money and get addicted to Valium like other moms?"

We laughed, and he said, "Yeah, not Toni Stern. She doesn't want any of that fancy stuff, like stability or joint bank accounts or trips to the grocery store. The dank weed and a nice eight ball, however ..."

When I was eight years old, my mother called me a fucking whore. I ran to my busted, cracked paperback dictionary, the same one my best friend Selena and I had used when we'd played the game "pick a random word and guess what it means" in first grade, and looked it up.

Whore:

noun
a woman who engages in promiscuous sexual intercourse, usually for money; prostitute; harlot; strumpet

verb (used without object)
to act as a whore

verb (used with object)
to consort with whores
obsolete: to make a whore of; corrupt; debauch

In January 1992, six months after my mother's HIV-positive diagnosis, I talked to her on the phone after a doctor's appointment. I asked her how it had gone.

"I told him my eyes have been acting weird and my leg hurts, and he said I might have something called cyta or cyto virus."

"Cytomegalovirus?"

"Yes! That's it. Is that bad?"

Yes, Mom. That's bad. That's awful. It's one of the most horrible, fucked-up, irreversible things you can get.

I wished I hadn't known about that virus at all.

"No, Mom. It's not so bad. They have a lot of drugs that can slow the progression. You'll be okay."

I met Aurora on an ordinary night. It was stuffy and unbearable, but the same as every other July in Indiana. It may have felt even more suffocating because I was in my old room at my mother's house. The TV was on in the living room, and I heard *The Arsenio Hall Show* playing. I couldn't be there. Couldn't stand it all. I was restless.

I walked into the living room, and my mom looked up, her eyes slightly confused but welcoming. "Good night, honey," she said.

I kissed her puffed-out, steroid-infested cheek and wondered who she saw in the mirror. I recognized her, like someone you've met somewhere but whose name you can't remember.

I pretended to go back to my room. Instead, I quietly opened the back door, the same way I'd done in high school, and left.

With nowhere in particular to go, I climbed into my 1978 Pontiac Catalina, the bumper still held in place by duct tape and two coat hangers, and lit a cigarette. I put in my current favorite mixtape. I kept rewinding the song "Day Ditty" by Shudder to Think in the dilapidated tape deck that was jerry-rigged through a crack in the dashboard and plugged into a random place under the hood. I decided to drive to my friend Susan's house. I'd known her since high school. We'd once gotten completely shitfaced on vodka and RC Cola, which, by the way, tastes exactly like bug spray and procures a vile hangover. We'd been in theater together, and although we'd never hung out consistently, we loved and accepted one another. I needed that. Susan's was also perfect because her sarcastic and alcoholic mom might be up, and there would be food. Susan would be home, because she was one of those people whom people went to. She was a bit of a sage—not so much for me but for many.

I'd moved back home in March to take care of my mom. Well, I'd also moved back because I'd started having sex with one of my roommates, and, yeah, that almost never works out. In my defense, I was endeared to him since I'd taken acid for the first time a month earlier. He screened the movie *Liquid Sky* in our living room, which turned out to be a way better trip than the drug. But it wasn't the movie that seduced me. It was a hot-and-heavy poetry reading at the elderly, chess-playing commie coffeehouse No Exit that spurred such bad decision-making. All of that abstract thinking and somatic responding can even make a totally-not-hot-James-Spader-at-his-absolute-whiniest roommate look close enough to Iggy Pop that you'll have sex with him. Well, that plus a bottle of Boone's Farm. I should have skipped the sex and gone straight for the headache. So, roommate sex led to weird arguments, which culminated a few weeks later in him shoving me after we were screaming at each other about dirty ramen noodle dishes and my hating to give blow jobs to weasels. Then I called my mom and told her that I hated my life.

"Just come home. I could use the help. I'll be there in an hour and a half. Start packing."

Right. The exact amount of time it would take to get from Northwest Indiana to Howard and Greenview on the far North Side, in rush-hour traffic—if you're my mother. On average, it took everyone else about two and a half hours. She still loved to drive, and she still drove like she lived—velocity hitting the pinball into orbit at every turn, plus music and cussing. She'd be in a good mood.

James Spader and I were still screaming at each other when she double-parked and laid on the horn. He tried to block me from leaving by spreading his legs and gripping the doorframe, but I gave him a sucker punch in the gut and pushed through, stopping only to turn back and throw my house keys at his head, which I missed. On the street, Mom popped the hatchback, turned up the dusties on the radio, and read *Vanity Fair* as I heaved in the big black garbage bags filled with books and clothes.

She looked tired but said she wanted to drive when I offered. When she asked me what the fuck had happened, I told her the truth. She laughed and told me I was an ass. I cracked up and said, "It's true," and put my hand on top of hers, where it was resting on the stick shift. She'd rescued me like a mama should. I loved her completely.

I slammed the door to the Pontiac and walked right into Susan's house. No one was in the kitchen, but I saw the light on in her room. Before I could knock, she opened the door. Her long red hair spilled over her tie-dyed T-shirt, which was spilling over her Stevie Nicks skirt.

"Emily, we were just talking about you. This is Aurora. She's bisexual, and so are you. I thought you two should meet."

"Yeah?" I said, and pushed the door open a little more.

Being bisexual in the early '90s meant two things: there were three books to choose from at your local feminist bookstore; and if you could get more than one bisexual in a room together, they were obviously soul mates. I looked past Susan's head and saw Aurora sitting on the bed in the corner against the wall. Her hair was all one length, just past her shoulders, and she had a long, slender neck. She wore camo pants, black combat boots, and a baggy, black Joy Division T-shirt. She looked up at me through naturally gold and auburn brown-flecked strands hanging in front of her face. Her eyes were the color of smoke from a steel mill shooting through the end of a sunset, varying layers of midnight blue invaded by swirly gray.

Aurora was the most beautiful broken bird in punk rock garb I'd ever seen. I immediately wanted to take care of her and ask her to dominate me at the same time. I walked into the room and sat on the other side of the bed. We smiled at each other. She was tall, maybe five-eight, and very thin. Her fingers were also slender and at first seemed delicate, almost dainty, until she pushed her hair behind her ears and adjusted the laces on her boots. She grabbed each side and yanked them tight and hard with a decisive snap. I chewed on my bottom lip and fixated on her muscley forearms as I watched her start the other shoe, until Susan interrupted the show to ask how my mom was doing. I said that there wasn't anything new. I asked her about her mom and her heroin-addicted brother. The three of us smoked pot and talked about music. Eventually, Aurora and I were sitting next to each other on the bed.

"Do you want a ride home?" I asked.

"Yes."

"Good," I said.

We got into my car and drove to her house in Munster. She played with my radio, fast-forwarding songs, and eventually pulled a tape out of her pocket. "Do you ever listen to Bauhaus?" she asked me.

I nodded and was excited that she knew how to say what she wanted, and that she didn't listen to shitty music. On the way, she said she was hungry, so I pulled into a gas station.

"Hot dog?" I asked.

She smiled. We both bought hot dogs and kept driving.

After a while, she told me to pull into an empty parking lot at the edge of a residential area.

"This is good. I don't want my mom to see me," she said.

She told me her dad was super religious, and her mom was oblivious. Aurora had been adopted illegally; her parents had bought her from a teenage girl in West Virginia when she was two years old. She had a recurring nightmare about a woman with long red fingernails ripping her out of someone's arms.

I told her my mom was dying and asked if I could touch her face.

"Yes," she said.

"Do you want to see me again soon?" she asked, her fingers wrapping around the door handle.

"I want to see you tomorrow."

"I'll see you here at six," she said and leaned into me.

Her hair smelled like a lady, which I hadn't expected. It was against my face and I felt it touch my neck, and I knew I was wet. We both cried out a little and looked at each other. I kept my eyes open as she kissed me. I wanted to remember every second of every moment.

I floated home, back into the house where my mother was dying, and into my room, where I stayed up and stared at the empty walls. I recounted every second of the night. I jerked off. I read Ferlinghetti poems until I fell asleep.

My mother had no idea I liked girls, and I didn't want to tell her. I knew it would hurt her because of my gay dad. Before she'd gotten sick, when she was being the most venomous, she always told me

I was just like him. Even though having AIDS trumped being gay in the societal hate-mongering stigma rule book, I knew she'd see only him, the man who had left her, and the daughter she'd hated. So I couldn't tell her I was in love.

My mom wasn't the only person I hid Aurora from. I didn't want anyone to know, not even Jason. I didn't tell him because I knew he'd talk me out of it, and I wasn't ready for that. When Aurora asked me to marry her a week after we'd started dating, I felt the push-pull of my entire body wanting to be pressed against her while my brain told me, *No! Don't answer! Run! This is insane!*

Instead, I said, "Yes, I'll marry you."

The only person I told was Scott, my old friend from high school. Scott didn't have the same authoritative impetus as Jason, so I felt I could tell him and he wouldn't be able to change my mind. Ever since our discussion about suicide in high school, he'd found me "fascinating," which was exactly the outlook I needed to make a bad decision. "Fascinating" was similar enough to "adventurous," which was the story I was telling myself. It also helped that Scott was hiding a relationship as well. His was with a blonde wild card with phenomenal tits who carried a razor in her purse to shave her long legs in the middle a date if she felt a hint of stubble. How could he say no to that? We'd go on our respective dates, drop them off, and then rendezvous at the Top Notch Restaurant in the middle of the night.

We'd laugh about how we were in over our heads. I'd tell him that I thought Aurora was bad news, a bad idea, potentially dangerous, but that I was going to date her anyway. He'd say, "Cheers!" and we'd clink our mugs of bad diner coffee.

The first time Aurora and my mother met was about three weeks after we'd started dating. Aurora was glued to the outer doorframe of my room, sulking because I didn't agree with her analysis of some Fleetwood Mac lyrics. My mom glared at her from the top of the kitchen stairs. I introduced them like there was nothing weird about a stranger coming out of my room in the morning, and Aurora mumbled, "Hello."

Mom gave me the old, familiar hostile eye that I hadn't seen much of since her diagnosis.

Exhilarated, I felt my old-school standby response reemerge as my lips formed an inappropriate and uncontrollable smile.

The last time my mother saw Aurora prompted me to move out of her house for two months.

Aurora and I were in my room, naked, in each other's arms, without blankets, and the door slammed open. My mother stood there, holding a large wooden spoon, and screamed, "Fuck youuuuuu!" with what must have taken a great effort for her body. She climbed onto the bed, wielding that fucking wooden Sicilian rifle back and forth in our faces.

Aurora and I grabbed our clothes and tried to wrap them around us as she chased us out of my room and through the back door, yelling, "Get out of my fucking house, you disgusting piece-of-shit queers!"

I yelled back, "Fuck you, Mom! That's fine! I'll move out this week!"

Aurora poked my arm and whispered, "Babe! Your mother just attacked us with a spoon."

That was when we got our own apartment.

I decided to go to college at Purdue University Calumet and take out a student loan. How else was I going to be able to pay for an apartment? I didn't have a job yet, and while my commitment to our amaranthine lesbian love was intact, my brain was aching for purpose, information, discourse, and structure. I chose communications as my major, hoping to cop skills to get the world to listen to why and how it was fucked up, and also to somehow reach inside of my girlfriend's soul and convince her not to kill herself because nothing else I'd tried was working.

One night, Aurora broke a beer bottle on the coffee table and shoved pieces of glass into her mouth while saying, "See how much I love you? See how much I love you?" over and over until the blood dripped down her pointy chin and into her hair, and I screamed for her to stop. Then she grabbed a butcher knife and ran into the bathroom and locked the door, screaming that she was going to kill herself because I didn't love her. I told her I did, and I huffed and puffed and bashed the door in. A September thunder-and-lightning storm exploded at the moment Aurora tried to push me out of the bathroom, and she shoved my elbow into the window. Glass flew, and then we were both bleeding. She started to slice her tiny wrists again, and I pulled her into me, and she begged me to never leave and to promise to love her forever. Which I did.

Aside from the chewing on glass ("Chewin' on, chewin' on broken gla-a-ass"—sing it to the tune of the Annie Lennox song "Walking on Broken Glass"; it's a classic), there were more butcher knife bathroom suicide attempts and begging for my undying love, which were both twice-weekly occurrences. It was exhausting but kind of endearing. I thought I could save her, and I knew I loved her. I called her my heroin girlfriend. The girl I needed in order to breathe. And she needed me. Since we were both damaged goods, and I was stronger, it was my job to tolerate it all until Aurora could pull herself together.

Because I could take it, I'd let her tiny fists punch me and push me and slap me.

Except when she screamed that I was going to end up a fucking dead whore like my mother.

Whore:

noun
a woman who engages in promiscuous sexual intercourse,
usually for money; prostitute; harlot; strumpet.

My arm shot out and my fingers wrapped around her skinny, delicious neck, and I lifted her body and held her against the door with her legs dangling. I looked her in the eyes and said, "Too much."

She nodded, and I dropped her in a pile on the floor.

We broke up. In the rain, on the doorstep of Samantha's house, the ex-girlfriend she'd slept with while we were together, I really said good-bye. I let her call me a liar. I let her call me stupid and fat. I let her call me a disgusting dirty prostitute who was going to hell. I even let her apologize and take it all back and beg me to stay. I breathed her in and let the exquisite chaos sink to the bottom, anchored. I stared at her upper lip one last time. I let myself think of going down on her. I let myself conjure the tongue and groove of her spine. Goddamn it. Her breasts and mouth. She still made me speed.

I told Aurora to always believe that I loved her and that I'd done my best. As I drove away, I saw her in the mirror behind me, throwing things and screaming, and so beautiful. I let that image move through me until I couldn't see anymore and parked by a creek and cried. I'd failed. I couldn't make her love me. I didn't inspire her to love herself. We didn't win. We couldn't hack forever, or maybe Aurora was right—I was a disgusting whore who didn't deserve it.

Eventually, my tears went beyond Aurora. They were ancient, circling inside me like a puppy chasing its tail. I was sitting still, though. I was sitting in the toxic Northwest Indiana grass and mud, watching it all happen in my mind.

Then I had to go. I had to extricate myself from the decomposing McDonald's wrappers and Marlboro Red butts. I was supposed to have dinner with my dying mother.

When I pulled into her driveway, I waited to go inside until my jagged breathing and tears stopped.

The day they'd met, my mother had told me she didn't like Aurora. I'd said, "You just don't like her because she's a girl," and she'd replied, "No. I just don't like her. At all."

But I hadn't listened. I'd heard only Aurora: her voice, the long-haired butch girl with delicate fingers who was both crude and soft. A girl, a real-life girl I could touch and love; a believable salve coating my insides, soothing my ulcerative, cavernous, historical gashes. Her voice spinning the story of our future had been the sweetest refrain.

Now I was here to see my mother. I had to suck it all the way up because I realized what a piece-of-shit daughter I'd been for wasting the last three months on a girl and how much it fucking sucked that this was the one time my mother had actually been right.

I walked in and smiled, kissed her hello, and asked if she needed anything.

Yes. To put the clothes in the dryer.

I walked down to the moldy basement that held her secret forty-year-old magazine-and-dust collection. When I was younger, I was afraid of going down there. I was sure ghosts who saw my vulnerability as weakness were waiting for me so they could suck out my soul and leave me a vacant, bobbing head with empty eye sockets. Now I was grateful to hide in the dimly lit laundry room as another wave of weeping hit me. I screamed into clean, warm towels that still smelled like my mother. I don't know how long I was down there, but when I finally looked up, she was standing with me.

She said, "What's wrong?"

And I said, "Nothing."

And she said, "You can tell me."

And I said, "No, I can't."

And she said, "Yes, honey. You can. You can ..."

And for the very first time in my whole shitty, fucked-up life, my mother wrapped her arms around me and held me tight like in a movie and told me I could tell her anything, and I felt her shoulder bone dig into my cheek and slide in and out of sharpness with the wetness of my tears as she said, "It'll be all right," over and over, and I shook her with months of my sadness, maybe years, while she touched my hair. Even though I could smell her rotting liver, I'd never felt so alive.

Andy Bell Made Me Gay

DAN CULLINANE

On July 3, 1981, when the *New York Times* published its first story about AIDS, I was fourteen years old, living in the last town in Idaho before the Canadian border, and thinking that holding Dawn Cowan's hand had to get me over my fascination with chest hair. My lust for men, fueled by glimpses of male nudity in the *Playboy* Sex in Cinema issue, was something I was hoping to get over, like bed-wetting. My penis would do what penises were supposed to do, because sooner or later, holding Dawn's hand would make me want pussy.

I advanced to a shoplifted copy of *Playgirl* the following year, after my family relocated to Upstate South Carolina, and because I now flogged my dick mercilessly over naked men, I realized I was done for. I knew this was something I shouldn't do, couldn't talk about, couldn't act on. At the same time, I knew I would take the very first opportunity, even though this was at best tragic and at worst an abomination. Honestly, I was okay with that. Sooner or later, I would touch a dick that wasn't my own, and even though I only had a vague idea of what would happen after that, I couldn't wait.

But then there was this:

I wasn't quite seventeen, when my brother asked me, "You know what gay stands for?"

"What?" I asked, feeling sick because I'd already heard the joke somewhere.

"Got AIDS Yet?"

And everyone laughed, and I laughed too, and my laugh sounded horrible in my ears because I was terrified and I was wondering why he'd asked me that. I wanted to scream at him, and his stupid friends who were supposedly also my friends, and I hated myself because I didn't scream at them: "I'm gay, you stupid motherfuckers, and I guess when I die, you're just gonna laugh your stupid motherfucking asses off."

I was going to die because I was gay. I was abominable and I was doomed.

I determined that getting drunk allowed me to feel okay, or at least allowed me to not feel. Semantics. Getting drunk is just getting drunk, but when being you means dying, then getting drunk is better. I had advanced from rural virginal closet case to rural virginal alcoholic closet case. I kept the alcohol, but in 1987, I left behind the rural so I could leave behind the virginal, too.

In Baltimore, I met a boy. A tall, loping boy whose hair caught the sun like an August wheat field. On our first date he opened the door of a derelict-looking building at the corner of Maryland Avenue and Lafayette, and we pushed our way through the shoulder-to-shoulder crowd of men with loosened ties and sleeves rolled up, celebrating the end of the week. Stephen knew them, and they greeted him and eyeballed me. He bought me a beer and then kissed me, pushing my head back over the bar, and I turned red but felt more excited and happy and at home than I could ever remember.

I met another boy. I met a man. Another man. I drank until I was comfortable, and then I fucked because I could.

I found Larry Kramer's *Faggots* and Armistead Maupin's Tales of the City series at Louie's Bookstore Café, and both revealed a playful vision of gay lust. But that was in the past. Now sex took place on a minefield of fear and judgment. There was still a shadow of abandon, but as I put together a circle of friends my own age I learned the rules.

Righteously, steadfastly, angrily, we rejected the notion that we were to blame for bringing the plague on ourselves, but we were cautious. Cautious and censorious. We would not indulge ourselves in those old and dangerous ways. And those who did would be reeducated or shunned.

"We can't do that," a boy told me as my eager, curious tongue found his asshole. So we lay side by side and jerked off.

"I'm not like that," a man told me one night, when I pulled him into an alley outside the Hippo and pressed myself against him. He kissed me quickly, guiltily, and we walked to his apartment. We lay side by side and jerked off.

Is my passion retrograde? I wondered. In this city, so far away from the Carolinas and my tattered *Playgirl*, where I am able to do more than imagine, are my yearnings a betrayal of myself and my community? Among my own, even, am I contemptible?

Before silence equaled death, desire equaled death. We drank, did lots of coke, danced until last call, then ate pancakes at the Buttery, and went our separate ways as the sun was coming up. We kissed and said good night. Sometimes we hooked up, sometimes we made out, sometimes we went home with someone we had just met. Usually I was too drunk to do much more than pass out naked alongside a stranger. We carried condoms scrupulously, but we rarely needed them because fucking was off-limits. The bars were booming, but now we watched New Order videos instead of porn in the back rooms, and we didn't touch. Or we cruised for contact, lips on lips, hands above the waist.

Being gay begins with fear and shame, and then blissfully turns into freedom from all that. In Mount Vernon, our neighborhood, we held hands, we kissed in public, we were loud and out and proud. We held each other as we danced, jumped atop the speakers and writhed together in sweaty pantomime, but resisted our impulses for more until we could no longer, and after that, we felt fearful and ashamed, and sweated out our next HIV test.

I met a man. He was lean and brown and sexy and coordinated volunteers for the Health Education Resource Organization, Baltimore's equivalent to the Gay Men's Health Crisis (GMHC) in New York, but with the far better acronym of HERO.

I volunteered in order to get his attention, and it worked because he lined me up for the next buddy training. It was a two-and-half-day crash course in HIV and AIDS, punctuated by grueling psychological exercises. For my first assignment as a buddy I did laundry for a guy in Bolton Hill, who had been in the middle of renovating an old row house when he was diagnosed. I tried to use my psychological training to get him to talk, but he really just wanted someone to help with laundry. He called HERO to let them know that I talked so much I didn't have time to fold his laundry, so I was reassigned.

My next pairing was to keep Joseph company while his partner, Dave, worked his night job or ran errands. Joseph was close to the end, suffering bouts of dementia, and couldn't be left alone. We sat and talked about everything but AIDS as I sorted his medications into appropriate doses. Joseph wanted to talk about my sex life but soon learned it was not very good conversation, so he told me his stories, which were so explicit, and so full of startling variety, that I began to think I had been trained in the wrong areas. "You need to get out there more," he said.

These were the first guys I knew personally who had AIDS. The gay community rose up in all areas to combat the disease, it's true, but for many of us who came of age after it had entered the mainstream, there was an us-and-them attitude. We didn't condemn them, at least not out loud, but we were afraid of them, so we circled the wagons and danced around our own campfire. That latency period allowed us to think that it wasn't among us—until it was.

At the Hippo, I leaned against the rail drinking a beer, watching my friends dancing below, and I saw skeletons. Volunteering for HERO had pulled me out of the safe zone, and now I grasped that there was no us and them. That night, instead of smiles, laughter, and the suggestion of sex, I saw a disjointed death throe. Just as I had back on that hot sweaty August afternoon under the Carolina pines, I realized that to be me meant I would die soon, unless I was a little less gay.

I met a man, and he was scared too. In 1989, the number of reported AIDS cases in the United States topped 100,000, so we ran together to the suburbs and bought a brand-new townhouse among thousands of other brand-new townhouses, on a brand-new cul-de-sac in Owings Mills. We had three bedrooms, one baby tree in the front yard, two cats, and a Blockbuster Video card. We darted inside and shut the door.

Bennigan's and Ruby Tuesday. Movies at Security Square. We stayed outside the beltway, steered clear of anything too gay. We went to work, came home for dinner, used our coupons at Giant Food on weekends, and socialized with family and, occasionally, the exactly two suburban gay couples we knew. Conversations and sex became less frequent and less satisfying. Hard work and focus achieved a stultifying heteronormativity that might have been a version of happily ever after until, at an Erasure concert in 1990, Andy Bell kicked me in the head.

With a ferocious in-your-face attitude he pranced across the stage at Merriweather Post Pavilion, in jockey shorts and fuck-me pumps, sweating like a stevedore. He was a cherub with an angel's voice yet seemingly ready to sodomize anyone who looked at him crossways. He appalled the straight boys who had discovered Erasure in college, but he set me on fire.

Politics fanned those flames. ACT UP delivered a coffin to Baltimore City Hall, and chained themselves to the doors of the Health Department, while we sat at home watching *Knots Landing* reruns. When Jesse Helms threatened the funding for the National Endowment for the Arts over Robert Mapplethorpe, I sat munching on a Cobb salad at the Old Post Office in DC, while outside the restaurant, at the doors of the NEA, protestors chanted, "We're here, we're queer, we're fabulous, get used to it!"

I had scampered to the suburbs because I was frightened. In my absence, fear had turned to fury, and it was catching. I ran because I didn't want to die, but I was dying all the same. My immune system hadn't turned on me, but I had. My quiet little world crumpled under the wave of gay men who were no longer asking for permission to fight for their lives.

Three levels of beige carpet and off-white walls, dress shirts and tidy sweaters, nutritious meals prepared at home, and quiet, quiet nights were cooling my blood and slowing my heart. I needed the heat of the fire.

We left each other. He stayed in Owings Mills. I picked up some booze and a fresh pack of smokes, and now, from my bed in my apartment in Mount Vernon, I could watch the silhouettes of rats climbing the fire escape. The tub barely drained, and tiles routinely popped off the bathroom floor. I parked my car on Read Street down by Never on Sunday so I could pick up a meatball sub on my way home. Chris Cornell and Eddie Vedder and Billy Corgan bounced off the walls as I read David Feinberg's *Eighty-Sixed* and learned about not giving a fuck what anyone thought. I read James Robert Baker's *Tim and Pete* sitting in the window of the Laundromat on Preston Street as the world grew dark and the city lit up, and I realized that rage and vengeance tasted better than victimhood.

I met a man, and we collided like grappling wrestlers, knocking pictures off his wall on our way to his bed. Chris and I went together to the March on Washington in 1993 and rode home on a train loaded with gays, my head in his lap, his hand in my hair. It didn't go anywhere and that was fine. Stephen, the lanky boy from my first days in Baltimore, reappeared in the doorway of a shop on Charles Street, and now we played pinball at the Eagle, and hearts, sitting cross-legged on the floor of my apartment.

I met Tommy at the HFStival in DC, drunk, stoned, muddy, and sweaty. Tommy came and Tommy went, always happy to share his weed at the Mt. Royal Tavern, or up on the Thomas Viaduct, or wherever we ended up. "He's positive," our friend Suzanne told me. I didn't care. I wanted his hands on my body and mine on his.

Winter came and Stephen called. "I tested positive," he said, and I hated my phone. Then Chris called and said he had too. Death danced around me again, and I danced back. Nights at Club 1722, walking home as morning crept over the city. Dancing with anyone, or no one, but always dancing. Waking up in this bed or that bed, until I decided I liked waking up in my own bed, so now they had to come home with me.

Michael knocked on my window and I let him in because it was cold outside and his coat looked thin. He took off his clothes, and because he had, I did too, and why not? I knew his body, skinny and knotted with muscle, blond hair so light it was almost invisible against his white skin. He lay on top of me and pushed into me and I knew that he wasn't wearing a condom, and I didn't care. He bit my neck and I felt him come inside me and I came too, without touching myself because giving up felt so good.

I'm not going to run. I'm going down with the ship, side by side with the men I love, our fists raised in defiance and triumph. Sex was counterinsurgency, a kamikaze dive. I knew what I was doing, and I did it because I was choosing sides. This is my world. These are my people. I had warmed myself back to life by their fire, and if that fire wanted to consume me in recompense, that was fair.

When February came, I was done with winter and wanted something warmer. I spent one last night with Tommy, smoked one last bong with him, and in the morning pointed my car west for California.

Tommy died. Stephen died. Dean died. Jeff died. I didn't. I didn't get sick. I tested negative. I tested negative again.

I didn't go down with the ship, so I decided to man the lifeboats. Another round of buddy training, this time with glossy visuals and heartfelt motivational metaphors. I drove the coastline of Laguna Beach on weekends delivering meals, but stigma abounded and men hid behind their doors, leaving a cooler on the steps outside. I joined the volunteer coordinator team at AIDS Services Foundation Orange County, and rallied high schoolers and University of California Irvine students for AIDS Walk.

I decided to move north, to LA, and split my time volunteering between Orange County and LA. *This is it. This is all it's ever going to be.*

And then it wasn't.

We were blazing diamonds in the night sky, destined to fall. And then we weren't. We were supposed to throw the biggest party the world had ever seen, those of us who survived, but we forgot.

Antiretrovirals revolutionized our world, almost overnight, and we fretted.

It's 1997. "Everyone acts like it's over," I say to my friend Shelly over dinner in Long Beach. We've been volunteering together for years, fighting side by side, day by day.

"It's going to be worse than before," she moans. "Infection rates are going to skyrocket and the new drugs are going to stop working."

Yet miracles abound. Tom's viral load is undetectable. So is Michael's. On August 13, 1998, I'm on the phone with one of the editors at the *Bay Area Reporter* in San Francisco.

"We don't have any obituaries in the paper." His voice is quietly awestruck. And then we are both crying. Then we're laughing because we're crying.

Imminent death, as central to my gay identity, is no longer imminent, and in my confusion I am all flailing anger and frightened judgment.

"I'm positive," Jon tells me one morning over breakfast. He wasn't yesterday; today he is.

What kind of fucking stupid asshole moron move is that? I think but don't say, giving him a hug. But I'm seething. How could you? We have been fighting this forever, and at the first sign of hope you fuck it all up.

I watch my friends discover the joys of online hookups, my thoughts jagged and condemnatory. *We've learned nothing about how to be,* I think. We survived, and now we're doing meth and fucking twelve guys a night at Flex.

I grab my bullhorn and climb aboard a school bus full of high school students. We head for the corner of Melrose and La Brea and chant and cheer for AIDS Walkers all day. Afterwards, the rally at San Vicente park in West Hollywood is deserted. Speakers address empty swatches of grass, as people gather swag and depart.

I have learned to dance, learned to fuck, learned to cry, learned to fight. I know how to act, and I know how to react. I know how to comfort and how to say good-bye. I know how to organize and how to march. I know how to shout. I have learned how to stand up for myself, and for my community, but now we're going in so many different directions at once. Over here, we're gentrifying low-income neighborhoods and driving the long-term residents into homelessness. Over there, we're pushing our diversity to the margins so we can convince straight people that we want to be boring and married just like them. We are suddenly appalling, and I don't know where I fit in. If anywhere.

So, I do what I know. I drink. A lot. I drink, and walk on the beach, alone in the dark, and think about dying. All the wonderful, colorful, magnificent ways I could die. I do that until I can't anymore, and then I get sober.

I meet a man. I don't know his name and I never will. We tear at our clothes until we are naked, and our hands revel in touching one another. Our lips celebrate our skin. I let myself kiss him anywhere I want, and he lets me. I push inside him and he shouts with joy. Then he is inside me, and I grab his head and stare into his eyes and say, "I'm so fucking happy that this is happening." We are totally lacking in self-consciousness, and savagely selfish, pushing for and extending our pleasure. We are laughing and breathing, and we howl our delight in who we are and how we can feel.

I am alive, and I am gay, and I am not abominable or doomed. We are not. We are ferocious.

Lucky

EDDIE WALKER

The day before Thanksgiving in 1995, I tested positive for HIV. It was my sophomore year in college at Kent State University. I had not been feeling well and had lost my appetite for a few days. I figured I was recovering from the forty-eight-hour flu. Nevertheless, as a sexually active twenty-three-year-old gay Black man, I decided to get an HIV test. When the doctor told me my results, I was shocked.

A week later, I went to my first appointment with an HIV/AIDS specialist—I'm sure he could see the fearfulness in my face, though I was trying my best to control my emotions.

When he asked, "How do you feel?" I said, "I'm afraid to go to sleep at night, because I'm afraid I won't wake up." I dropped my face into my hands and wept as I tried to silence my sobs. He said, "Don't cry. You're lucky it's happening to you now."

Growing up gay in Canton, Ohio, was challenging. I did not know anyone who was gay until I went to college, so I had to figure out how to be gay on my own. Occasionally, a gay character made a cameo appearance in a television series, but that was all there was in the '80s. Much of my education came from watching the news about gay men dying of AIDS, wondering if this tragedy was my destiny. Or from the gay romantic comedies and movies about

AIDS on VHS that I ordered from TLA Video. I could imagine myself in the happy moments, but everything was about gay white men. So I thought I couldn't be Black and gay. But trying to be straight always felt unnatural, awkward—I knew I wasn't pulling it off.

When Magic Johnson announced he was HIV-positive in 1991, it brought the epidemic to my front door. My dad never talked to me about sex, until Magic Johnson. He said, "Use a rubber when you have sex so you won't get AIDS, because once you get AIDS, you're sick for two years, and then you die." In order to end the conversation, I simply said, "Okay." I was sixteen when we had "the talk."

The first time I had sex was one week shy of my eighteenth birthday. It was the end of my senior year. I had just left a graduation party because I was bored. I decided to take a long walk and ended up in downtown Canton. Outside a late-night pizza parlor, an older Black man struck up a conversation. He looked as old as my father, if not older, and had a bit of belly. I did not find him attractive at all, but he was familiar. He could have been one of my older male cousins or uncles I'd seen at an annual family reunion or summer BBQ. He knew how to flirt without being overt, and I realized I knew how to flirt, too. I don't exactly know how I learned, but flirting with men just came natural to me. After talking for a few minutes, he asked if I wanted to "hang out."

He drove. We stopped for beer—and condoms, at my insistence. I wanted him to see me as responsible, even though I forgot about the condoms as soon as they were in the bag. We drove to the Blue Moon Motel in East Canton. When we got into the room, I was nervous and excited at the same time. He got me to relax, and eventually we were both naked. He took his time with me. We started kissing, and then he told me to suck his dick—nothing felt more natural or heavenly, which made it official: "I'm gay!"

I started having sex regularly when I went to college. I hardly ever used condoms, unless the person I was with insisted on it. I felt like condoms stole the sense of intimacy from sex, and I was starving for intimacy. My father loved me, but it was always at arm's length. We never hugged. I couldn't even call him Dad, Pa, or Pops. The words seemed alien on my tongue. I've always called him Big Ed, for as long as I can remember.

The majority of the men I slept with reminded me of Big Ed. I guess it was my way of loving a man the way I couldn't love my father. I just wanted to be as close as possible to a man, not just in the physical sense but also on spiritual and cerebral levels. I felt like condoms blocked that intimate exchange from happening.

One thing I learned from Big Ed was that it's possible to love more than one person—I had numerous stepmothers over the years, and he seemed to love each one in turn. And by the end of my freshman year, I had numerous lovers. That said, I didn't sleep with everyone; I had standards. The golden rule for me was "Never sleep with anyone who looks sick." I remember one time, in the summer of 1995, I thought I saw a lesion above the left eye of a hookup. I didn't ask him about it, and I dismissed it as a scar, but after I tested positive I was certain that was the time, even though I'd made many exceptions to my golden rule, and we all know that someone can look healthy and still be positive.

The doctor told me I was lucky that I tested HIV-positive when I did. He explained that the first protease inhibitor medication had been approved for use by the FDA. This gave HIV-positive individuals the option of a "cocktail" treatment. The cocktail was two antiretrovirals (AZT and 3TC) taken with the protease inhibitor Crixivan. At best, I thought it would slow the progression of the disease. In my mind, Big Ed's two-year timer was ticking, and I needed to make some moves.

The first thing I had to do was figure out how to pay for my medication. Since I wasn't tested anonymously, my HIV status was considered a preexisting condition, which meant the cost of my medication wouldn't be covered for one year. Luckily, I was a student at Kent State, which allowed me to charge my medications to my student account at a monthly cost of $750. I used my student loan money to pay the balance of my account at the beginning of each semester.

When I tested positive, I was still commuting daily from my father's home in Canton to college and work in nearby Kent. In less than two months, I decided to move to Kent. I left home because I didn't want to risk anyone in my father's household seeing my medication or the medical insurance mail I started to receive. I did not want anyone in my family or hometown to find out my HIV status.

I come from a hyper-macho Black family. It was bad enough that I was gay—everyone in the family knew this, but no one would dare utter a disparaging word about me for fear Big Ed would break their jaw. My father taught my three younger brothers and me that we had to "be men," and that included handling things on our own. That's what I felt I was doing. I would not let my father bear the stigma of having a gay son, and certainly not a gay son dying of AIDS. I felt it was my burden alone. That's why I decided to move out of my father's house, and eventually move out of state. I looked at a map, and said, "What's the farthest place from Canton, Ohio?" The answer was Seattle, Washington.

Moving across the country was no easy task. I would never have been able to move if it weren't for the generosity of my dear friend Drew. We met like most gay men met back then, at the local gay bar. We both attended Kent State, and it turned out he lived only a few blocks from me. We hooked up a few times and always had safe sex, at his insistence. Eventually, we became best friends. Not only did he drive with me cross-country, but he also loaned me $2,000 to help with my move. I added this to the $400 I had saved, and we set off for Seattle in my car. Two weeks after graduating from Kent State, I arrived in Seattle. It was June 1998.

I had a job set up and an apartment with my cousin NeeNee, who had recently graduated from high school in Yakima, Washington, and decided to move to Seattle with me in order to escape her difficult mother and seven younger siblings. But once I arrived, my job offer was pulled after they did a background check. I had felonies from 1992 for aggravated arson and attempted murder, after I set a boy's dormitory room on fire because he gave me a black eye—I couldn't let him get away with that.

NeeNee had found the apartment for us in Seattle—she passed the credit and background check, but I failed both. We didn't learn this until we arrived. So the three of us ended up staying in a seedy motel on the outskirts of Seattle.

I didn't think my criminal record would follow me. It had been six years since the incident. After my arrest, I was released to my father's charge. My family was poor, so the court appointed an attorney. He explained that I was going to be convicted because I'd confessed and given a full statement. He said the judge was going to sentence me to five to twenty-five years in prison, and five years' probation after release. It took my breath away when I heard this; I couldn't talk.

Luckily for me, I was a first-time offender and a college student, so I qualified for Ohio's Scared Straight Program. Instead of doing five years minimum in prison, I would only do six months, and then be released early on probation. If I stayed out of trouble for five years, the conviction would be expunged from my record. I did my time, finished probation successfully, and earned my bachelor's degree. The only thing I didn't do was get the conviction expunged from my record.

After several days of looking for an apartment in Seattle, we were all starting to get a little nervous. We couldn't afford to keep paying for a motel because then we wouldn't have enough money for a deposit. I was trying to keep a positive attitude and tried to assure NeeNee that everything was going to work out.

That's when NeeNee snapped. "We would already have an apartment if you would have told me you had felonies on your record!" she yelled. "I could have got an apartment in just my name, but no, I had to find out from a landlord! How the hell you gonna get a job with felonies when you can't even get an apartment? And, on top of all of this, you tell me you got AIDS, but that you're okay, and I'm not to worry about it. That's some shit. That's a whole lot of shit to deal with!"

I felt like I had just gotten punched in the gut, but in a calm voice I said, "I do not have AIDS. I am HIV-positive." I paused and looked at her as if it was the last time I was going to see her. And it seemed like she was looking at me the same way. When NeeNee woke up, she packed all of her belongings into the car, and Drew took her to find her own place.

Drew was the first to speak when he returned. "So, what are you going to do?"

"I don't know. Do you think I should go back to Ohio?"

"Eddie, you can't afford to go back to Ohio."

I just put my hands over my face and started crying. He was right. I was broke. And there was no way I could ask Drew to loan me more money.

Drew came over to the bed where I was sitting and put his arms around me. After my heavy crying had passed and there were only silent tears running down my face, Drew asked me, "Can't you get some help because of your condition? They helped you in Akron. I'm sure Seattle has places that will help you, too." Drew had a point. It was ironic that the thing that made me leave Ohio would be the same thing that would help me make it in Seattle. I stopped crying and fell asleep in Drew's arms.

When I woke up, my head felt clearer. I was over the shock of realizing I was on my own. I had no choice but to look for assistance with a local HIV nonprofit. I grabbed the phone book and looked up HIV in the Yellow Pages. I ended up calling a place called the Northwest AIDS Foundation. I talked to the receptionist and explained my situation. He said they did offer emergency housing, but I had to come in for an intake interview. I got on their schedule for the following morning.

The Northwest AIDS Foundation set me up with state insurance to cover my doctors' visits and medications. They also gave me a two-week voucher for the Seattle YMCA, and I was very excited—I thought it was going to be just like the Village People song, full of young men passing through town or just starting out. But once I settled in, I realized there were no hot young men to speak of, just transients and displaced families.

I dealt with my stay by telling myself it was all just a grand adventure. But then I had to figure out a way to get some money coming in fast. I figured I had three options: hooker, stripper, or server. Because of my HIV status, I didn't want to put anyone at risk, so I ended up getting a job as a server at Denny's. It was at this point that Drew wished me luck, said good-bye, and jumped on a plane back to Ohio. I was all alone in the big city, but I wouldn't be alone for long.

To Say Good-Bye

ANDREW R. SPIELDENNER

I do not like coming back to the Bay Area. This is where the ghosts are, where I came of age, where I started learning some truths about myself, and where I told lies—lies meant to show what I wanted to be and become. This is where I made my first faltering attempts to connect with others, and where I failed and lost. I recognize these as queer tactics: the strategic truths and the mythmaking, the activism and resistance, the attempts and failures to connect. I see these same maneuvers in the broader community as we create memories that include some people and exclude others. The lies take a shape; they have a weight. If the lies do, then surely the lives do, too. I am haunted by the mistakes I've made and the people I've lost, even the ones forgotten over the years.

> *Good-bye.*
> *Thank you.*
> *You made an impact.*
> *I want to touch you again.*
> *We will miss you.*
> *I wish future generations would meet you.*
> *I wish I could remember what you sounded like.*

In the United States, people have a hard time with the end of life. We do not see dying as a natural part of the life cycle. We have morgues where no one has to see the dead, funerals where no body is revealed. Morticians want pictures to see if they can return the body to its "best" state. Dying is something to put off, to fight until the last breath—as if struggle were proof of the value of the life.

When someone reveals that they are dying, we are shocked, unsure what to say or do. Is it okay to hug them? Do we talk about our own fear of death? How our friend's absence will affect us? We want reasons for it—a cause brought on by something that we can avoid. Suicide is pathologized and not seen as an option. After the death, we say, "I'm sorry for your loss" or "Condolences," and then stand in awkward silence. Sometimes we bring food.

I am from a generation of gay men who came of age well into the HIV epidemic. HIV/AIDS media coverage was both stigmatizing and tragic. When I wanted to handle another dick—anywhere on my body—I thought a condom was mandatory or I was doing something wrong. Was this piece of latex required for a blow job, for mutual masturbation, for bondage and role playing? The messaging was overwhelmingly "Use a condom!" But it wasn't clear what the parameters were. Dicks tasted and felt better without latex, but it felt risqué, producing anxiety. I went for HIV tests regularly, until my test came back positive in 1998 or '99 (I can never quite remember). My capacity for friendship and intimacy emerged in the context of a dying generation. We learned how to attend funerals, to accept that some relationships go unresolved, and to say good-bye.

I first read "When My Brother Fell," one of Essex Hemphill's poems included in *Brother to Brother: New Writings by Black Gay Men*, when I was a sophomore in college. The words felt prophetic.

Essex Hemphill's parting poem to Black gay activist Joe Beam recalls the suddenness of Beam's passing, the gaping hole left where Beam's vision was. The call for action was a resonant one, especially around HIV. And with HIV, for many of us, came activism around race, sexuality, gender, economic justice, and ability. When Essex says, "it's too soon / to make monuments," I hear a critique of passivity and nostalgia. The process of building some kind of monument, a marker of some history, does not sit comfortably with the urgent need for activism and social change. The monument is a testament to a past, it locks it away for us to walk by and admire, to be moved by the sacrifice(s) it represents.

I hear you, Essex.

I was living in fast-forward, trying desperately to have a life before I died. This poem was part of my matrix, swirling with *This Bridge Called My Back*, *Sister Outsider*, and poems from June Jordan and Chrystos. Women of color feminism led me to gay men of color writers like the Black gay collective Other Countries, James Baldwin, Assotto Saint, and Reinaldo Arenas. This was a new language, one that held me, rooted me firmly. I wanted to know more—about these men and their struggles. The idea that there were men like me in the past seemed to be too much to ask for. It was the first time I was conscious of a community for me outside of my family. I am of a generation that met AIDS head-on—in the bars and bathhouses, as lesions on the skin of men I slept with, and lying under the sweet nothings whispered in bed.

Oakland and Berkeley are different worlds from San Francisco: more so before the tech boom, prior to the massive gentrification of the Bay Area. In Oakland, several Black gay and lesbian bars thrived, places where queer Black culture, music, and people were centered and celebrated. On weekends, there would usually be someone throwing a cookout, filled with family, neighbors, friends, and potential or ex-lovers. Across the Bay, the few spaces where people of color congregated seemed to mostly be about finding a white partner. The clubs were bigger in San Francisco, but the communities of color seemed smaller, more tightly concentrated in these spaces.

In the early '90s, Black gay filmmaker Marlon Riggs was a professor at UC Berkeley and deep in his collaborations with his East Coast friends, Essex Hemphill and Assotto Saint. Chicana lesbian playwright, poet, and essayist Cherríe Moraga taught intermittently at Berkeley, and Chicano gay sociologist Tomás Almaguer had pushed for the packed Sociology of Sexuality class there. The innovative LGBT periodical *Out/Look* was being published, and I eagerly sought every issue on campus. The faculty still remembered the turbulent social movements of the '60s and '70s; many of them were already teaching or active in the movements then. There were small independent presses and bookstores that carried writings from a diverse range of feminists, theorists, community organizers, and survivors. It was entirely possible to read the entirety (or close to it) of LGBT literature in the United States. I was fascinated by the people behind the images of lesbian and gay life at the time: the men in porn, the models featured in gay or lesbian calendars, as well as those in the International Male catalog. Who were they? What kinds of people did they date? Would they like me?

When I see the master narratives of AIDS history today, I cannot find my friends. We did not appear on the covers of gay media or in the burgeoning HIV media worlds. The records of people of color, especially queer people of color, remain beyond the scope of much of this work. History remains a mostly white and normative endeavor where only these stories are repeated. So I remember.

Carmen and I came out to the Oakland gay bar the White Horse when we were twenty. Goofy, mixed race, holding fake IDs—we were sure we were cute, or we tried to look that way. Through the years together, we dated near each other, sometimes overlapping, always friendly. After Carmen's transition, we spoke less as our identities settled in other places. We still kissed hello, would share a cocktail, but our paths diverged. I cheered Carmen on when she started performing at the Sunday show: I did not know how to cope with her death at twenty-three in 1994. She had a fierceness and beauty that attracted the sexiest men in the bar. She would walk fearlessly in the day through the downtown mall, turning heads and marching through the whispers and catcalls. I wanted to be her, but she was larger than me: her life was full of elaborate sets and melodramas. Carmen could have been her own opera.

Darren was a middle school teacher. He was tall and thin like a willow; his hands were long and spindly, from his grandmother, he told me. A sweet, attractive, conservatively dressed man who hung out with a group of lesbians; only a few gay men bitterly claimed to have dated him—and these were mostly Asian or Latino. At that age, I lit up when I discovered a guy's multiracial romantic history because it meant I had a chance. I pursued Darren mercilessly until one night, when his friend was having sex with my roommate, he sat in my room. He wouldn't let me near him: we sat on opposite parts of the bed, naked, furiously masturbating, while we talked about the things we wanted to do. His best friend had died of AIDS, he told me, so this was the only sex he had. We never spoke again outside of casual greetings. I looked at his stream of Latino and Asian guys with pity after that.

Vince brought me into the HIV industry—at first, just volunteering to support weekly HIV education events before landing a full-time job of my own. He's always been his own kind of man, unpredictable in his conversations, choices, and moods. Once a waiter and a massage therapist, until finding himself widowed in San Francisco, and then working in HIV. He took me on my first trips cross-country as a gay man—to DC for the 1993 March on Washington, and later to New York. We started dating because

I looked like he did at my age, a resemblance that all his friends would comment on. We both had a dating history of racial difference; it was weird finding the sameness sexy—the smoothness, the hair, the gawkiness and floppiness, even the love of comic books. For a year, we did.

Leon was a remarkable liar. Everyone he dated knew a different story about him: he was a gangster, he dealt drugs, he used to be a fashion model, he used to date a celebrity. For me, he said he was a mixed-race Black and Filipino man. He came with me to a few college parties; we had sex a lot. He claimed me in ways that were charming to me then: "My man," "Baby," "All mine." A few years later, a friend is going through my photo album and finds a series of pictures with Leon. "Oh, you dated him, too? You know he died?" After checking with a few others, it turns out that Leon had passed in the same web of stories that I had known him to spin: he was homeless, no one claimed the body, his family didn't have a funeral, he was back to dating women.

I did not know what I was doing in sex. It was new and strange; I was too used to being an awkward boy to be cute or sexy, or any one of a number of things that seemed so easy for others. My lessons came from people in my orbit. Carmen taught me how quickly people forget, no matter how big your living is. From Darren, I saw the cost of fear, and the need for touch; from Vince, I was inspired to be in the world, to venture across it; from Leon, I realized that everyone has a version of you, and most never bother to learn more. There are vague impressions of other people behind how I do things, paths I've been down, and falls I've recovered from.

These ghosts come forward when I think about the '90s. They get more solid as I recall the pre-social-media past. I promise to do more, to create interventions in history so that their lives, and our moments together, continue to exist. I have never knitted a quilt panel; I tell the stories over and over. So many people I know, so many I had never met. I want to hold sacred the spaces where we danced, where we found and even failed each other.

A 2013 email from a peer who moved across country:

I am SO glad this is over ...

I am also regretful about many choices I have made in particular [over] the last 5 years but grateful you tried in small and big ways to offer loving support; it made [a] HUGE difference [in] making it as far as I did.

Ultimately there was too much pain and baggage to extricate and try to fix and/or ameliorate. I will miss all the fun and transcendent experiences we shared together. Please cherish those and keep them close to your heart, as I will ALWAYS!!!

With love and admiration till we meet again ...

My partner at the time and I considered him a friend: he was, in fact, the person who had introduced us. We phoned him immediately. He was loopy, clearly high. He talked about the clear sky and bright sun, the sound of children playing in the background. It was enough, he said, life is enough. I soothed him, then asked for confirmation. He said he was sure—this is it, good-bye—then he hesitated. We spoke about the children playing and the park he was in. "Help," he pleaded, changing his mind even as he felt himself slipping from the drugs already in his system. I had my partner keep him on the phone while I tried to get first responders to our friend. Eventually, we did and he spent the next month in a treatment facility.

After the incident, my partner looked at me with anger, disgust, and horror. "You would have let him die? You're a monster!" He was nearly yelling. "I was respecting his choice," I tried to explain. "This is the third time he's called me like this." We argued. "I can't want him to live more than he does," I said, exasperated. "No one can do his life for him." My partner, seven years younger and coming out in a different place, did not have the same experiences I had of weekly funerals and drag shows to raise money for them. "Would you do that to me if I was dying? Just let it happen?" I sighed. "If that was what you wanted." He took the dogs for a long walk, needing some space from me. I do not think he will ever forgive me for my honesty.

With love and admiration till we meet again.

At some point, people began turning to me in an emergency: family rejection, an accident, a vandalized car, a robbery, a beaten lover, an eviction, an overdose, impostor syndrome meltdown, any of the myriad troubles that come from being a queer person of color in the United States. Listening became a practice, rehearsed until my body was still, carefully unfazed, regardless of the news. Some people just want contact, a moment to stabilize in the chaos. There is power in a hug, to—as Essex Hemphill writes in his poems—"hold tight gently." We are more than one, yet so often we are split.

I can't hold on to everyone; none of us can. There are losses and damages that are beyond our arms. When this friend sent that email, did he expect me to save him? Or had he made peace with this ending? Suicide was familiar to him, so this choice was not unexpected. His email signaled both his need for help and his farewell. It was sent to a group; I was the only one who called.

Rarely do we get to say good-bye. We do not know when things are breaking away or when death comes. To be unresolved is a constant state. If I had not phoned after receiving the email, my then-partner and I would not have been able to be with him, and talk him through this moment. He would have died without anyone with him, he would not have been able to change his mind, and he would not have been able to live past that day. My then-partner's anger at me is a mystery. One lesson from the '90s is to say good-bye when you can and accept when you cannot.

Does this make me a monster? For my then-partner, it was the beginning of a growing disgust with me. My sense of humor has a sinister edge. I find deaths interesting in ways that make others uncomfortable. There is a coldness to my crisis responses. For my generation of gay men, I've found this to be normalized. Our experience in the HIV epidemic produced specific understandings of health, sex, loss, governmental neglect, stigma, and community. Calling us monsters denies that AIDS happened in the way that it did, that the epidemic continues to thrive in Black, brown, and poor communities because the HIV response did not change the world for everyone. The movement surrendered the need for structural change around racism, homophobia, and capitalism and instead settled for neoliberal solutions that included HIV medication.

If we be monsters, then I bid farewell to notions of civility and respectability. We do not need to play nice but can instead rain fire on the people and institutions that would mark us so.

Each era of HIV has particular characteristics that impact the ways that we come to know our bodies and each other. For me, the early '90s in the Bay Area taught me to value touch, to sit with disgust, and to commemorate events and people before we fade away. For a decade, whenever I returned to the Bay Area, I was greeted on the street and in bars with "Girl, I thought you died." At some point this stopped, because those familiar with me had either passed or moved away from the gentrified city. But the memory lingers.

We are a generation of witnesses, and this weight shapes how we love, how we fight, and how we break away. I hold this personal version of an AIDS memorial within. It comes between me and other relationships. I know what loss means; I approach people knowing I will say good-bye.

I do not know if I will ever be comfortable in the Bay Area. This city discomfits me, the layers beneath and all around us. This is where the ghosts are, for me. And until I find a way to make peace with those missing, I remain haunted.

Rea

HUGH RYAN

Have you ever been struck so suddenly that your body enters a momentary state of shock, where it acknowledges the sensation of what is happening but not the meaning? That is—when you know that you've been hit, but you don't know yet if you've been hurt? Time dilates; a single second yawns open and swallows the future, and you know that when reality returns you may be changed irreparably.

Throughout my college years (or from the fall of 1996 to the spring of 2000), I lived in that paradoxical second for two weeks out of every semester, in between my appointments with Rea.

Rea worked out of a small, taupe-on-beige office in our college student health center. Now, more than twenty years later, I can't remember much about the center itself. Not the building, nor the area of campus it was in. Was there a lobby? Did I make an appointment, or did I just show up? Other people must have worked there, but gun-to-my-head, I couldn't tell you a single thing about them. All I remember from my biannual pilgrimage was the hot, wet flop sweat radiating from my pits, and the fear balled in my gut—and Rea's voice.

That voice! Rea had a voice like the words were being scratched out somewhere dry and deep in her throat, not in her mouth at all. Low and firm, no bullshit, she instantly commanded every room she entered. People hopped to like hers was the voice of God—if God were a fifty-something dyke with emphysema (let's hope):

"ELISA is a test for the antibodies produced as a response to the human immunodeficiency virus. The results of this test will be confirmed using a Western Blot. The whole process takes about two weeks. This is a confidential test. I can no longer give you an anonymous test because of some horseshit from the CDC."

No one—no one—had ever before talked to me about sexual health and treated me like an adult at the same time. Once, the father of a high school friend had given me the first dose of the hepatitis vaccine while we stood awkwardly on my parent's suburban porch. He showed up with no warning, and he was a radiologist, so in retrospect, I have questions about the legality and safety of his actions. But it was the closest anyone had ever come to talking to me about the sex I might be having, instead of lecturing me about how homosexuals die of AIDS—a lesson I had already learned from movies, books, TV news, AM talk radio, Cardinal O'Connor, Ronald Reagan, George FUCKING Bush (George W. FUCKING Bush would come later), church, family, friends, teachers, and a particularly gruesome educational cartoon that depicted the virus wearing pointy World War I–era German helmets (an image indelibly burned into my mind).

Maybe that's why Rea's voice stayed with me—because it could cut through the homophobic Greek chorus that was always singing in the back of my head. Throughout my childhood I was convinced I would one day get AIDS; by the fourth grade, I already had a recurring nightmare in which I died of AIDS—during a Russian nuclear attack (it was 1987).

But never was the anxiety so bad as during the two weeks while I waited for my test results. Two weeks! Two weeks was a lifetime—a lifetime spent going over every sexual interaction I had ever had with the granularity of a crime scene investigator. I would stare at my hands, looking for cuts that could have provided the virus a way into my body, and only belatedly realize I was in class, wasn't taking notes, and had no idea what was being said. All I could do was wonder. Wait. Wanting time to speed up, so I could get my results. Wanting time to stop entirely, so I would never get them. Just wanting time, more of it, a full human life-span's worth, not the measly crumbs that gay men got. At eighteen, I didn't know any older gay men, but the media had shown me an endless parade of twenty-somethings who looked sixty-five. Fear was a well with no bottom, and I tumbled in free fall for weeks at a time.

When the worry got to be too much for me and I couldn't sleep (I could never sleep), I would let Rea's voice fill my head, assuaging my fears with risk factors and new medications: evidence that I didn't have it, and that the world wouldn't end if I did. It was like a mantra made out of gravel, and maybe that was why it worked. I don't think hope can be something fragile. If it were, it would break right when you need it. Rea didn't spin fairy tales and never minimized anything. She dealt in facts and sarcasm. In her mouth, AIDS wasn't an apocalypse or a personal failing; it was a medical condition.

Rea taught me about transmission, phlebotomy, RNA, viral loads, spermicidal lubricant with nonoxynol-9, AZT, the triple-drug cocktail, making a homemade dental dam out of Saran Wrap, the uselessness of laetrile, Kimberly Bergalis, night sweats, the powerlessness of positive thinking, the difference between confidential and anonymous testing, and a million other things, small and large, that turned the immensity of AIDS into something I could handle. But for all the times we met, I never learned much about Rea. She was that kind of professional. Years later, I discovered that she had been a sexual health activist for decades, and had worked with Planned Parenthood and fought for abortion access all throughout the '70s and '80s. I'm pretty sure she knew a thing or two about fear, uncertainty, and moral judgment.

I stopped seeing Rea around 2001, and shortly thereafter, the first rapid test for HIV came out. By this time, more drugs had been developed, and those who had access to them suddenly had access to the future. Silence settled in around AIDS—a different kind of silence than the one I had grown up with but a silence nonetheless. I still hear Rea's voice whenever I get an HIV test, but I hear it more now when I'm trying to help someone else in a moment of need. Some of the lessons Rea taught me, I didn't even realize at the time: What we live through, we can learn from. What we know, we can teach. And one voice can stop an epidemic—at least for one other person, for a few weeks at a time, when they need it most.

Lie Back and Get Comfortable

LIZ ROSENFELD

My dad is at the microphone: "This is now the moment in the evening when the bat mitzvah girl will announce the charity that she has chosen to donate a portion of her gifts to." I look up at him in panic. My heart races. I'm not at the point where I love performing yet. "We are so excited," he continues. "She wanted to keep it a secret until now." He leans in, and asks me to whisper it in his ear.

"Are you sure?" he asks, shit-eating grin even wider than before. I give him a silent, stern nod, as the room full of his friends and our extended family waits with bated breath. "Liz has decided that she would like to donate a portion of her gifts to ... Gay Men's Health Crisis." I have to hand it to him, his enthusiasm is consistent; he is a committed performer. I smile awkwardly as the guests around me clap diligently to hide their confusion.

I imagine the banner headline internally scrolling through the minds of the people in the audience:

HOW THE HELL DOES A THIRTEEN-YEAR-OLD GIRL FROM THE UPPER EAST SIDE KNOW ABOUT GAY MEN'S HEALTH CRISIS???!!!

Post-announcement, my mother's searing look from across the room says it all. When we fought about my weight, she would often admonish me by saying all her friends were thinking, *How could Naomi and Steve allow this to happen?!* And now I was not just a fat thirteen-year-old, I was probably a queer one, too. A queer kid who knew about AIDS. My future was clearly doomed.

Little did my mom know, I paid attention. One of my earliest memories is of eavesdropping on her talking with her best friend T right after his partner passed away. I remember them whispering to each other in the living room. The stress. The sadness. I later found out that the family of T's long-term boyfriend was threatening to cut T out of the will because they were "illegitimate partners" in the eyes of the law. Early morning, probably before he and my mother went to work, hiding behind the doorframe in my pajamas ... hearing his soft cries. My mom, sternly and silently listening to him, holding his hand, while also uncomfortable with the reality of her own position concerning Homosexuals and the AIDS Epidemic.

There was no question that she cared for and loved her friend. "At least he has his own money," she would say. "He is a brilliant business-man and genuinely loyal person. But it would just be so much easier if he wasn't a fag." A few decades later, I thought about this memory as I sat next to my mother, holding her swollen hand, while she lived out her final days in an induced coma. I wondered if she felt the same way about me: "She has a pretty face and a good education. It would have just been so much easier if she wasn't a fag."

BABY, LET ME BANG YOUR BOX

It's late. Very late. I am protected by the tent of my duvet, except for a small opening that I have made just big enough for my eyes to peek out. The TV turned down as low as possible, so I can still make out the sound and not get caught by the babysitter. It is tuned into Manhattan Neighborhood Network. *The Robin Byrd Show.*

"Lie Back. And Get Comfortable. Snuggle up next to your loved one. And if you don't have a loved one, you always have me, Robin Byrd."

Live strippers. Live voices you could talk to. Live boobs, pussies, and cocks. Live bodies and genders. People living with HIV/AIDS. I can still remember the call-in number flashing across the screen: 575-1550. Mostly men called in. Calls of admiration for Robin Byrd and her guests. Calls to find out where one could get safe sex supplies and HIV testing. I remember a gay man calling once. In tears, he thanked Robin for being supportive of queers. I never called her, but I thought about it a lot. There was so much I wanted to say to her, to ask her about. I wasn't just hot for her; I was also inspired. She made me feel. I wanted her to know this. She was the first person to encourage me to shamelessly jerk off and experiment with different ways to do so. Sexuality could be anything and everything. Everybody was a body. Fat, curvy, skinny, flat, femmes, butches, muscle queens, queers, heteros, and all and every gender in between. Her idea of sexual freedom read as an urgent need to move away from the compartmentalization and dehumanization of sexuality and the sex work labor force by creating a platform where people could talk to one another and feel inspired to fuck however they fucked but always with encouragement to "wear a rubber and use a dental dam."

Besides Robin Byrd, my initial insights into the AIDS crisis came from *AIDS Community Television*, a weekly show by members of ACT UP. Often the discussions centered on the impending threat to health care for people living with HIV/AIDS, local housing policies, a breakdown of recent protests, and discussions remembering community members who had passed away that week. The tone was always urgent and angry. Pragmatic and strategic. There was also a weekly call-in show called ACT UP Live, where, similar to *The Robin Byrd Show*, viewers could speak to members of ACT UP.

My sister, K, eight and a half years older than me, rich-Jewish-teenager-turned-anarchist, had left home for college, returning during the holidays when she would bring me to protests, political events, and "inappropriate films," against my parents' wishes, as she had throughout my childhood. K was great at looking out for me while not hiding anything and was next in line after Robin Byrd to show me how to use a condom, to introduce me to queer people, and to stand up to our parents: do-gooder liberal capitalists who threw money at the causes they cared about without having to get their hands dirty. She took me with her to the infamous ACT UP Stop the Church protest in 1989—my most vivid eleven-year-old memory is of feeling very, very small and holding her hand so tight. I can remember the overwhelming feeling that being there mattered. It was possibly the first time I felt urgently needed.

YOU WILL DIE ANYWAY

"I'm worried," my mom says to my father, as the three of us shuffle toward the cinema exit, shoulder to shoulder in a crowd after a screening of *Philadelphia*, the blockbuster movie where Tom Hanks plays a gay lawyer who dies of AIDS in the '80s.

"Huh?" I say. "What did you say?"

Over her shoulder to me, in an unnecessarily loud and slow voice, my mother says, "I. Am. Worried. About. Your. Sister."

K had recently come out as a lesbian in her college graduation speech. "Mom, why are you worried about K?"

"Well, Lizzy, you saw the film. Is there anything you want to ask me about? Anything confusing? Do you have any questions? Are you scared?"

"I think you are the one who is scared, Mom," I responded.

My mother always went silent when she was angry. The angrier she was, the deeper her silence became. Her silence was so loud that it would also silence the voices of everyone around her. She taught me that any woman who showed emotion in public, even at home in front of her family, was weak, and a weak woman would never thrive in a world fueled and defined by men. She was always winning. Even when she was dying of cancer, on and off, throughout the last decade of her life, she was still winning. Because knowing everything about your disease, before any medical professional gets to tell you, means power, even if it's temporary power over terminal cancer.

"You know Nancy Reagan and Rock Hudson were best friends," my mother would say. "And when he called her up to beg for access to drugs because he was sick, she just threw her hands up. I suppose it was business for her, you know? And friends and business, well ... In a way, he did it to himself, you know?"

No, I don't, Mom. I really don't know.

Sometimes I wonder if my mom had known as much about HIV/AIDS as she did about her own illness, would she have been able to help T, her best friend, through the death of his partner? Most likely not at that time, but I also think she wouldn't even have tried to support him, because she probably believed T's partner did it to himself.

My mom was the daughter of Holocaust survivors, anti-Zionists who met and fell in love in Palestine after they had both fled Germany, and then fled again with my mom when she was six years old, the year the State of Israel was established. They left everything again for New York City and settled in the Upper East Side in the early '50s. However, my mother was certainly not a queer person dying of AIDS. She never had to fight for her right to health care or to feel seen by the medical establishment. She was a rich white lady who got to decide for the majority of her life how she was allowed to touch the world and how it touched her back. She was a tough broad. An inspiring one in many respects. She hung on and fought through an illness that literally devoured her slowly from the inside out.

I don't regret much. I really don't. However, I do regret not standing up to my mother as much as I could have. In her most homophobic, anti-fat, anti-queer moments, which were all the moments, I could have fought back, I suppose. But I was also young. Too young to be taking care of a dying woman fighting to use her access and power to stay alive in the face of a disease that just wouldn't relieve her.

I also regret not saying "I love you" more. Saying it as a form of resistance to my mother's opinion that to say "I love you" was just another form of weakness. Is feeling loved, knowing you are loved, hearing you are loved a position of privilege? Over the past decade, many of my friends have tested HIV-positive. A few times some have referred to sharing their status with me as a second coming out. We were kids in the '90s, and we started our sexual lives with more accessible knowledge about sexual health on university campuses, even in some high schools, in urban centers, in popular culture. We knew that one could live a long and healthy life with HIV. Yet my friends who tested positive still felt afraid to tell their communities, I think, because of a fear of being judged for "reckless" behavior. A belief that they, as politicized queers capable of fighting for justice in the streets, should also be able to take care of their sexual health, and that becoming HIV-positive made them unworthy of compassion. We are a generation of queer people who are ashamed to admit that our politics are not synonymous with our desires. As a dear once expressed to me when coming out as HIV-positive, "What if our friends stop loving me? What will I do then?"

Shortly before my mother died, I was on duty at the hospital, trying to get her to walk around the room, as I had been instructed. "When did you get to be such a tough bitch?" she asked me with a tinge of love.

"Takes one to know one, Ma," I said.

"You're damn straight," she replied.

And I said, "Actually ... no ... I'm not."

As I placed her slippers on her feet, and tied her robe, she responded, "Well, it's awfully fashionable these days, darling. I always knew it would become fashion, ever since the gays started to survive."

I managed to get her to walk across the room ... just once ... but she did it.

In a 1997 *Washington Post* interview, Robin Byrd says, "I'm as tall or as young as your fantasy. That's all we really have these days—our imagination. If we lose our imagination, then we lose our drive to live."

I think this is just as true now.

Leaving Atlanta

STEPHEN H. MOORE

It's 1985 or 1986. I'm a nine-year-old kid in a girl's navy plaid school uniform jumper, with a Mary Lou Retton haircut, and it's late on a winter Friday night. I am *definitely* out after my bedtime. I am at the Majestic Diner. It's a community landmark in the Midtown gayborhood of Atlanta, but I don't know that. I just know that I've never been here before, and my beloved uncle Lester is taking me out for dessert, and he seems to know everybody.

We started the evening at his apartment, with a home-cooked meal more unusual than anything I had ever eaten: shark steak, egg noodles with butter and poppy seeds, and fresh green peas. Lester is an adventurous chef; he owns a wok, which no one else I know does. I've never seen a studio apartment before, growing up in the suburbs; his place is basically just a bedroom, with a tiny bathroom and a galley kitchen. The largest wall, above the bed, is mirrored. As an adult queer thirty-plus years later, I have all kinds of speculations about that decor feature and what his tricks thought of it. As a child, it was merely exotic.

I didn't know Lester was gay. I knew that he was my mother's youngest brother by three years, and I knew that he was my friend. And he knew that I wanted to be an astronaut when I grew up, and he wanted to help make that happen. After dinner at his place, we went to the Fernbank Science Center for an evening show, and then stood in line to look through the observatory telescope in the chilly night air. I remember the cold; I remember that we never made it to the front of the line, and that was how we ended up at the Majestic, looking at the list of pies. I don't remember whether the pie I ate was lemon meringue or coconut or chocolate cream. What I do recall is how friendly he was with the waitress, like he was a regular. What I do remember is that my dinner was too rich for my little-kid stomach, and that after I got home I threw up in my bed and was too ashamed to wake up my parents to change the sheets. What I do remember is that the night at the Majestic Diner was the last time I saw Lester alive.

Within a few months, I knew that Lester was sick with "pneumonia," that he was in the hospital in Columbus, where my grandparents lived. I remember my mother and her other brother meeting up to make the two-hour drive together while I stayed overnight at my friends' houses. I don't remember how long he was in the hospital. I remember my father pulled my sisters and me out of school in the middle of the day and started the long drive to Columbus. We were halfway down the road to my grandparents' house before he told us that Lester had died and we were going to his funeral. I had never seen a dead body before. I just remember looking into the casket, like the adults told me to do, and how beautiful Lester was in his good suit, and how I cried until I couldn't cry anymore.

I don't remember how many days of school I missed for the funeral, but when I returned, the other kids taunted me about how my uncle had been a "faggot." At the time, I didn't know what that word meant except that it was bad. I just knew, in my grade-school innocence, that there was no way Lester was a monster. I didn't know then, but I know now, that someone at my private school run by God-fearing women of the religious right must have explained Lester's death from AIDS to them, and probably said that it was "God's judgment on homosexuals."

Years later, I tell my therapist the story about my classmates taunting me, and her face falls in horror. For me, that story is just the wallpaper of my life; it's normal, like the way I've been a feminist since I was seven or eight. It's normal, like the corporal punishment that my father called "godly discipline" because the Bible said that to spare the rod was to spoil a child. It's normal, like the fact that I was a girl-child too smart for my own good. It's normal, like the fact that whenever I told an authority figure no, I ended up on the receiving end of a belt or switch to the ass.

Somehow, against all likelihood, I survived, made it out of the South, got higher education, lived to come out as nonbinary, and transitioned to the queer male life I live today. At the same time, some part of me will always be eight or nine years old, standing in the cold outside the planetarium in Atlanta, waiting to look through the telescope at a faraway star. And some other part of me will always be a child standing at Lester's open casket, unable to stop crying.

I wish I had more clear memories of Lester than that night at the Majestic Diner. I have to make them up, because my family refused to know the parts of him that I would know, now, if he had lived. Lester was born in 1953; he would have turned sixty-seven in the fall of 2020. The details of his death were the cautionary tale I didn't hear until I was sixteen, when I started to edge my way out of the closet as a queer young woman. All my Southern Baptist father could say when I told him I was struggling with my sexuality was, "Don't get AIDS and die; it would devastate your mother."

I didn't know a fuller story about Lester's death until another twenty years later, when my grandmother was on her deathbed, and my family insisted I come see her. That's when I met Linda, her home hospice nurse, who recognized Lester in the photos of ancestors arrayed around my grandmother's bed. While my grand-mother drifted in a fentanyl haze, metastasized stomach cancer ravaging her body, I sat with her and Linda, and I learned the ways of caring for a dying person. Take her vitals every few hours, write them down, note what's going on, make sure she knows where her morphine button is, and hold space for her to complete her unfin-ished business. And in this case, what she needed to do was hear Linda tell me stories from thirty years before.

Linda was a young woman in the mid-'80s when the thirty-two-year-old with the strange illness was admitted to her hospital. That hospital had never seen an AIDS case before. I learned that they were extra careful with Lester; the only medical staff who worked with him had volunteered for hazard duty. Linda had been his nurse, one of the only ones who trusted that she wouldn't be infected by caring for him. She told me that they put Lester in a ward with a separate negative-pressure ventilation system, just to be safe, but I knew that meant it was an isolation ward. No one could go in who wasn't willing to take the risk, even though HIV isn't an airborne virus.

I don't know whether family members were allowed in to keep him company, to hug him and make his last days as comfortable as possible. I don't know whether his gay friends were allowed to visit from Atlanta, assuming they could make the two-hour drive south from the city. Maybe only "family" visitors were allowed. Maybe no one was allowed into that isolation ward until the very end. I can't ask my mom or her homophobic brother, so I can only speculate.

I do know that when I went to that funeral as a child, it wasn't in a church. The Southern Baptist theology my family believes in says that "the wages of sin is death," and I don't remember the details of the funeral sermon from thirty-plus years ago. But I do know that my grandmother held on past the time I had to go back to my job, and that I'm bitterly glad not to have been at her funeral. Apparently, after her death, the preacher delivered a hellfire-and-brimstone salvation sermon to all the mourners. Was that the kind of sermon preached at Lester's funeral? I may never know.

I have no pictures of Lester other than his high school senior portrait. There may be some decaying VHS tapes somewhere of him at family events, but if so they're in the possession of his homophobic brother. I know he liked to cook; I've inherited his wok and his artisan-made, traditional wooden biscuit-making bowl. I still use both of them.

I know he had a motorcycle, and a vinyl rainsuit trimmed with blue and white, and fingerless gloves. His fashion sense included cuff links. The rainsuit has long since fallen apart, but his fingerless gloves are in one of my storage boxes. They're three sizes too large for my hands, but they tell me something about the adulthood of a man I never knew in his fullness.

By the summer of 2014, I was far from my childhood as a girl in Atlanta. I was in a different gender and a different city, with a different name. And I was on some gay cruising app or other, where the first thing I saw of Keith was his tattooed cock, because that was his user icon. I was turned on and fascinated. His trans etiquette was flawless, and he was open about being HIV-positive, and I figured we would of course use condoms, so I decided to take a chance. He turned out to be a handsome, hot silver daddy, and a perfect gentleman with a thing for trans guys that didn't cross the line into being a creepy chaser. He was twenty-plus years my senior, close to Lester's age, if Lester had still been alive, and I was hooked. I threw caution to the wind. This was what I'd been waiting for years to be able to do.

The first time we met, Keith came to the place where I was house-sitting for the summer, and I talked shyly with him for longer than anyone who's trying to hook up ever does, before he suggested we move to the bedroom. He was gentle and trustworthy, except when he wasn't gentle at all. His hands filled both my holes, spreading me open; his voice told me what to do with the poppers he brought. When the time arrived, there was a condom, and the moment was perfect—me facedown, his arms around me, his cock in my holes, first the front and then my ass, and the basement bedroom meant that I could cry out in joy and pleasure as loudly as I wanted without disturbing the neighbors. When I felt his cock throb and shoot, it was like coming home to a life I'd never dreamed of.

We kept hooking up. The sex was hot, and I was infatuated, even though I knew this wasn't going to be a Relationship like it would be with someone my own age. We pillow-talked about our lives, about the fact that his live-in partner was HIV-negative and took a drug called Truvada that kept him from getting HIV. This was the summer of 2014, and I didn't yet know about preexposure prophylaxis (PrEP). Keith told me about the science of HIV treatment and prevention. He was on effective medication for HIV that reduced the viral load in his blood and made it impossible for him to transmit the virus. We were in a city with some of the best HIV care and research medicine in the United States, and I was intrigued. I didn't even know undetectability was a thing, and Keith was telling me something miraculous. At the same time, I knew enough to know that nothing in my previous thirty-eight years had prepared me to take the sexual health risks of a queer man, so I went looking for help. After several doctors' visits, I lined up pregnancy prevention, an HIV test, and a prescription for PrEP.

Dear reader, condomless fucking was every bit as hot and delightful as I had hoped. Every time I have sex without barriers,

I feel connected to my queer forebears from before the plague. I know sensations and feelings that Lester knew, and I know them in my body and soul and spirit. Even now, writing about the joy and ecstasy of condomless gay sex feels transgressive to me, like it's something I shouldn't be saying out loud. There's no good reason for this. My friend Damon L. Jacobs points out that all of us got here because our parents barebacked, yet so many queers are still given the idea that the pleasure of condomless fucking is something we shouldn't desire, except at risk of horrible disease and death. That idea is part of the moralism I grew up around that called itself "Christian" while blaming queer men and injection drug users for their own deaths.

Using PrEP, I've experienced things I could not have imagined as an adolescent or young adult. I've used condoms when I wanted to, and much more frequently *not* used them because that's become a comfortable option for my level of risk tolerance—at orgies, in bathhouses, or wherever I can find the sex that feels pleasurable and liberating.

I recently started seeing someone new, a trans boy a few years younger than me who just started testosterone a few months ago. As part of getting to know one another, I tell him that the queer men I know who survived the plague years are some of the best people I've ever met. "I don't know any," he says, and I think, *We have to fix that.* Within a week, he's in Keith's barber chair, asking for "something more masculine" as part of his first professional men's haircut. They carry on a polite and friendly conversation, and my boy walks out into the sun smiling, a little more secure in his gender. For the first time, I feel like maybe the plague hasn't taken everything from us, like maybe there's a future where we all will know queers our parents' age who are as fearlessly, joyously sexual as we want to be.

Old Testament

ALEXANDER MCCLELLAND

I have had HIV my entire adult life. I found out in the late '90s, when I was eighteen. It was about a year after the major treatment breakthrough, the introduction of antiretroviral medications, that began to curb the massive death rate. But still, my doctor told me I wouldn't live past thirty, and public health nurses told me to refrain from sex altogether. The Canadian national news that year featured a story about a man being criminally charged for not telling a sex partner that he was positive.

I had grown up during the heyday of condom campaigns and was told many times that I should have known better; getting HIV was my fault for being reckless. Then, in 2008, something called the Swiss Statement came out, announcing to the world that people with HIV could get treatment to make the virus undetectable, meaning they would no longer transmit the virus through condomless sex. I theoretically understood this news, but I didn't act on it. I didn't know how to. I had been told for years by medical experts, campaigns, nurses, the media, and my peers that I was an infectious threat.

For most of my life, I have not been interested in advances in HIV prevention. Public health campaigns always manage to make it sound like the lives of HIV-negative people matter more. People like me are framed as scary risks from which others must be protected, as helpless charity cases, or as the sole people responsible for ending the epidemic. It was hard witnessing an ever-changing onslaught of messages meant to scare people away from becoming like me.

Many of my friends living with HIV avoided sex altogether, and I mostly slept with people who were also positive. The shame around sex after a diagnosis—what we were all told was the worst thing that could happen to us—was a lot to handle, especially coupled with the social hysteria. Sometimes the cuts went deeper: one ex, who was HIV-neg, told me this was his reason for dumping me. After a year of dating, he sat me down on a park bench during a summer afternoon and told me he couldn't be in a relationship with someone when he knew they were going to die. I said, "But we're all going to die." He walked away and stopped talking to me for years. After that, I mostly swore off HIV-negative guys altogether.

Of course, I worked to ensure that I couldn't transmit to others, but protecting my HIV-negative sex partners wasn't just an individual moral decision. It was part of an ethos of queer collective care I have learned over the years, an approach that grew from the early days of the HIV response, when HIV prevention was conceptualized as a shared responsibility. This feeling of community led to milestones like the 1983 booklet *How to Have Sex in an Epidemic*, which helped invent the idea of safe sex for gay men as a way to promote mutual affection, sexual expression, and joint responsibility. The primary authors, Richard Berkowitz and Michael Callen, were radicalized in college in the '70s as part of gay liberation, feminist, anti-war, and racial justice movements, and although *How to Have Sex in an Epidemic* was debated intensely among gay men at the time, the ethos behind the text nonetheless inspires me to imagine the collective trust I want for all of us.

Still, for me, it was a full five years after the Swiss Statement that I again decided to give an HIV-negative guy a chance. He was persistent and a bit younger; things had changed, and he had grown up with less hysteria. He wasn't scared of HIV or of my body. He understood, in a way that even I hadn't quite accepted, that I couldn't transmit, and he was totally uninterested in condoms.

Living with HIV is now a common human experience. There are as many people around the world living with HIV as there are residents of Canada, the country where I live. In 2019, an HIV-positive man in Portugal celebrated his hundredth birthday, and doctors say the life expectancy for HIV-positive people is close to average when, like me, they have the privilege of being connected to treatment, housing, and a decent income. For some, life with HIV has been radically transformed to a state of near normalcy.

But that doesn't mean all the underlying problems have just disappeared. Despite some recent progress, Canada is still one of the world's worst countries when it comes to criminalizing people living with HIV—creating criminal repercussions, in certain jurisdictions, for people if they don't tell a sex partner they have the virus, even if medication has made them uninfectious. As a result, the only HIV-related bodily harm I'm likely to face is from the police or from people's hatred. It has often seemed to me that the fear that has made HIV criminalized is the same fear underpinning HIV-prevention campaigns. To many of us living with the virus, fear is the real problem, not HIV. As a result, I've never understood my sexual life as an adult outside of the parameters dictated by the police and the criminal justice system.

Having HIV means living with a sort of cognitive dissonance— holding multiple contradictory ideas in one's head at once. Although I can't stand the capitalist ethics of pharmaceutical companies, I must also take my once-a-day pill to stay alive. And now there is Truvada, a once-a-day pill for people who are HIV-negative. Yes, in initial trials, Truvada had been tested on female sex workers in sub-Saharan Africa, including some who had been displaced when foreign-owned oil drilling forced them from their land. Yes, it can feel counterintuitive to be advocating for a preventative pill for HIV-negative people when there are still more than 10 million people globally living with the virus without access to anti-HIV drugs. Yes, that pill is now being marketed primarily to wealthy gay men in the Global North, including the settler-colonial state of Canada. It seems to be the epitome of globalized capitalism, patriarchy, white supremacy, and medical apartheid wrapped up in one not-so-tiny pill.

It's undeniable that the pill, in certain parts of the world, has the potential to radically reduce new infections. Canada could be one: gay and bisexual men (and other "men who have sex with men," as the epidemiological buzz terminology goes) still represent 55.5 percent of all new HIV infections in this country. We make up approximately 2 to 3 percent of the population, but are 131 times more likely to get HIV than straight men. Surprisingly, although HIV infections have decreased in many countries, Canada's rates are still on the rise; experts believe the new infections are linked primarily to people who don't know they're HIV-positive (and sometimes linked to transmissions that happen outside of sex).

So let's not overstate how far we've come. But for guys having sex with me, PrEP is, in a way, redundant. It is already impossible for HIV-positive people on treatment, like myself, to transmit to anyone. More than that, it's basically all the same drug: PrEP is one of the same chemical compounds taken by people living with HIV, the same drugs that make us no longer infectious. PrEP wouldn't exist if HIV treatment hadn't already been made effective. This is something most people, including HIV-negative guys, don't often seem to know.

I'm forty-three now. Some have said that the PrEP era means we are all "HIV equal," dispensing with the negative and positive. This so-called new era can be confounding, at least to me. Just a little over a decade ago, in 2008, a man known as the "Berlin patient" was famously cured of HIV through an extremely expensive bone marrow transplant. The news traveled around the world, and although the procedure proved not to be viable for mass application, it was considered a triumph. The man became HIV-negative, and in 2017, he announced he was on Truvada. In other words, he was taking almost the same medication as when he was HIV-positive. The announcement hurt my brain. Was this scientific progress? Was this queer sexual liberation?

A few years ago, a friend emailed me a link and a note: "Check this out!" It was a blog post. I immediately called him so we could read it to each other, both in shock from what it said. The blogger was reclaiming a "whore" identity, a "Truvada Whore," because he believed people thought that PrEP encouraged promiscuity and that society was judging his choice to have sex without condoms. He went on and on about his sex life. "He thinks he experiences stigma," scoffed my friend, who works in HIV prevention. "Tell him to call me once he's lost his job or housing or been sent to jail because of HIV."

PrEP was allowing HIV-negative gay men to explore new possibilities in their sex lives, and some white, cisgender HIV-neg guys suddenly had a space to unleash all their sexual entitlement, not to mention some narcissistic exhibitionism. This was still well before the PrEP floodgates had fully opened, and blogs like this were only starting to trickle out.

More was still to come. Since PrEP was launched on the American market in 2012, it has become impossible to avoid. The powder-blue Truvada pill has joined the ranks of mainstream pop culture iconography, so ubiquitous is it in queer male spaces.

Gilead, the company that makes Truvada, funds NGOs across North America that routinely launch new social marketing campaigns. Convincing people to take medicine as a preventative drug when they are not yet sick is notoriously a challenge. But encouraging people to champion that drug by linking it to their own empowerment—that's a next-level marketing feat. This has happened with PrEP to an extent not seen since the birth control pill.

The astonishing production of PrEP-themed merch includes, but is not limited to, T-shirts, posters, key chains, and tote bags. Unlike people with the virus who take anti-HIV medications, those on PrEP seem to flaunt their pills. I see them prominently placed in people's apartments, posted on social media; in gay bars guys take their pills publicly, as if to say, "Look at me; I am taking care of my health," or in other words, "Let's fuck; I'm desirable." On Instagram in late December 2018, artist and musician Casey Spooner posted a pic of a Truvada pill on top of a Bible, with the caption "NEW TESTAMENT."

That first blog post I saw was replicated over and over, shaping the idea of PrEP as a whole new identity. The homo blogosphere has been flooded with first-person narratives of the trials and tribulations of being a "Truvada Whore," with such pieces as "Please Feel Free to Call Me a Truvada Whore," or "You Say 'Whore' Like It's a Bad Thing."

Many of the writers of these posts call upon histories of queer sexual liberation—but those times were about demanding changes to oppressive social structures, such as anti-sodomy laws. The current movement is instead about demanding individual protection from people in their own communities.

PrEP's popularity goes beyond social media. Medical professionals have also championed the drug, with the World Health Organization now recommending that a large portion of sexually active gay men go on the drug full time. Similarly, PrEP is also now targeted at men of color, trans men, and trans women. Many of these communities have started to articulate similar individual self-empowerment messaging about the pill.

As one of my exes put it, "Either you have the AIDS, or you're on the PrEP." He is HIV-positive, rarely talks about HIV, and when he does, only as a joke. Still, he's right: the barrage of marketing and hype means there has been little room for conversation or dissent about what PrEP means, let alone the decision to take it. The drug has been framed as a polemic: either you are against it, meaning you are sex-negative, slut-shaming, and against gay male liberation, or you aren't. But I worry that zero-sum games have high stakes.

Like most gays, I go through phases of using hookup apps: I delete them, use them, delete them, use them. The last time I re-added Scruff onto my phone, it was a Friday night and I was newly single. That's when I came across new profile options. One, called "safety practices," included checkboxes for "condoms," "PrEP," or "treatment as prevention"—meaning you have HIV and are taking treatment rendering you uninfectious. Additionally, under the "I am into" section, I could now indicate if I was looking for someone else who had HIV, listing "poz," and under the "I am" section, I could include "poz" as a self-identifier. Although I appreciated the new options, they also kind of creeped me out. I'm old-school, wary of the consequences of technologically mediated sex and how information could be used in a future of omnipresent surveillance. Ultimately, I decided to avoid the new ways of publicly labeling myself. I filled in what I felt comfortable with and began scrolling through profiles.

I found a guy nearby who was hot; we expressed mutual attraction and shared the usual introductory, inane, flirty small talk. The conversation moved to sex, and I asked what he was looking for. He responded, "Vers, open, mostly into bb." I responded, "Same, I'm undetectable."

The chat ended there; he immediately blocked me. This response to a guy disclosing his HIV-positive status is a common one, and it still stings, but I just move on. The block is much better than the moralistic diatribe that some HIV-negative guys feel entitled to spew: "How dare you, trying to still have sex, you sick fuck!" was one of my favorites. I moved on to a few other options on the grid, deciding, in my next chat, to say that I'm undetectable as soon as possible to avoid wasting time.

Another guy initiated this time: "Hey, how goes?" I disclosed my status within the first few minutes. He responded, "It's ok, I'm on PrEP." The discussion then turned to logistics—as far as he was concerned, we no longer had to talk about risk.

I've heard this from guys many times: that my viral undetect-ability is of no interest. They are on PrEP, so it doesn't matter what's going on with anyone else. One of my exes, who is also HIV-positive, often deals with this when hooking up with new people. "Before PrEP, as a poz person, I would have conversations with guys," he told me over dinner. "We talk about ourselves and responsibility and HIV, build a human connection. It was a process, a way to get to know and be accountable to each other. Now they are like, 'I'm on PrEP, who cares, let's fuck.' It's like choosing from a catalog."

Taking the pill can mean more action and less talk, but is it the sexual revolution we're looking for? PrEP is emancipating some of us from the legacy of AIDS hysteria, but sometimes I think it's also dividing us. The moment to have a bonded connection over our shared relationship to HIV, negative or positive, is no longer on the table. For some of us who have lived with HIV for a long time, this can be refreshing, and for others, disconcerting.

One problem is that basics about HIV or STI transmission are still rarely taught or understood. The rise of PrEP, and people's disinterest in talking, means that, in some cases, I have to do the work of educating HIV-negative men about their own sexual health while I'm looking for action. This is a conversation that most guys don't want to have, and they think PrEP means they no longer need to. I decide to pass on lecturing this guy tonight, and we arrange to meet up, me traveling to his place, a few blocks from mine.

Anti-HIV medication has had a tremendous impact on my physical and mental health. No longer being able to transmit the virus has given me a sense of freedom and a moment to breathe. But enabling greater sexual freedom is not the same thing as addressing stigma and fear.

PrEP has become a dual-purpose regimen; its second purpose is to manage HIV anxiety among gay men. My roommate is HIV-negative, sexually active, rarely uses condoms, is not on PrEP, and has never had an STI. I often call him an enigma, the last unicorn. "PrEP is as much of a mental health drug as Tylenol is," he says. Surely every drug is partly a placebo, after all.

I spent New Year's Eve in New York City with a lover of mine, and early in the morning, on a packed train from Brooklyn to Penn Station, I talked to him about how much I've been thinking about fear.

"What would it mean if we started taking the fear of gay men seriously?" he asked. "How are we to make sense of the history of AIDS and death when we have not had space to ever do that?"

I agree—fear is a rational response to the traumatic legacy of AIDS, but it's still disconnected from the realities of HIV today. My friend continued thinking out loud: "The pill isn't enough to help us address the root causes of our fear," he said. "But what else do we have access to?"

The collective trauma of the HIV epidemic has been passed down through generations, but we rarely contend with it as a community. There has not been room for healing; that's not how the world is organized. How do we grapple with the past grief of a group that was largely ignored and marginalized? People died while everyone else continued to go about their business. The grief and deaths of thousands of gay men, trans women, injection drug users, sex workers, immigrants, people of color, and other marginalized people were not taken seriously then, so how can the grief and fears of subsequent generations be taken seriously now?

I think of the shared moments our communities have established, like annual AIDS vigils—times to come together and mourn. In the past, these events have been helpful for me in working through this history. But one evening a year can't fix it. The idea of a silver bullet continues to persist in responses to HIV because it avoids the messy complexities of rebuilding broken parts of society. Taking a pill might be soothing, but in the end, we can't avoid facing the past. However painful, it's part of us, part of what made our community what it is, for better and worse. With the advent of PrEP, discussions about an end to the crisis through other means have halted. It's almost as though PrEP is regarded as a cure itself.

Change, though, is often incremental. I think back to when that lover of mine, the one who helped me talk things through on the train, first told me he was on PrEP. One night, he called me out of the blue. I was on my way to a friend's place in Montreal's Gay Village. It was a warm night and I sat on the sidewalk of Sainte-Catherine Street, which had been made into a pedestrian-only main drag, and looked up at the strings of colored balls that hang overhead each summer. He was about to visit me for the first time and told me he was anxious about the trip and anxious about sex. He had never slept with a positive guy—at least, not one he knew was positive. Our first real date was happening in a high-stakes, long-distance scenario.

I wondered if I was setting myself up for another negative guy letting me down. His general anxiety about the trip was warranted; I was anxious, too. But his HIV worries weren't. I felt overwhelmed by the usual fatigue that comes with being asked to manage the HIV panics of negative guys. I was concerned that through taking PrEP he was buying into an individualistic way of thinking—a way of thinking that regards my body as a problem, when it isn't.

I realized that wasn't the case with him—he did understand the critiques of PrEP. Yet he still felt like it was right for him at this time in his life. Perhaps the way forward is to throw away all the meanings ascribed to PrEP, to people who choose to use it and to those who choose not to. I simply told him I thought his worries about HIV were unfounded, which he knew. I tried to listen and understand instead of react. He was being honest about his dread and was naming his anxiety in order to move beyond it, not entrench himself. It was a way to become closer.

Ultimately, as I sat on the curb and it got late, we had a good talk: I overcame my initial reactions, and he was less worried. When he visited, we had great sex, partially because of the closeness we'd established in that talk. In the end, it was a moment of connection that can so easily be lost.

The Conversations We Need to Save Each Other's Lives

CHARLES RYAN LONG AND
THEODORE (TED) KERR

We met in the hallway of a fancy Mexico City hotel. It was 2008, and we both were contributing to an activist blog for that year's International AIDS Conference. We were early to the meet and greet before work began, and we started talking. Twelve years later, our conversation continues.

Throughout our friendship, we've worked on many projects together, including a 2012 performance for Visual AIDS entitled *We Didn't Talk about This*, and, most recently, RAGE IS SUSTAINABLE ONLY WHEN SHARED, a series of workshops we hosted in 2018 in New York City and Chicago.

Ted is white, forty-one, Canadian, and HIV-negative. charles is Black, forty, living with HIV, and was born in the United States. What emerges from our conversation is an interest in the middle, the space between the AIDS crisis that was and the crisis that is.

charles: I think people say hurtful things about AIDS when they have been told how to feel about it and have not had the time to sort out their own feelings. Living with the ignorance and ignorant is dangerous, and toxic, not just for me, as a person surviving, but also for the person holding the thoughts.

Soon, I will have been living with the virus longer than not living with it. I remember, as a baby gay, going to give blood and I was blocked. This was pre-diagnosis. Being turned away from offering up what was inside of me cemented this sensation that I grew up with that as a gay man I needed to be contained, and that I would always have to wear condoms. I was disgusted—in a political way—with the idea of having to wear this barrier for the rest of my life solely because of my attraction to penis. I was a Black gay kid on the South Side of Chicago, so I was at the intersections of homophobia and racism, coupled with the sketchy medical industrial complex's history with the Black body at large.

Ted: I grew up seeing communities bound together by AIDS on TV, or at my city's AIDS Walk—and that access to AIDS communities shaped me. Yet it wasn't until the summer when I met you, and so many other great people, in Mexico City that I felt like I had a real AIDS community that I could grow into. And it was after that when I began asking questions, especially in terms of what I did with my body.

charles: Do you think a young person now in Edmonton would be able to see communities bound together by AIDS?

Ted: Not as easily. I came of age sexually in a period of time I call the Second Silence. Starting around 1996, with the release of life-saving meds, the epidemic went quiet. People were still diagnosed, and caring for each other, but AIDS went from a public concern that activists had kept on the social agenda to something overtly private. I think the visibility of communities bound by AIDS was lost during the Second Silence. It left me, and people our age, to feast on scraps from the immense cultural production from the decade prior. This experience has made me almost pathologically focused on making noise about HIV. And I see that in you, especially around talking about HIV through a larger lens of justice.

charles: Do you feel like, if you had the magical power, that you would want to either be born earlier and be part of that decade of Keith Haring and Larry Levan, or be born later, and come of age post–Second Silence?

Ted: I am grateful I was not a young adult in the First Silence, those early years before ACT UP, and I am specifically happy I came of age before PrEP. With Truvada not on the table, I had to deal with my thoughts about HIV in a way that I think PrEP helps people avoid. I was told as a young person to be afraid of HIV, and I knew that this way of being wasn't going to work for me. I refused to be afraid of AIDS.

charles: Because you knew that it would paralyze you as a person?

Ted: I knew I couldn't be afraid of HIV and be the person I wanted to be in the world. I worked to not fear the virus, because I never wanted to be in a position where I was afraid of someone with the virus.

charles: I feel similarly. I got into prevention before I sero-converted. I was also taught to be afraid of HIV. I was taught that there's this killer looming. But I remember the first poz person I met, and what that person meant to me—as a person. At the place I worked at, prevention meant coming together and doing the work to separate the virus from the person so that we did not stigmatize the positive identity. And I think we have lost that step. With PrEP, people can just avoid HIV, which means avoiding a part of a person. And this relates to the grand othering that has been happening for too long where people do not identify with people. Instead, we make bonds based on race, sexual orientation, gender, size. I feel like people are looking to align more than connect. And so this has an impact on everything from dating to HIV.

Ted: The only time I get nostalgic for an AIDS time is when I see old-school HIV activists kiss wet on the lips. I do it now, too, because somewhere along the way I learned that this was an act—not of solidarity but of belonging. Instead of the unknown causing fear, the activists used the unknown to bring them together. It's good to embrace the positive unknowns. The activists learned it from each other. I learned it from you!

charles: What? When?

Ted: It was 2012-ish. We left a Midtown roof dance party to go find the piers. Under the glow of the pizza parlor awning on Eighth Avenue, as we waited for our order, I thought it would be really cool to say to you, "Let's talk about all the things that we're sad about." You were like, "No, I'm sick of people doing that. I wanna talk about the things that bring us pleasure and joy, and I wanna talk about where we can start from."

charles: Damn, I'm smart! I think it relates to what is missing with PrEP. It is what I was trying to say earlier. The people in prevention, myself included, in the late '90s and early 2000s, were trying to get people to learn how to negotiate their best sexual selves, and too little of that moment caught on or survives. Instead, we only swapped condoms for a biochemical intervention, right? So people are still largely unaware of what they are doing with their bodies, and what they want to do. This sucks because I think AIDS can propel us into deeper exploration, beyond and through penetration. On the apps I see guys advertising themselves as cum dumps, and I am like, okay, but maybe just let me know on your profile why you are doing this, some hint of intention. I like the boldness, but I guess I just want it to have the same sense of awareness as when, for example, you kiss a fellow AIDS activist on the lips.

Ted: I mean one of the things that meeting you and our friends in Mexico City did for me was question my sex. For example, for a long time anal sex was not something on my mind. For a long time I didn't even fully understand what it was.

charles: Wait, what?

Ted: I mean, I knew what it was in theory, but in terms of practice, and desire, it was kinda fuzzy to me. But in this relationship anal sex became important, and related to it was condom use— even though we were two HIV-negative people, in a monogamous relationship.

charles: I don't understand. Why were you using condoms?

Ted: For a lot of reasons. First, because as a kid I grew up in the age of AIDS in Canada, with a decent education system that, while not LGBTQ-friendly, did drill into us this idea that condoms were the responsible and expected thing to do.

Second, as I have come to understand, for me, condoms were less about HIV and more an emotional layer around my then-complicated feelings around anal sex. It was, for me, some misbegotten sign of gay citizenship.

charles: Ha! I am certainly the opposite. I've always found condoms to be annoying, I did not like them and I think they complicated the pleasure I was able to get from intimacy. Like, I don't think I had really good anal sex until my early thirties. I didn't know how to activate my butt. I did not think about my own desires because, first, as a person with HIV who grew up in a society that doesn't honor my Blackness, it was just enough that someone desired me. After I let that go, then I could actually dig into my own desire. And that means that right now I can say I want seven people to run a train on me, and I can actively identify what that is about, versus thinking it was hot because that is what I had been told or saw on MyVidster.

Ted: I think I didn't put myself in positions of desire because of early childhood stuff where rejection could lead to a lack of survival. I think as an older person who has sex, at first I didn't question why I was topping. I was too focused on the other person.

charles: And you were hoping that people would just be satisfied with your dick?

Ted: I thought they would be satisfied because of a shared moment.

charles: What did you want?

Ted: I spent a lot of time suppressing fantasies about being crushed. Only when I was nearly inconsolable would I find the language, with my first boyfriend, to have him lie on me, to feel the weight of full-body contact. To me, kissing and hugging and bearing the wholeness of a person is the thing I ache for.

charles: And, ultimately, the greatest sex comes from that combination of what you're talking about with connection and the ability to express those full desires.

Ted: Right, and this is where it gets tricky. I want a fulfilling sex life, and I want that for others. But I am turned off by people who work to obtain sexual pleasure without any consideration of people beyond who they want to fuck. What makes it worse is this pursuit is too often framed as a radical politic in the name of AIDS. For me, radical sex comes with earthly costs. Not in the sense of punishment or illness, as our haters would have us believe, but in terms of fleshy compromise: the space between fantasy and possibility.

charles: Say more about the relationship to AIDS.

Ted: In a romantic view of the epidemic, AIDS is this thing that robbed the world of young gay men, and then put restrictions on who and how we, the living, could fuck. And of course this story is true and ours to wrestle with. But AIDS is also actually more insidious. The struggle of gay men in relationship to AIDS sits in the larger story about medical apartheid and misogyny.

charles: Not to mention drug use, stigma related to drug use, poverty, all forms of racism, and so much more.

Ted: Right. I mean, AIDS is a very alive topic in the twenty-first century; I just think we are not yet having the conversations we need to have to save each other's lives. Nor are we being intersectional enough when we do talk about HIV.

charles: Wait, and this is why you can't fuck?

Ted: You are a jerk. But yeah, kinda. As I have gotten older, I have become better at being vulnerable, but I am not so interested in being vulnerable with someone who is ignorant about male privilege, gay exceptionalism, and white supremacy.

charles: So the price of good sex for you is what?

Ted: I don't know. I think the price we pay for good sex is how we figure out what to do with what we can and cannot have. I think the best sex happens because what ends up transpiring is different than what we had been anticipating.

charles: Do you have an example?

Ted: Well, remember that time you came back to New York after you moved? We hung out, as friends, fellow artists, and organizers on a stoop in the West Village. And then we hugged on Fifth Avenue as you went to jump on the subway. In that hug there was electricity between us.

charles: I remember.

Ted: I could feel the weight of our bellies against each other. I was at the point in my life where I was pretending that I was still 120 pounds. But to have our tummies navigate one another that way was hot. We walked away from each other, turned around, and we were like, "Did you feel that?" I had to admit that my body was not the body I wanted, but actually, the body I had felt good with the body you had.

charles: I am coming to love this idea that desire comes at a price. When you first said it, I was like, "Oh man, that feels like a bummer." What I am thinking is that the cost is the price of negotiation. You have to do the work internally to figure out what you actually need or want.

But I have to say, I think you are assuming people know what they want. And I don't think they do. I think we have created sexual cultures that have allowed people to become less connected to personhood. Negotiation requires an ability to hold up a mirror, to see yourself and feel your feelings when confronted with yourself. Negotiation is even better when people having sex can share in the confrontation, the distance between fantasy and reality.

Ted: And maybe riding that compromise is also the experience of an artist.

charles: Yes! There is a connection between art and sex. And let me say, when it comes to art, I am negotiating my annoyance around our current culture's limited idea of wokeness. This comes from my own understanding that there is no wokeness without having a love for people or community.

Ted: Meaning?

charles: Wokeness comes from intimate confrontation. Many people within the art world and activist spaces can't handle this. They get away with slogans and hashtags, and that distracts us from the nuance, the lived, messy, complicated cultural and emotional impact of the systems. Things get treated with a blanket. During the Second Silence, AIDS was hard to see in a museum. Now, you go, and the write-up about any artist who ever lived in the East Village in the '80s is seen through the lens of AIDS, with no real reckoning of if and how AIDS impacted that person's life. So, what is interesting to me is work about AIDS rooted in a wholeness.

We need this work to be rooted less in identity and more in ongoing practice that lets people dip in and out. I can do the right thing in some direct action, and then unwind and watch the problematic and lovable Golden Girls.

Ted: I agree, and yet I have my limits. A commitment I have is to privilege the voices of the people living with HIV over anyone else. This is a kind of essentialism I can get behind. And it is an inherited wokeness that is as old as AIDS activism itself. People with AIDS know what they are talking about because they are People with AIDS.

charles: Well, I think we too often don't challenge that. There are people living with the virus who can't scream their desires and stories, and while there is a lot of room for the problematics of people representing other people's stories, it can be done with care and consideration. It does not make sense for us to talk about the ongoing role of stigma on one hand, and then assume and demand that all AIDS representation come from people living with the virus on the other.

Ted: Maybe we—or I—need to be careful about essentializing people with HIV. While lived experience is real with the virus, I think what you have been asking is what happens when sex, activism, and art are rooted less in rigid ideas of identity and more in practice and exploration.

charles: I appreciate that. But let me also say, at the same time, if we don't create a negative status that doesn't stigmatize the positive person, we won't move ahead in our work. Too often AIDS work is just prevention. And that is not really for poz people. That is for negative people.

Ted: I think, throughout our conversation, we keep coming back to a middleness, a shared space of possibility where we can bring in everything, including politics, race, HIV status, sexuality, artistic practice, attraction ... I mean, maybe everything ...

charles: The middle is powerful.

Ted: I have to tell you something—we never found the piers that night after we got our pizza. You let me lead, and I got us stuck at the base of some overpass heading to Jersey. On a concrete barrier, long after the sunset, we sat near some dead greenery, drinking soda, burping, talking about possibilities, and breathing in car fumes.

charles: I think it was the entrance to the Holland Tunnel. And here we are, still in the middle of that conversation, waiting to pass to the other side.

Scar Tissue

ADRIAN RYAN

Some stranger just came in my ass.

It was the night after Christmas. The second time in my adult life that any guy has come in my ass. That I remember.

"Hey, faggot! How does it feel to know your own death?"

Fifth grade, some seriously nasty little jerk called Mike Dennehy screamed that at me across the classroom. And everyone laughed. Including the teacher.

This was in 1985, just after Rock Hudson was diagnosed with AIDS and every tabloid on the planet exploded, because nobody knew he was gay and he had just deep-kissed Linda Evans on an episode of *Dynasty*. And people still thought you could get AIDS by kissing.

The stranger who came in my ass two weeks ago was on Scruff. He messaged me, wanting to hook up. No face pic. I didn't care.

I had come home to Southwest Montana to celebrate the holiday with my family. The guy who came in my ass drove twenty miles from some rural outlying nowhere place in the middle of the night to bareback me. We did it in the alley behind my family's house in the back of his tacky, tricked-out monster truck. The sex was filthy and dangerous and incredible.

And I am terrified.

I scheduled a test with Kaiser two weeks ago—a full STI panel. Kaiser is conveniently located only two blocks from my apartment. But I don't have the courage to go in yet.

Lately, I'm sweating at night when I try to sleep. It's probably just my radiators—they are ancient and run very hot at night. Or the new comforter. It's heavy and thick. Also, I've kind of been drinking a lot.

I grew up on a steady diet of AIDS fear, and AIDS grew up with me. The terror of it still lives inside my brain, my stomach, my bones, everything. When a headache happens, a mysterious bruise, a fever, a sneeze, I still think I am going to die ugly in shit and shame.

I'm so fucking pissed at myself. I am not on PrEP anymore, and that dude came in me. I let him. *I asked him to.* I want to throw up.

PrEP is a fucking miracle. All the new HIV medications are.

As part of the PrEP protocol, you have to get tested every few months. When I finally mustered up the courage to join the program in late 2014, it was the first time I'd been tested in more than five years. Negative. I wept with relief. And so I went on the program.

PrEP was the best antianxiety medication I ever could have taken. The terror I had endured my entire life wasn't there anymore, like a broken car alarm suddenly unstuck, just like that. Even the nightmares—dark, sweaty dreams of sores and sickness—gone. I felt free for the first time in my life.

For a while. I made a valiant attempt at PrEP. I tried my best. But I had to stop taking it. My guts can't handle it. For nine months, PrEP shredded my stomach and gave me an interminable case of the shits. So, I made a hard choice: freedom from fear, or eat and poop again normally, ever. I chose to eat and poop.

I grew up in a small, mean town in Montana. A mining city. The only other obviously queer kid my age was Joseph McQueen. Joseph was mean and conniving, and he and I could never admit to each other that we were gay; it was too dangerous, and we were both smart enough to understand that.

Joseph used to make up lies like it was his personal mission from God. Childish lies, like that scientists had discovered that AIDS is caused by bacteria. Every guy on earth has this peculiar bacterium on his penis—you're magically immune to your own, but if you dared touch some other guy's dick ... WHAM! AIDS! So stupid. He was trying to clock my reaction. He suspected I was messing around with Calvin, the kid across the street. He was right.

I moved to Portland in 1992 with my best friend Justin and his fiancé Mikey so we could be gay. I was just out of college. We all knew that being gay in Montana was dangerous and pointless for us. The comparative risks of living in the big city seemed worth it.

Justin suddenly became very sick, with a scorching fever that caused mad hallucinations, like his oven jumping away from the wall to attack him. The fever went on for so long that he lost his job for missing so much work. He was unable to support himself anymore. I suspected the worst, but his pride would never let him tell me. He broke it off with Mikey, packed up everything in his new apartment, and moved home to his family back east. We'd only been in Portland for three months.

Soon after, Mikey started coming down with strange things, too. Thrush on his tongue. That's how it started. A vile creamy white fungal infection that looked like rotten vanilla pudding. A primary symptom. I knew he was positive before he knew. I gave him gentian violet for his tongue and begged him to take the test that I was too afraid to take. Mikey is still alive today, but what the virus, and the early toxic treatment, did to his body is terrifying.

I navigated my lifelong hatred of condoms by twisting and pruning my sexual activities like a bonsai tree. A guy and I could go all the way to pound town and back again, but no exchange of semen, one way or the other, ever. Not by mouth, not by ass, not by anything. Verboten.

Primarily, I had to convince myself I was a top. That took some serious mental gymnastics.

One in three gay men in Seattle was HIV-positive in 1994, when I moved there. Every week the obituary section of the *Seattle Gay News* was endless. Friends who tested positive went to crazed, desperate extremes. My friend Chris used a machine he constructed from blueprints he got God knows where that would generate an electrical current to zap the lymph nodes in his neck, crotch, and armpits to kill the murderous bug. He died around 1997.

I knew guys who douched with bleach or Listerine after getting fucked. I knew people who drank vile mixtures of aloe vera and hydrogen peroxide from the GNC at the mall. It was supposed to kill the virus. My first ex tried that. David. It gave him an ugly rash on his legs and back.

Keith was my last friend who *officially* died of AIDS. He did not go down without a fight.

Keith claimed he was one of the first identified cases of AIDS way back in the early '80s, and he hung on by his fingernails for decades. He had a tattoo in gothic script on the back of his neck that read "McNasty." He was funny. But funny wasn't enough to save him.

Keith never went on the pills. No AZT or interferon or anything else. He chose to kick the virus's ass with herbs and organic food and good intentions.

Keith did pretty okay until 2006. But by then, when he got sick, it was too late for the new pills or affirmations or anything else to save him. He got a fever one day, and slipped away. Gone. He used to have a bird, a sassy-ass cockatoo called Blooper, who used to yell, "FUCK YOU, BITCHES!" at random. I wonder what happened to that foul-mouthed bird?

My first real boyfriend has AIDS. Has—present tense. David. Even now. He was among the guys who drank the cocktails of aloe vera and peroxide. Still alive somehow. A miracle, really.

We didn't know David was positive when we decided he should move into my place in 1993. I'd been in Portland for a year. But after just a few short months with David, I knew something was deeply wrong. Intuition. I threw down an ultimatum: get tested, or give up sex with me. He got tested.

I remember Darren. Darren had the body of an underwear model. He was short and tight and blond, with abs that could grate Parmesan and a voice deep like the Mississippi. He made my dick harder than Cocteau Twins karaoke. We dated for a hot minute. It didn't work out.

He ditched me. The rejection stung. We lost touch. I found him, months later, on the cover of a porn DVD at a video store. (It looked pretty hot.) So that's what he'd been up to! I was still bitter, so I didn't rent it.

Soon after, I found him again. Darren was just there, randomly, on the street in front of me. Surprise!

I hugged him. The lymph nodes in his neck were as big as golf balls.

His beautiful blond hair had fallen out, too, poorly hidden under a baseball cap. "What difference would it make if I got the test?" he asked. I told him I was worried and alarmed by his appearance. "The test wouldn't change anything anyway ..."

I never saw him again.

My ex, David, got his positive results on his birthday in 1993. I can still see it: David is entering our apartment with shopping bags filled with birthday presents to himself on the day of his test results, and I am waiting, chewing my nails and fearing the worst.

He has a big smile on his face, and he's carrying several department store bags full of shiny new things. *Birthday boy! Hello! Huh. Was my intuition wrong? It must have been. Thank God. He's okay?*

"And your HIV test, David?" I had to ask point-blank. He wasn't offering, and he seemed so happy.

Positive. It hit me like a gunshot.

He had to be joking. He seemed so stupidly okay. He was in such a good mood!

"I'm positive." Bang, bang.

The first guy who came in my ass, long before the stranger in the truck did last Christmas, was Vlad. He was a fresh expat, new in the country from Russia. This was in 2001.

Vlad was hotter than Satan's bicycle seat—lush, shoulder-length black hair and as uncut as his wavy locks. I met him out dancing at a gay club in Seattle. Probably Neighbours. That was my prime hunting ground at the time.

Vlad shoved his uncut penis in me and came without asking, almost as soon as he got through my front door. "Did you just come in me?" I demanded. He had. At least he was honest about it. I'd specifically asked him not to.

The whole carnival of terror began again: fear, anger, a desperate visit to Harborview hospital for emergency tests and "the day after pill": a new rigorous three-month protocol of toxic antivirals that made me shake and shit and feel like my skin was crawling with fire ants. Almost exactly how I felt when I was later on PrEP.

I forced Vlad to test, relentlessly pressed the issue, lied that we might remain romantically and sexually involved afterwards. I demanded documented proof of his results. But, of course, those results would take weeks.

I suffered the side effects of the prophylaxis for almost a full month—until Vlad got word back from the lab.

Negative.

My relief was indescribable. I threw the prophylaxis pills away. Two more months of that toxic stew would have wrecked me. I couldn't have endured it. The adventure cost me $2,000 in hospital fees (out of pocket), and I never spoke to Vlad again. The bastard.

When my then-boyfriend David told me he was positive on his birthday in 1993, and I was finally able to set aside my denial and believe it, my entire world tilted sideways.

I begged him to be joking. Begged. "Please take it back." I fell on my knees. I'd been having sex with him for four months solid, no condoms. But he wasn't joking. It was true. I made up my mind then and there that I probably was positive, too.

I forced myself to get tested—a few weeks of torturous uncertainty after I had my blood drawn, my results came back. You had to go in to the doctor's office to get them, back then. They were afraid that if they gave you bad news remotely, you might kill yourself. I marched into the clinic, braced as best as I could for the very worst news. They called my name.

The doctor tap-tapped herself into the room. "Hello, Adrian, you've had a recent scare?" I wanted to vomit.

She flipped open her clipboard chart, squinted and furrowed her brow, scrolled down the page a bit, blinked, and broke the news, as gravely as she could.

"You're ... *negative*."

Negative.

I danced around the room like I'd just won every beauty contest in the world. I hugged her. "Thank you, thank you, thank God, thank you!"

Then she burst my bubble.

"I mean, negative ... for now. Please come back in thirty days for another test, to be sure." Then again, thirty days after that. I could still be infected, they just couldn't be sure yet. "We just have to wait and see ..."

A few days later, I got the flu. Bad. Glands, sweats, fever. Hallucinations. Vomit. All of it. I was convinced this was my seroconversion.

I did not go back to the doctor in thirty days. I didn't go back to the doctor at all. I didn't have the courage to retest. I just couldn't do it.

I delved manically into my own "research." I studied everything I could lay my fingers on about HIV—the latest research, speculative articles, quack theories, European studies, autobiographies of AIDS survivors, trance channelers, Louise Hay ... everything. And I discovered the Immune Enhancement Project in Portland.

The Immune Enhancement Project was a clinic set up early in the epidemic to practice and study the effects of traditional Chinese medicine on HIV. My boyfriend, David, became a patient there. I made damn sure of it. They offered intense herbal protocols, acupuncture, shiatsu, remedies for ailments chronic and acute, all on a super-cheap sliding scale. I couldn't join because I hadn't tested positive. But I used to bogart all David's pills—and I tried to mimic the program's treatments and protocols as best as I could. I got a little obsessive.

Meditate seventy-two hours per day. Yoga for breakfast. Booze was worse than Hitler. Coffee? Not even that. Juice every meal. Immune tonics, Chinese herbs, stress elimination, ionized water, weeks-long fasts, tai chi. Acupuncture twice per week, chiropractor once, shiatsu on demand, everything my co-pays could bear. I even drank the peroxide and aloe shit from the mall (and got the horrible rash). I couldn't bring myself to go in for the test again.

And if I stuck to my rule and didn't come in anybody's ass or mouth, I wouldn't hurt anybody, right? Like Clark. For a full year, we dated, and I pretended to come in his ass, 2012 through 2013. I hadn't been tested in who knows how long, and neither had he. All Clark wanted was for me to fuck him and come. His big thing. He was much younger. He didn't care that I didn't know my status. Or that he didn't know his. He didn't care about the risk.

I did care.

I faked flooding Clark's guts for months, to make him happy. When at long last I confessed that I had never actually come inside him because I cared for him, and had not been tested in years, he was furious. He broke up with me for trying to save his life.

"If that's true, you must have the best fake O face in the fucking world," he spat at me.

So true. Years of practice. I do not regret my decision.

William and I worked at a five-star hotel together in the early '90s, became lifelong friends, and he still lives in Portland. I was crushed when he tested positive, in 2007. I went barreling back down there to support him. I gave him my desperately optimistic, "HIV DOESN'T HAVE TO BE A DEATH SENTENCE!" speech that I barely believed myself. I immediately signed him up for the Immune Enhancement Project, just like I'd done with David so many years before. I always figured the IEP might be the primary reason David was still keeping body and soul together on this planet.

Which reminds me of James, who was a ridiculously sexy graveyard bellman at a fancy downtown Portland hotel circa 1993. I was a graveyard bellman across the street, at the rival hotel, where William and I worked together. Sometimes, when the night was slow, I'd sneak across the street and James and I would find a deserted spot somewhere and smash it out like coked-up spring rabbits. Epic kisser, he was. I remember doing it on the roof of his hotel one time, twelve stories up, overlooking the downtown city lights, blanketed in a blinking ocean of stars.

James died of AIDS-related cancer the year I moved to Seattle, just a few months later, in 1994. I ran into an acquaintance from Portland at Neighbours, and he screamed the terrible news at me over the deafening music. I started to shake. James had no idea he even had HIV, as far as I know.

Why did I let that stranger come in my ass? After all this time? Why did I want him to?

I was going to go in and take the test today after work. I swore to myself I would. But what if I get fired and lose my insurance? What if I'm positive and my body rejects the medications, like it did with the post-exposure prophylaxis back in 2001, or with PrEP? It seems likely. What if Martin Fucking Shkreli or someone at Gilead jacks the price up $3,000 and posts a YouTube video about it? What if Trump's Nazis ... do something ... worse?

But my friend just texted, and he's meeting me here with a bottle of wine to hang out and watch the new season of whatever's on Netflix instead. These old scars run deep. I really need to go in for that test. And I swear I will. Soon. I'll walk the dreaded two blocks, bite my lip, and just fucking get it over with. As soon as I can.

Got AIDS Yet?

AARON NIELSEN

As a kid, every news report about AIDS, every magazine cover, every made-for-TV movie, every televised AIDS benefit, red ribbon, et cetera, seemed to be screaming at me, *This is your future!*

My first memory of making the connection between myself and all those men I saw dying on *60 Minutes*, the nightly news, wherever, was in an airport bathroom in the late '80s. I was eight or nine years old, and on the wall of the stall I found the following:

> *Got*
>
> *AIDS*
>
> *Yet?*

I remember being frozen in horror. I was old enough to know what gay meant, old enough to know that label applied to me, and of course I knew about AIDS. It didn't take me very long to connect the dots and understand the implications.

Fast-forward a couple of years, and the older I grew, the more the anxiety increased. The panic began to set in because the closer to sexual maturity I became, the closer I got to this disease. It became less abstract, not just something I watched on TV but something I would in fact have to navigate in my life. It didn't help my anxiety any that when I came out at fifteen or sixteen, the first thing my father said to me was, "Well, don't get AIDS."

When I first gained access to the internet in the late '90s, of course the first thing I searched for was porn, but back then the only images I found palatable were of men by themselves or jerking each other off. Butt-fucking terrified me. I didn't even like seeing it in porn. I abstained from anal sex until my early twenties, and when it finally did happen it was with my boyfriend at the time, after we had been together for about a year.

Starting in my teens and continuing into my early adulthood, AIDS was such a constant worry that I would have nightmares about contracting it. In one nightmare that particularly stands out in my memory, I was being chased by a man with a large syringe full of AIDS-infected blood, the needle curved almost into a hook. He was feral and terrifying; he caught me, pounced on me, sat on my chest, held my arms down, and then slammed the needle into my chest.

I finally went to get tested when I was twenty-three, or maybe even twenty-four. I put it off for so long because it was too terrifying. My mind-set growing up was that I would rather just not know. But my boyfriend at the time and I decided to go because, after having been in a monogamous relationship for more than a year, we let our guard down, and our condom usage became, well, intermittent at best. Even though our risk was relatively low (neither of us had had many sexual partners and we had been exclusive for a while), we still felt some anxiety, and so we decided to get tested just to put our minds at ease. When we went in for the results, the clinician, who knew we were a couple, called us back together, and told us both at the same time that we were negative. It was a relief, but it was just the start of a cycle that would play out again and again over the years. Our relationship lasted four years, and after we broke up there were new boyfriends, dates, the occasional one-night stand, and every time I went to get tested, the fear was just as acute as the first time. Actually, it might have been worse, because I didn't always have someone to go with me. But I went dutifully, every few months, once the anxiety became too much to bear.

I usually went through a spell of abstinence after getting tested because I wanted to be able to enjoy the relief that I didn't have anything to worry about. Another tactic I tried to help myself cope was volunteering at an HIV/STI clinic. I figured if I was regularly in a setting where HIV was the main focus, I'd become a bit desensitized to it; it would become less terrifying. It worked. Sort of. I started off filing test results and scheduling appointments. I didn't think I would progress beyond that, because the idea of actually testing someone was just too much. I didn't think I could handle it. Well, filing and reception work became very boring, very fast, so I asked to go through the HIV test counselor training. I still wasn't entirely sure it was something I could handle, but I felt compelled to directly engage with what frightened me the most. Besides, I had been tested numerous times for free, so I figured it was my time to start giving back.

There were a couple tense and upsetting moments in the five years I was a volunteer, but the majority of the time it really wasn't terrifying and I learned a lot as a test counselor. Most notably, I found out that HIV-positive people with an undetectable viral load cannot transmit the virus. Which was frankly difficult to believe—that drugs could suppress the virus to such a degree that the body no longer detects it, no longer makes antibodies against it. So treatment provides HIV-positive people a life expectancy on par with those who are negative, and, oh yeah, as a bonus, on these meds the virus can't be transmitted.

In tandem with the discovery that undetectable meant untransmittable, came PrEP, another not-quite-miracle but, compared to where we were when I was growing up, a pretty fucking amazing development. But when PrEP debuted in 2012, there was a lot of misinformation about it, in particular about how effective it really was and about the potential side effects. So, I was dismissive of it. But in 2014, the clinic where I volunteered hosted a panel discussion with the group of researchers from the University of California, San Francisco, who were responsible for the iPrEx study that resulted in PrEP. The researchers presented their findings and discussed how effective it really was and how minimal the side effects usually were. I called my doctor the next day, and I was on PrEP by the end of the week. Suddenly, I didn't have to be afraid of sex anymore. But decades of fear don't just immediately dissipate once you start taking a pill.

Smash cut to three years later when I started dating someone who was HIV-positive. I had an inkling before we met that he was positive, because he didn't have his HIV status listed on his dating profile. He told me on our second date. He became pretty choked up, told me that he liked me but that he needed to tell me something, and I went cold. I knew. I knew what he was going to say, and, yes, I do remember feeling afraid, and I remember sitting on his couch while he struggled to find the words and I just kept thinking to myself, *Hurry up and say it. Let's just get this over with already.* And when he finally got the words out, I hugged him and told him that it wasn't a deal-breaker. I told him that I know that people who are undetectable are fine, healthy, that it can't be transmitted, and besides, I'm on PrEP, so we're good.

Three days after that, I broke down sobbing in my therapist's office. It all came gushing out, the years of generalized fear and anxiety, as well as the guilt over the specific fear and anxiety around dating someone who is HIV-positive. I say guilt, because I fucking knew better, yet I was still scared. Scared and ashamed, because in spite of all I had learned while volunteering, it wasn't enough to completely unfurl the layers of terror that had slithered around me over the last thirty-plus years. Because even though he was undetectable and I was on PrEP and there was zero chance of transmission, I was still afraid to sleep with him. I liked him, though. He was cute and kind and a sweet guy, so I found a way to push past it. Dating is hard, no one is perfect, and I wasn't going to let my anxiety over his status dissolve our relationship before it really even began. After about a week or so of dating we fucked. We decided to forgo the condoms because both of us had been screened for STIs recently and hadn't had any new sexual partners since being tested. The longer we dated, the more my anxiety waned, until I didn't even notice it anymore—or so I thought.

When I went to my regular PrEP follow-up a couple months into our relationship, I was pretty much at ease. I discussed the situation with my doctor and he told me it should be fine. He also added that if my boyfriend was undetectable, I didn't need to be on PrEP. When my doctor said that, the ease I thought I felt just completely evaporated. Even though I thought I was okay with dating someone positive, the thought of fucking him without being on PrEP brought the terror roaring back. I told my doctor we hadn't been together for that long, but if things continued I would for sure consider it. A blatant lie, but I was too embarrassed to tell him the truth, that despite all I knew, I needed to cling to the safety blanket of PrEP in order to be comfortable with this relationship. Yeah, on some level, I was afraid of my boyfriend, or rather the undetectable virus inside of him.

As it turned out, though, I wasn't the only one a bit tense about the situation. I don't recall exactly how long into our relationship this happened, but we had been together for a while, which is why I was rattled. We were sitting on his couch, searching for something on his iPad—I'm pretty sure we were looking for the menu of a nearby takeout place—when a previous search he had done popped up in the search field: *how to bareback safely in a serodiscordant relationship.* I immediately felt embarrassed. I didn't know how to react. I had never once stopped to think that he might have anxiety over sleeping with me. It had never crossed my mind.

In hindsight, I feel like I fumbled in that moment, handled the situation badly. I asked him if I we could look at the page he'd browsed, and he agreed. On the page were the three options one would expect: condoms, PrEP, and the HIV-positive partner having an undetectable viral load. I remember pointing to the section about PrEP and saying, that's me, then pointing to the section about being undetectable and saying that's you. So we're fine, I added, we're doing everything right, and then I kissed him, and that was the end of it. But I think I should have tried to actually have some kind of dialogue about it, instead of just pointing at a website and saying all is well, when clearly it wasn't, because even though the meds work, the fear remains.

Please, We All Gonna Get It

Trans Women on Inevitability, Health Care, and the Cure

RORY ELLIOTT
WITH ALYSSA PARIAH AND GAYSHA STARR

Alyssa Pariah and Gaysha Starr grew up a decade apart on opposite coasts of the United States. Alyssa Pariah is a thirty-four-year-old Afro Puerto Rican trans woman who came of age in the early 2000s in New York City, and Gaysha Starr is a forty-eight-year-old Filipina trans woman who came out in the drag scene of Seattle in the early '90s. In this conversation, they share their experiences accessing health care, their thoughts on trans representation and chosen families, their relationship to the HIV/AIDS crisis, and their struggles to live, date, and thrive as trans women in a world without a cure.

Alyssa Pariah: I was raised by a single parent who did the best that she could, but she was dealing with drug addiction, and some of the people she brought around me were having health complications with their HIV diagnosis and were trying to keep living despite dealing with racism, sexism, homophobia, and many other kinds of oppression that made their diagnosis and their health that much worse. At the time, it was hard for me to understand the gravity of this, since it was a normal and nonsensational thing in my life; there were just some people who were dealing with a health issue. And when I learned about the virus outside of that context, I also learned about the stigma, and I felt embarrassed for these people in my life who I knew didn't deserve it. And it made it a little bit more diffi-cult for me to come out later, because queerness was paired with the threat, or the scare, of the virus. And that's just not the kind of soup that you want to be blossoming in, in terms of your gender or sexuality while growing up. But there it was.

Gaysha Starr: I came out in January of 1993, when I turned twenty-one, and then by April I was doing drag, and that was the way I was expressing my feminine side. I didn't know very much about the trans community, and the girls back then in the '90s who were trans-identified, no one would hire any of us. We didn't have health care, we were discriminated against, so we did the shows, or we hustled.

I learned very quick about HIV/AIDS. My drag mother Hiram, she had a house of eight of us, and it was very much like what you see on *Pose*. We would all be in a tiny apartment, mostly African American—my drag sisters Ivonna, Dianna, Sable. Then Bianca actually died of HIV right in my first year. So, I would say Bianca, who lip-synched Sandra Bernhard—she was the white star and was really, really talented—was the first person I met and knew who died of HIV/AIDS.

So, to be in our house you had to fundraise. We worked with POCAAN (People of Color against AIDS Network), which made sense for us because all of us with the exception of Bianca were— well, I'm Asian, Jasmine was Latina, Sable, Dianna, and Ivonna were all African American, and Hiram was Native American, and then we had the boys. We would find a balance of doing benefits and shows, go to the drag balls, but then also volunteer in offices and help out any way that we could. We fought very much for funding. We worked with Chicken Soup Brigade, which is now absorbed into Lifelong, and we marched up and down Broadway, which is still the gay area, and I live a block off it. So HIV was always a part of me coming out, even before I came out as trans.

I became positive somewhere around the early 2000s. I kind of grew up in my gay adolescence and drag adolescence just assuming everyone was HIV-positive, you know? It was hard because back then we didn't have the medicines and the health care that we do now. I mean, I'm undetectable; I've been on pills for over ten years. I take Descovy and Tivicay and I get my blood drawn and we're working on it.

I started my hormone replacement therapy in January 2019, and we have to watch a lot of the blood clotting and other health concerns. I am definitely telling a lot of the younger queens now that HIV/AIDS is always a big part of whatever LGBTQIA+ umbrella you sit under, and that is always going to be the basis of our work until we find a cure and until the stigma is gone.

COVID has really re-realized a lot of that shame and fear. I contracted COVID in March 2020, and a lot of the shame and a lot of the guilt and a lot of the work that I had to do and the questions I had to answer both with my health care provider and King County, and the state of Washington, like "Where were you, and who were you with? You have to contact all of the people you were in contact with." It reminded me of back in the '90s and 2000s, when you had to go back to your partners. I think being trans and a person of color, it is already an insecure thing to be, and then when you have a disease, regardless of if you're undetectable or you are cleared from it, you kind of still have that shame and that guilt and those feelings.

AP: When I got older, when I was an adult, the woman who pumped me with silicone—and for the record, I don't recommend it; I am not endorsing illegal silicone injections—the woman who did it, she made a joke, she made a lot of very dark jokes, and I guess when you're in her profession you better be comfortable with some of the darker aspects of life, but my trans mom, her name is Nicoletta, she took me to her maybe a year and a half into transitioning. I saved up the money.

They were talking about girls who they used to know back in the day, who they used to hook with, who are now dead—and who died, and how. Some of the girls died of complications related to them having HIV, some not. But the way that they were joking about it made me reassess how I should be talking about it and thinking about it because she jokingly said—and this is one of the phrases that gets stuck in your head and that is in there forever—she had really long nails and she said, "Ey loca, please, we all gonna get it," and it was like a punch line. It was funny, but like I'm also learning at the time, I don't know, I haven't been through what they've been through, I'm just trying to figure this out, and I guess if you know these older queens who have been through more, if that's the level that the jokes are on, and if that's the shared understanding, then, okay? There was some inevitability there, but at least there would be some community there, some shared support if it did happen. This was the early 2000s in Brooklyn, New York. I was eighteen.

When I was growing up, I used to watch a lot of talk shows, trashy talk shows—a memory that I have that was formative was when I was watching *Ricki Lake* with my cousins, and it was one of the trans episodes. I think I was like nine, and my cousin said, "That's going to be you when you grow up." And he didn't say it in a nice way; he was making fun of me. And I just thought, *Well, okay, you're right, but I know you don't mean that as a compliment.* So even though the women on these shows—*Ricki Lake, Jerry Springer, Jenny Jones, Richard Bey, Montel*, oh my God, all of them!—they were all disrespected, and openly disrespected, I know a lot of them just wanted the exposure so that they could make more money on their ads or whatever, so it was a trade-off.

I'm a chronic underachiever, and I don't really put a lot of effort into improving my own life 'cause, like, that was the expectation that was given to me. There was nothing about my life that made me think I could strive and do great things. So, I'm pretty comfortable with just chillin' and whatever. As long as I can get by and pay my rent and eat enough, I'm like what the hell? I'm not going to strive to do well in the capitalist economy, no! I'd rather help people strike against it; whenever they need someone to scream at protests and stuff like that, that's my main thing. And I know for a fact that that is having an impact on young trans girls, because just recently, I've been in correspondence with a mother who has a trans daughter who is struggling to come out, and it looks like I'm about to start facilitating a support group for trans children.

So, I hope that I can be a decent representation for them. There are youth who see me when I'm out agitating for any number of causes for social and economic justice, and I'm very impassioned, and they see me and it makes them feel a little bit stronger.

GS: For me, there is a duality of being Filipina, or Asian Pacific Islander, in the gay community because you are the "good minority." You get the car, you get the white boyfriend, you do all that. I haven't really ever experienced a gay relationship, because especially back then, the gay boys didn't want to date effeminate men. Or if they did, I wasn't attracted to those kinds of men. But when I was in drag, I started to learn what I could look like, and learned about the effect—the power—that sexuality had on men. Then, you know, you're feeling lonely and empty and you just want intimacy, of course your guard is down.

And when I got older in drag, I started learning about what it was like to get drunk in drag and do drugs in drag, and then you're putting that together with being this female. I guess, looking back now at my self-expression of feeling like a caged animal getting free to go out at night, of course you're going to make questionable decisions and feel invincible and feel even worse the next morning. It breaks my heart that I don't know who I got HIV from.

It is even harder now because as you date as trans, you say that you're undetectable, and most guys will drop you because they aren't interested or don't understand. But we grew up around it, we know the health care, our counts, our doctors and nurses and those within our support system. But when you are meeting people outside your community, and you put it out online or you tell them, there is that fear of rejection because in the straight world they're just like, "Nope, never mind." It's a weird place to be in because as you come out as trans, you are being yourself. You are finally being able to express yourself. I am having a second adolescence, and maybe it's the hormones, as we've increased them. I'm feeling like I'm fifteen going on sixteen all over again, and then sometimes I definitely feel like I'm forty-eight and I don't want to make the same mistakes I made when I was twenty-one.

Rory Elliott: You both were talking about houses and having mothers and that specific support system. Could you talk about that system of a trans/queer family and how that influenced growing up queer with the inevitability of the AIDS crisis around you?

AP: Nicoletta is ex-Xtravaganza. I think she left the house some years ago—we've lost touch—but I'm very, very grateful for how she prepared me. She's very funny, she deals with sad stuff with humor, and whenever we were hanging out with other groups of people it was very much about her. She helped people to feel welcome and seen and was always ready to flash her titties at any moment. We would all get something out of seeing people reacting to how outrageous she was. And her laugh was like very guttural and, well, evil, but in the best way.

The other side of it, though, is that she offered me some mixed ideas of how you're supposed to carry yourself, which now I might identify some of them as being regressive and definitely very problematic, but she really was trying to protect me because so many of her friends were dying, and she didn't want that for me. So, she gave me a bunch of tools, like only use my sexuality to make money. She felt like, you're going to spend all this money putting it into your look, your transition, your womanhood, and you're going to let some dirty piece of trade come and fuck you and give you nothing and leave you feeling used? She thought it's better to just take some extra hormone blockers and learn to regulate your libido if you're feeling that horny. Take a Spiro and a Xanax and go to sleep at the end of the day of hoeing. Don't stay up late into the night playing with the boys. Part of that was her fear of getting a little too loose with the boys, and then boom—now you're a statistic. She made me pretty afraid of that, so I didn't want to fall into the traps that she was telling me were out there. And it's had a profound effect on how I see myself now, all these years later.

GS: So I have four drag mothers that, in each stage of my career and my experiences, have helped shape me. I have my mother Hiram, she's Native American, she'd be the mother that would give you her very favorite dress just so you could wear it to make you feel good. We were the kind of house where we borrowed each other's clothes. We didn't have a lot of money, but our talent and our heart made up for everything.

So, then I got into pageantry, and at twenty-two I went to Portland and competed at the Femme Magnifique International and won, first winner from Seattle, at Montgomery Park and brought the house down with "Proud Mary" by Tina Turner in everyone's borrowed wardrobe. That's where I met my second mother, Coco Vaughn. She won in '86, and she groomed me and cleaned me up so I wouldn't look so "street drag," I guess.

Then my next mother, who is really one of my best friends now, still to this day, and I'm still good friends with all of them, was Kahlua Ice. She's a former Miss Gay Seattle and former Miss Gay

Washington. She taught me a lot about life and about the nightlife scene, and we'd go to shows together at Neighbours, the big bar up here. And she really taught me what to do about my drag and to be the queen with the boys and the importance of men, of gay boys.

My final mother, she actually lives in Portland. She's a Rose Empress; her name is Cicely, she's a legend there and is still breathtaking. We all have different relationships. It got to the point when the daughter, or the child, does more and supersedes maybe what the mother has done. I have my own kids and some of them are fantastic, and some of them I forgot were my kids and haven't talked to them in forever.

When you are in our community, it really is your chosen family that teaches you about yourself and gives you a purpose to be more than yourself. I think when it comes to HIV/AIDS, if you never feel like you can talk to anyone, hopefully one of your chosen children or mothers or sisters is there for you and you can have that kind of support.

RE: Yeah, I think one of the things I'm thinking about is the common narrative that with the development of protease inhibitors and the cocktails, and then later PrEP, that AIDS ended and it was over, right? How does that conflict with what both of you are talking about—growing up poor, growing up hustling, in houses, and fundraising to live and work? I'm wondering how that narrative really interacts with your own and how the ability to access medical care in the medical institution as trans women, as trans women of color, how that interacts with the idea that the AIDS crisis was over in 1996, when the cocktail came out.

AP: I'm just thankful for everybody who did activist work in order to get us whatever semblance of dignity we have come to expect in the health care industry now. Because I know I wouldn't have it if it wasn't for them throwing down like they did.

I don't feel safe going to the doctor or engaging with my insurance, but if it really gets bad, I know that it's there, and when I really have to suck it up and engage with it, I do. I know it would be a hell of a lot worse if I had no access at all, if it wasn't for the people who came before me, so I'm very grateful and know I am in a better position because of their sacrifice for the movement.

GS: I think for me, you know, I've been with my job now for nine years, and over this past year is when I got really serious about transitioning at work. I am the first openly trans employee with my company, and without that health care, without that card, without ENDA [Employment Non-Discrimination Act], and looking at the benefits—I know, just in talking with my girlfriends who don't have jobs, who COVID hit especially hard, that I am one of the lucky ones. In some ways it delayed me coming out at a younger age. Would I have liked to come out at thirty-eight? Absolutely. But I don't know if mentally I would have been as ready as I am now, trying to get my things in order with finding the right health care provider, making sure I'm undetectable, making sure that mentally and emotionally I can say I'm trans, even if I'm not presenting full time yet.

I just went through my name change last Wednesday, and that was a lot of, I don't want to say sadness, but it was a lot of stillness, saying good-bye to my male identity. I go in at the end of the month to get my driver's license and social security card, and then going through all of the checks that one of my girlfriends gave me. I am lucky that I'm having a smoother transition, between the electrolysis I started in October of last year and growing my hair out, I wouldn't be able to have all of those things if I didn't have a job, if I didn't have health care, didn't have privacy and different kinds of laws to protect me, and I know living in Washington that I'm protected, but it's still scary to work and start presenting full time.

Before it used to be about passing and not getting clocked, and that was the ultimate goal and the ultimate ticket. Now, as I've gotten older, if someone sees me, I just want them to say, "Oh, well, she looks good." That is more important for me: to feel healthy and just do the right thing for me and the others around me. I could care less if someone clocks me; I just want to be left alone so I can live my life because I've waited for so long to live it. I know there are a lot of girls who I have referred to my doctor who have had to go to the state or go to Country Doctor, which is the public clinic here, to get help, and that breaks my heart. I don't even know how many of them may or may not be HIV-positive, and that's just another layer in trans health that is very much there.

RE: Gaysha, what was your experience like with accessing health care when you tested positive in the early 2000s?

GS: It was a very dear friend of mine; he's a physician assistant at Dr Peter Shalit's office on First Hill. Dr Shalit's office is an LGBT, mostly gay men's, office, and so I went there—I didn't feel shame, I didn't feel guilty; I felt very related. They were like, hey, we're here to take care of you. I went through different types of treatment. I would go and get my blood drawn and they would teach me about my cell counts, and then they took me off—hold on, let me get my pills—I was on different pills, so now I take, every morning I take the Tivicay and the Descovy, and then I take in the morning 4 milligrams of estradiol, and then at night I take two 400 milligrams of progesterone. The health care was great, going to a gay clinic, or a gay-targeted clinic. I'm lucky now that my nurse practitioner Janna is trans, and she's walking me through the entire process, upping and keeping my levels where they need to be, 'cause I don't know anyone else who's HIV-positive who's also transitioning. Most of the time it's the other way around. I had a very positive experience, but that's also living in Washington. If you don't live in a major city that has a healthy gay community, I think it would probably be a different story.

AP: In New York City they have some clinics that are geared toward us. Like Callen-Lorde and Apicha, so if you didn't mind waiting a long time, you could get an appointment.

GS: What's a long time?

AP: I guess a few weeks or more than a month to get in.

RE: That's just for general care?

AP: Yeah, yeah. My impression was that it takes a lot of work to get all of your ducks in a row to get to the point where you can be seen by a doctor and pursue being healthy? It felt out of reach for me, and also just like too much work, and I'm pretty lazy, so I didn't even try. I just figured, "Well, if I feel sick, I'll go to the emergency room if I can't take care of myself." And it wasn't until I needed to pursue mental health care that I even started to put in the work to make appointments, to show up to the appointment, to follow up, to do all of that stuff in order to get that access. So, I was just lucky that I didn't suffer any major physical health problem or diagnosis that needed medical attention until very late. I think I might have been like twenty-eight when I started to feel safe enough to even go and talk to a doctor about this stuff. Even now that I should be better, and I thought I would be, but honey, Miss Rona got me like, "Stay home, and if you feel sick, you can call, but don't be trying to get a bunch of appointments that you probably won't be able to keep."

But I also just don't feel like the LGBT rainbow is really for me. You know, all of the oppressed people of the world are gonna have to band together and fight against oppression if we have any chance of surviving, and if you simply don't feel like you are a part of the oppressed masses, then I guess you're not going to be on my side, and you know, see you when we roll up the guillotines, baby.

GS: I think that people keep saying that the AIDS fight or the AIDS crisis is over—it's not over, there's no cure for it, there's just this medication, and I get this every month, every thirty days I get my supply from the CVS, and I have to take those every morning, and I can't meet a man, or I can't have a purpose 'cause this is hanging over me. So, it's not over until I don't have to take a pill every day. I'm not ashamed of it anymore, but I'm definitely shy, and I don't lead with it. If someone was to ask me, I definitely would tell them, 'cause most people don't know someone, you don't go around and ask, "Do you have it? What do you have?" I would say we need to say that it is not over 'cause you can still get it.

AP: And to the girls who think that just because you're on PrEP you're good to go—that's not true. So, don't feel like you're invincible just because you're on PrEP. I understand that people who were in ACT UP, like Larry Kramer—he was on *Democracy Now!* recently, and it was a clip from a speech that he gave at Queer Pride in New York City, I think it was last year or the year before, and he sounded very, very angry specifically because of that. He felt like people who should be in the fight for a cure are stepping back and not doing their duty because we have PrEP now. That hit me really hard, so I wanna support any actions that people take that are fighting for a cure from here on out so that I'm not abdicating my responsibility—just because I have PrEP, it's not over.

GS: It drives me crazy. How many years have we had this disease? How many billions of dollars have we raised for it, and they still can't find a cure? And I don't know how much of it is the government, I don't know how much of it is politics, I don't know how much of it is each administration, I don't know. And it makes me sick to my stomach that in this lifetime we still won't have a cure for it. I've got friends who are millennials, I've got friends that I'm meeting now who are Gen Z, and I hope that in their lifetime there is a cure for this disease so that they don't have to do what we did, or fight what the people before us had to fight.

Fearing El Sida

MANUEL BETANCOURT

I was born in 1984, the year when the first case of AIDS was reported in Colombia, the year when the Centers for Disease Control in the United States developed a blood test for HIV.

I have not known a world without AIDS.

Except, for much of my life, it was not AIDS I knew but El Sida. Where the English acronym for acquired immune deficiency syndrome felt like a morbidly ironic piece of linguistic schadenfreude, a disease that called out for aid even as its sufferers received none, Spanish speakers personalized the síndrome de inmunodeficiencia adquirida into a kind of villainous subject; he was to be dreaded and avoided at all costs.

Growing up, whenever anyone spoke of El Sida, my mind would conjure up images ripped straight from the television shows I used to watch after school. Of course the syndrome was a "he," our gendered language tacitly reminding me that it was men, *certain* men, who should be feared—El Sida was both mythical and mundane. At times, he was an armored deity, like something out of *Los caballeros del zodiaco* or *Dragon Ball Z*, a powerful adversary who showed no mercy when openly challenged. His body was all rippling muscles and bulging veins, an enemy you couldn't outrun, only succumb to.

He was terrifying precisely because he seemed unbeatable. I had no superpowers at my disposal to vanquish him. All I could do was hope that we never came face-to-face.

This type of personalization was, for a closeted gay teen growing up in Bogotá on a steady diet of anime, *Buffy the Vampire Slayer*, and *ThunderCats*, the only way I could make sense of the obtusely abstract way HIV and AIDS were discussed around me during my formative years. AIDS didn't feel like the health crisis it had been in the late '80s, but it hadn't yet faded to the background—neither present emergency nor ancient history, its specter hovered over my budding awareness of my sexuality. Which is why, when I didn't imagine El Sida to be a cackling Big Bad intent on destroying me in one fell swoop with his impossibly ripped body (even in my imagination, death and desire seemed one and the same), I imagined him as a lurker in the shadows. El Sida was the kind of villain who, if given the opportunity, would take your body hostage. Decades before I read Susan Sontag's *AIDS and Its Metaphors*, I understood the way my own concept of this disease was conditioned by how we talked about it, by the images we used to describe its effects on bodies, and by the figures of speech we deployed to make sense of it. El Sida wasn't so much a reality for me as a fantasy fed and nurtured by the discourses and institutions around me.

Just as I never knew a life without AIDS, I was never taught any kind of sex education without a requisite discussion of El Sida. In 1993, two years after Colombia ratified a new constitution, the government passed a law making sex education mandatory, requiring schools across the country to provide teenagers with the information they needed to curb what was becoming a growing epidemic on Colombian soil. The move couldn't have come at a more urgent time: 1994 would see the number of HIV/AIDS cases reported in Colombia almost double from the previous year.

By the time I hit puberty, the government's educational out-reach programs surrounding sexual health were ubiquitous. Moreover, my private school so prided itself on offering a holistic education that every semester of high school was peppered with endless special sessions on everything from drug use and religion to career counseling and, yes, (hetero)sexual health. That's why, from the time I was twelve, I often found myself cramped in my school's auditorium, overheated by the restlessness around me, listening to sexual health professionals talk about STDs, unwanted pregnancies, and El Sida with an all-too-clinical attitude. What was key, my schoolmates and I were told over and over again—and here a string of unplanned pregnancies across various classes no doubt made the matter more urgent—was to always wear a condom when having sex. This was also the core messaging of a nationwide sex ed campaign launched by the Colombian government by the time I turned twelve in 1996.

If this all sounds like a utopian progressive vision of what sexual health education for teens can look like, let me dampen your awe when I describe this TV and print campaign. The slogan was simple enough: "Sin preservativos, ni pío!" In essence: "Nothing without a condom." Except you really need to get the line's use of slang to better understand the concept of the ads that flooded Colombian prime-time TV: "Ni pío" ("not a peep") is the kind of vague expres-sion you'd use to signal that you wouldn't say a word, that you wouldn't budge on any given topic. The message was clear: you shouldn't engage in any kind of sex without a condom. The slogan was corny, sure, but you really couldn't begrudge the campaign's attempts to make such a lesson as blunt as possible.

"Blunt," though, is not a word you'd use to describe the prem-ise or the tenor of these ads. Owing, perhaps, to the misguided belief that talking frankly about sex is somehow immodest, the creatives behind this government-sponsored TV campaign chose to illustrate their on-the-nose tag line with puppets. Not just any kind of puppets: chicken puppets. The concept behind them was probably something like "PG-rated Muppets," only the chicks (not hens or roosters; the implication was that they were still young) were less Big Bird and more *Fraggle Rock*. The choice was not without a cause; the imagery riffed on the wordplay of the tag line ("pío" is Spanish for "chirp"), but that didn't make these humanoid chicken puppets any less terrifying, even when the messages they were spouting were earnest and urgent in equal measure.

In one such ad, for example, a couple's plight at a pharmacy sought to dramatize the way shame was but one obstacle many young people had to overcome in order to engage in safe sex. In it, a young couple walk in with one goal in mind: buying a condom. But the young boy, nervously taking the lead, gets flustered right away. He stalls and asks the pharmacist whether he has gum. Whether he has mints. Whether he has chocolate bars. Whether he has hand cream—anything to avoid asking for what he really wants. Eventually, his girlfriend gets fed up and asks outright whether the pharmacy sells condoms. "How many?" she's asked, prompting the young lovers to blush (or, well, shield their faces to denote a puppet-like blush).

Designed to remove the stigma around condom use, these ads nevertheless depended on a distancing effect that reinforced that very stigma. Colombian families couldn't be exposed to *actual* teenagers walking into a pharmacy and gleefully ordering a pack of condoms; instead, these scenarios had to be simplified and turned into comedic skits featuring laughable puppet characters that echoed the didacticism of *Sesame Street*. That many of them depended on puns and wordplay (another took place in a pool where a conversation about "taking the plunge" and "having brought a lifesaver" was clearly code for going upstairs to have sex) further suggested that these PSAs, though well intentioned, merely showed the limits of what the Ministry of Health could feasibly get Colombians to openly discuss.

For a campaign intent on removing shame from safe sex talks, its own artistic trappings laid bare just how much more work still needed to be done. It wasn't long before these various ads became punch lines in themselves, with "Sin preservativos, ni pío!" quickly emerging as a popular catchphrase used for schoolyard humor, deployed whenever my classmates wanted to nail a raunchy joke or a tired put-down. It never reached the ubiquity of, say, "marica" ("faggot"), which was used with abandon to punctuate any kind of sentence, sometimes serving as a noun, other times as an adjective, other times as a cruel form of endearment, but most definitely always functioning as a normalized homophobic slur. But their contiguity always reminded me how much uncomfortable laughter was wrung out of sexual shame: it was easier to laugh off these all-too-earnest PSAs and to turn faggots into punch lines than it was to engage with either seriously.

The two came head-to-head in one of these ads, the only one I remember tackling same-sex desire in any way. In this one we follow a male chick (that word coupling will never not sound ridiculous) as he waits expectantly at a restaurant for his date. He's beginning to worry that his date may not show up when a pair of feathered hands cover his eyes. This leads into a funny bit where he tries to guess who might be so playfully greeting him: "Martita?" he asks. Then, upon getting no response, he tries again: "Monica?" Much to the dismay of the entire restaurant, he gives it yet another go: "Maria Claudia?" And then another: "Amparito?" Here's where the choice to have these chicken puppets be both gendered but also rather genderless (with only a hairstyle and a voice making clear which ones were male and which ones were female) helped set up this mini comedy of errors. For, as it turns out, it wasn't a girl after all. "No," he's told by the unsuspecting stranger. "Charlie!"

The reveal is supposed to be surprising but also kind of reassuring. Here was a government-sponsored ad at least gesturing to bisexuality, even if it had to do so in the abstract in order to make it palatable for prime-time television.

That's all the support I received as I entered my teenage years and began to sense that my own sexual identity was little more than a cruel joke to those around me. I should add that when Charlie introduces himself his tone of voice is low and conspiratorial, as if the director of the ad had insisted the actor make it clear there is a level of shameful lasciviousness at play here, an "on the down low" kind of vibe that is much more obvious to my thirty-five-year-old self than it could (or should) have been to my twelve year old self. Moreover, the lack of expressivity in these puppets all but negated the necessary nuance this scene depends on. As the guy lists the names of his many female partners (and possible dates), the bartender at the other end of the restaurant looks aghast, slowly becoming more and more shocked as additional names are listed—he even takes a gulp from a liquor bottle once it's clear this may go on for some time. Right before Charlie reveals himself, we see the bartender collapsing at the bar, a bit of lighthearted slapstick comedy whose very point is unclear: Is he repulsed by what he sees? Is he so shocked? The on-screen messaging that followed was inclusive enough ("In all types of sexual relations, a condom is an effective way to prevent AIDS and STDs"), but all I remember was this feeling that men having sex with men was begrudgingly acceptable at best and shamefully ludicrous at worst.

What fascinates me now in looking back at this particular ad campaign is the way it's aimed almost exclusively at a heterosexual audience. This was, of course, by design. Unbeknownst to me, a 1994 Supreme Court decision had made this necessary. In 1993, the same year the Colombian government had set out to formalize sexual health education across the country so as to better combat the growing AIDS epidemic, an ad featuring a gay male couple kissing with the requisite "please use a condom" message—"We hold no prejudices, but use a condom, the only cure against AIDS," it read—was refused airtime by the Consejo Nacional de Televisión. Such censorship led to a lawsuit that eventually landed in the Supreme Court and yielded a curious ruling that's emblematic of how progressive ideas about sexuality were used to erase and outright ignore the gay male community in Colombia at a time when gay men most needed to be seen and supported.

The 1994 ruling sided with the Consejo Nacional de Televisión, arguing that the council was in the right to refuse to air the ad. Furthermore, it argued that doing so in no way constituted a discriminatory act. This was the decision, despite the judges making clear that homosexuals were protected under the law from discrimination. As the ruling would have it, this particular case didn't fall under discrimination (or censorship) because the ad itself—and here's where it gets more and more revealing—solely addressed gay men as its audience, neglecting the mainstream audience it would be made privy to.

In just focusing on a safe sex message that targeted gay men, the ruling suggested, the ad irresponsibly made it look like HIV/AIDS only affected the gay male population. Or, worse, that it tacitly endorsed the idea that homosexuality itself was the cause of HIV/AIDS. It's as befuddling a ruling as you can read, self-congratulatory in the way it writes into law how gay men are protected, all the while noting that—and this is an actual quote—"homosexuals cannot be discriminated against because of their status as such." It's a circular argument that allowed Colombian law to refuse sexual health outreach to the gay community because doing so would actually be treating them unequally when they deserved to be treated equally under the law. This explains why teenage me was stuck with puppet PSAs that danced around the specific sexual health concerns of gay men.

Watching those "Sin preservativos, ni pío!" ads, I remember thinking that the glaring absence of gay male chicks spoke volumes. On the one hand, it told me that boys like me, the kind who were laughed at on the soccer field for being "maricas," were not worthy of being taught sex ed that would keep us alive. On the other hand, it told me that maybe I was correct in thinking that there was an immutable relationship between El Sida and men who liked men. Just as the Supreme Court argued that gay men couldn't be seen on TV advocating for safer sex because it would add to their misrepresentation, I felt their absence all but confirmed the urban myth that my own sexual desires were always already dirty and diseased. Why else would they not be fit for scrutiny during prime time? Why else would they always be couched in hushed whispers and schoolyard taunts? Why else would I have internalized this message by age thirteen, if it wasn't already so prevalent around me?

I took my first HIV test in 2003, when I was eighteen years old. It was a mandatory part of my Canadian study permit application. Back then, the Canadian government required a full medical examination for all applicants from Colombia (the country has since been exempted from such demands). From what I gathered back then, Canada couldn't deny you a visa if you were HIV-positive. Nevertheless, one's status was a key piece of information they required when assessing your application. This meant that my mom spent an inordinate amount of time driving me around Bogotá as she dropped me off at various doctors and labs where I got asked plenty of uncomfortable questions and had my blood drawn more times than I could count.

Despite not being sexually active, taking the HIV test was a nerve-racking experience. Intellectually, I knew that I had nothing to fear. But there was something about finally coming face-to-face with El Sida (or, in this case, his henchman, El VIH) that made me have to reckon with how uncomfortable I was with my own homosexuality. In my mind, I couldn't think of my same-sex desires without associating them with this most terrifying of possibilities. If so many in the generation before me had lost their lives because of lack of pertinent and disseminated information, my generation had to unlearn the ways in which same-sex desire was conflated with AIDS. Much of our basest instincts were irrevocably tinged with a shame that was hard to shake off.

As I sat there, looking away as vials of my blood were taken, I found myself reflecting on the many ways I'd internalized the message that same-sex desire and AIDS were the same. Porn, for example, which I'd only just begun seeking out furtively whenever I got to be alone with the computer in my mom's office, began to feel too dirty. It wasn't just that toggling between windows in case my sister suddenly came in was a chore. Or that I'd become sloppier and sloppier about scrubbing browser histories to avoid letting my mom find out I'd been searching for "gay porn free" on AltaVista. There was something about how those all-too-pixelated images (this was the early 2000s, after all) of sweaty men felt illicit in and of themselves. It's why I'd begun to search instead for porn stories rather than porn videos. I was much more at peace with my own desires when they remained in my imagination, when short narratives about strippers masturbating all over clamoring fans or horny jocks fucking one another in steamy locker rooms felt safer precisely because no actual bodies—and no fluids, except my own—were ever involved. That's the sort of mental gymnastics I became all too adept at. I compartmentalized my sexual hunger so as to dissociate from the possibility of putting my own body in contact with that of another man. Soon, my journeys down porn story forums led me to cruising men on gays.com message boards. The written word was a safe haven where bodies could be coveted but never touched. I became consumed with the desire to find men who would cam with me, yet another example of how comfortable I'd become with limiting my sexual urges to virtual arenas where desire, but never sexually transmitted diseases, could be communicated.

A few days after getting my blood taken at the lab, I went in to get my results. I was handed a sealed envelope to deliver to an embassy-approved doctor, whose note I needed to attach to my study permit application. When I handed the doctor all of the paperwork he needed to sign for my application, he noticed that my HIV test had been opened. He understood what had happened and didn't berate me for breaking protocol. Instead, he instructed me to remind my mother that test results like the kind she'd so blatantly opened were meant only for myself and my doctors. I could feel my face burning with embarrassment, both for not noticing that she'd torn the envelope open and for knowing exactly why she had. She was working from that same facile kind of math that was all too common then, and that I myself couldn't let go of: gay = HIV+.

Did she hope to reassure herself that I wasn't gay if I was somehow HIV-negative? Did she fear that my test would come back positive, a confirmation of her deepest fears about who she thought I really was? My own inner fears were finally laid bare. Why else would she have chosen to look at those results if not to answer a question I didn't even know she was secretly asking herself?

We never did discuss it. I brushed it aside and chose to live in denial about what that breach of confidence really said about how my mother saw me. Like much of our relationship back then, we both chose to ignore the incident. Even now, close to two decades later, we've yet to sit down and unpack how that moment made my coming out soon thereafter even more painful. That unspoken moment with my mother is but one of the many emotional scars

I carry with me still, a reminder of a time when my sexuality was legible to myself and those around me only as it concerned a virus.

Thankfully, the villainous El Sida never did show up to knock me out in my sleep, but my fear of him remained. And the absence of concrete talk about the impact of AIDS on gay men like myself left me terrified of El Sida in ways that made it all the more difficult for me to come to terms with my sexual identity. Coming out didn't vanquish him—he still runs amok and rears his head in my mind whenever I go in for a routine HIV test—but it stripped him of any power he had over me, over how I understood my sexuality and how I chose to live my life. I even refashioned those cheesy PSAs into my very own motto: "Sin orgullo, ni pío."

Looking for Gaëtan

RYAN CONRAD

Gaëtan Dugas died on my first birthday in 1984. He was the flamboyant, promiscuous Quebecois fag erroneously described as the man who spread HIV throughout North America in Randy Shilts's disingenuous and sensationalized 1987 book *And the Band Played On*. The Patient Zero theory promoted in his book has been debunked by researchers and activists alike, but as a young small-town queer coming of age in the markedly homophobic and pre-/ proto-internet '90s, I knew nothing of this critical response to Shilts, just that I was a fag, a fag was the worst thing a boy could be, and I was going to die of AIDS—God's punishment, or something. As a young teen, I remember seeing the made-for-TV movie version of *And the Band Played On* and feeling an inescapable sense of impending doom.

I was raised in a family of six in a moderately conservative Irish Catholic enclave in southern Rhode Island, home to the Naval Undersea Warfare Center where my father worked, a small Catholic university, robber barons' Gilded Age summer homes, and an international elite vacationing on their gaudy yachts and twelve-meter sailing boats. I'm the youngest of four kids, the only boy, and—disappointment of all disappointments—the gay one.

My three older sisters had the unfortunate luck of having to attend Catholic school until it became financially untenable in the wake of the '80s Reagan recession and the early-'90s banking and loans scandal. My gay ass was spared the Catholic school experience by the mere chance of being born last, but weekly mass and Sunday school were compulsory while I lived under my parents' roof. Being born last in 1983, as opposed to first in 1974, like my oldest sister, also may have saved me from an early death. Protease inhibitors, the drugs that finally pushed HIV into hiding in the human body, came out when I was thirteen, but kids in high school still regularly made jokes about fags dying of AIDS.

As soon as I could manage it, I moved from my deeply alienating Irish Catholic hometown of 16,000 to a poor post-industrial French Catholic town of 35,000 in central Maine to attend college. The prevailing conservative moralizing attitudes about sex, drugs, abortion, and homosexuality between the two places were parallel, despite the more than 200 miles and class differences that separated them. I barely knew anything about queer culture and never met an out gay man until I left home. As a post-pubescent adolescent, I had consciously limited my exposure to anything queer to evade the perception that I was gay, especially once my friend circle disintegrated after the realization that the mutual masturbation and sexual play we innocently engaged in as Boy Scouts had deeper meaning to the adults around us. As soon as our playful behavior had a name, it also had a history, pathology, stigma, and associated disease. If we kept this up we were going to lead unfulfilling lives and die of AIDS like all the poor, emaciated, KS-pocked faggots we occasionally saw on the nightly broadcast news—and go to hell.

No one taught me anything about being queer until I was in my twenties. There were no gay-straight alliances, PFLAGS, or queer-inclusive sex education classes. There were no queer clubs, bars, or bathhouses. There were no activist, artist, or subcultural scenes outside of urban centers where I could find my proverbial people. There was one sexuality-themed course in college, and I took it, but that was it.

Thankfully, Emma Goldman, punk rock, and movies saved my life. Emma for writing with such eloquent, exacting rage against the violence of social controls and disenfranchising-by-design economic systems in a way that remained accessible to disaffected teenagers like me nearly 100 years later. Punk rock for not only giving me a sense of what's possible through collective organizing and shared passions but also for calling out the limitations. Punk also showed me that I didn't have to be a boring rainbow flag–waving pink dollar consumer like the boys of *Queer as Folk* and *Will & Grace*. Instead, I could be a queer anti-capitalist punk, though the urban centers of queer punk culture (San Francisco, Los Angeles, Toronto, etc.) were places where I had never been and all the punks I knew were conspicuously straight. And, finally, movies, for connecting me with the gay history I so desperately wanted to know but couldn't find.

When Netflix began its DVD-by-mail subscription service in the early 2000s, I devoured everything I could get my hands on. I was a film studies student of my own making, following a self-directed syllabus based on Netflix's then-expansive DVD catalog. The anonymity of the mail-order system meant no longer interfacing with and outing yourself to potentially hostile cashiers at movie rental stores, greater access to unrated and NC-17 queer films that Blockbuster Video refused to carry, and a selection of queer films far greater than any brick-and-mortar video rental store I had ever encountered.

Through Netflix, and the painfully small video library at the college I attended, I watched queer film classics alongside a slew of queer AIDS movies on glitchy degraded VHS or DVD digital transfers: *An Early Frost* (1985), *Parting Glances* (1986),

Common Threads (1989), *Longtime Companion* (1989), *Tongues Untied* (1989), *Silence = Death* (1990), *The Living End* (1992), *Blue* (1993), *Philadelphia* (1993), *Silverlake Life* (1993), *Totally F***ed Up* (1993), *It's My Party* (1996), *Love! Valour! Compassion!* (1997), *After Stonewall* (1999), *Angels in America* (2003) ... Despite deficiencies in representation, constraints of genre, and other shortcomings, these movies were where my HIV/AIDS and queer historical education took place, as there was nowhere else for me to start. The AIDS crisis has always been a crisis of representation, not just a medical and/or political crisis.

After graduating from college, I cobbled together a life through a mix of low-paying part-time social service and agricultural jobs while also starting a mostly queer collective house with friends. Together, in various combinations of ever-changing collective members, we volunteered our time and skills to help reenergize a fledgling queer and trans youth drop-in program, organized drag shows to raise much-needed cash for local youth HIV and STI prevention efforts, fought to reestablish a needle exchange, antagonized local Christian zealots at every opportunity, fought gay bashers and racists in the streets, defended low-income housing, traveled to regional and international activist gatherings and protests, and organized an AIDS Walk—a tedious nonprofit industry complex event for big-city folks but groundbreaking in our socially conservative working-class hometown where the Catholic hospital that was paid by the state to provide case management for people living with HIV refused to participate because we planned to distribute condoms.

The experience of being a part of this collective was equal parts exhilarating and exhausting. We were doing what we could with the limited experience we had, and the conspicuous absence of older queer mentors, save a few rad dykes—thanks, Penny and Erica. This absence of older queer mentors, particularly queer men, would set me on a different path, forcing me to abandon the collective I had co-founded and relocate to the urban centers I found so alienating and soul crushing.

There's an entire generation of queer men missing from the present-day frame, and many of those who are still with us are deeply traumatized from decades of watching their friends and lovers decimated by a deadly virus made more virulent by homophobia and medical negligence. When I heard that Roland Blais, the owner of a defunct gay bar in Lewiston, Maine, inconspicuously named the Sportsman's Athletic Club, was retiring to Florida, I hastily interviewed him so there'd be some sort of official record. Mid-interview he made me turn off the video camera and wept while describing what it was like to lose bartender after bartender to AIDS and what loss on that scale meant for gay men like him living in small cities and rural towns. I didn't realize what kind of trauma I was prodding. I didn't know any better. The history of HIV/ AIDS that I had learned up to that point had been an urban-centric one, where small-town queers were unaccounted for—or, worse, unimaginable. The presumptive lie was that the only way for queers to survive and thrive was to move to the city, a lie that continues to circulate today.

By 2009, I grew restless for greater intellectual stimulation and queer mentorship with older gay men that I couldn't connect with in central Maine. The economy had just tanked, so, like a lot of un/underemployed millennials, I headed back to school that September. Uniquely, my studies were paid for in part by settlement money from the city of Miami, where I was beaten unconscious by riot police and illegally jailed as part of the anti–Free Trade Area of the Americas (FTAA) protests in 2003. Through my studies, I would be paired with an advisor from outside the school, my main reason for applying to the program in the first place. I fought with administrators so that I could work with James Wentzy, a video artist and long-term survivor of HIV living in New York City.

As part of my studies in queer history, cultural memory, and HIV/AIDS, I met with James monthly in his basement apartment in the bowels of lower Manhattan. His apartment was filled with thousands of videotapes and pieces of AIDS activist ephemera that, at the time, you would never find in a museum. On my monthly visits he would fill me with stories, tea, and biscuits while we reviewed hour upon hour of video footage, both raw and polished. It was through my time with James that I learned inspiring queer histories I had never been taught, particularly the work of AIDS activist video projects like Damned Interfering Video Activists Television (DIVA TV), AIDS *Community Television* (ACT), and the Gay Men's Health Crisis's *Living with AIDS* series. I watched, in awe, the raw power of his unnarrated collage documentary *Fight Back, Fight AIDS: 15 Years of ACT UP* and the performance poetry of David Wojnarowicz that James had captured before David's death in 1992. It was through my time with James, the exposure to his work and the work of his friends, that I'd come to understand the AIDS crisis as a genocide committed by a government against its own people. In particular, his experimental short, a 1994 collaboration with Kiki Mason entitled *By Any Means Necessary*, shook me to the core.

I've always understood the AIDS crisis, both in the past and present, to be deeply political. It wasn't until this moment with James, however, that I began thinking through what it means to understand this history as a history of genocide. Why don't we remember the AIDS crisis in the same terms as it was described at the time by the people who experienced the mass death and destruction firsthand? What's lost as metaphors shift? How is cultural memory passed from one generation to the next? Of course I'd never know loss on that scale. I'd never know what it was like to drag a friend's coffin through the streets, enraged and exasperated. I'd never know what it felt like to throw fistfuls of ashes of dead friends and lovers onto the lawn of the White House in protest. There are limits to what I could know of history, no matter how hard I wished otherwise.

For me, history has always been about understanding how we got to the very moment of the present we inhabit—to understand how we've survived, who our enemies and allies have been, which activist strategies have worked and why, what is made (im)possible through shared collective experiences and moods, how the queer political imagination expands and contracts to render certain futures viable and others impossible. To think through these ideas I made a short film, *things are different now ...*, in the fall of 2011. I was at a particularly low point in my life—depressed, broke, recently uprooted, heartbroken, full of self-doubt, deeply alienated from living in a city for the first time in my life, and burned out from a decade of activism that never seemed to produce lasting structural change. At that moment, it felt like nobody gave a shit about queers, poverty, or HIV/AIDS, while the upwardly aspiring gays and lesbians were clamoring for marriage, open military service, and hate crime protections. I could barely get through my day most weeks, but making this film gave me structure and focus.

My short film struck an apparent nerve and was picked up by queer film festivals in North America and Europe, most excitingly, MIX NYC, where it premiered on opening night in 2012—the same film festival where James Wentzy's *By Any Means Necessary* screened for the first time when I was just a kid. What I didn't perceive was that I was part of a new wave of HIV/AIDS historicism in film, art, and literature. Suddenly, lots of people seemed interested in the history of HIV/AIDS. Documentaries and historical dramas came out every year for nearly a decade, some winning mainstream accolades and awards. Retrospectives of AIDS activist art were suddenly in vogue. New biographies and memoirs dotted the shelves at mainstream bookstores. It all felt a bit strange to be swept up in this moment, especially as a largely unknown artfag from a small town in central Maine who made irritatingly experimental short films that hardly anyone had seen.

This wave of HIV/AIDS revisitation projects was the subject of much criticism, some of it pointedly directed at me—my work was dismissed as merely nostalgic, and I was put on blast alongside famous and/or well-resourced artists, curators, and writers. I remain sympathetic to many of the critiques of the whitewashing; the self-aggrandizing, questionable hero narratives; the historical revisionism, misogyny, and lack of engagement with historiography itself. There were so many things to discuss, but it felt bizarre to me that any interest in the past was being dismissed as merely nostalgic.

History is how I understood myself. I had no sentimental wish for the good old days of mass death and hopelessness, and I continue to have a hard time believing that one can't engage with history while also being involved in activist projects in the present—the very thing myself and others were doing. Importantly, though, this conflict over concentrated attention to the past was a symptom of a larger issue: How do we balance the urgent need to remember rapidly disappearing HIV/AIDS activist histories with the bifurcated urgency of HIV/AIDS in the present?

Surely, the imagined fortieth anniversary of AIDS in 2021 will create new waves of HIV/AIDS historicism, for better or worse. Of course, how we tell stories about the past tells us just as much about the present. The renewed interest in critical and artistic work exploring HIV/AIDS speaks volumes to the desire in the present for a better understanding of recent history that younger queers and activists aren't getting through formal and informal education. Thankfully, we now have a plethora of tools, both visual and textual, to continue thinking through how histories come to bear on the present. These tools are not simply part of a clichéd directive not to forget the past lest we repeat it but also an injunction to recognize and deal with the traumas of the queer past that will always haunt the unfolding present. History is not a luxury.

Lying in bed talking aimlessly after sex the other day, my francophone poz lover revealed that he had never seen an HIV/AIDS–themed film, and that he had never even heard of Dugas or the Patient Zero myth that preoccupied my youth. At thirty-seven I carry the baggage of lived and historical trauma into our relationship, whereas at twenty-two he carries the burden of unrelenting stigma and criminalization wherever he goes. We've grown close quickly, flipping the cliché of the wiser older poz gay man educating an ignorant younger neg man. Without guidance or experience to fall back on, I find myself trying to be the person in his life I wished I had when I was a young queer in search of a history: kind, loving, generous, fierce, and knowledgeable—a friend and mentor.

Jason & David

DAN FISHBACK

I'm in my bedroom, staring at a drawer filled with notes and drafts from *thirtynothing*, a performance and writing project that dominated my life from 2009 through 2013. In that final year, I sent the book version of *thirtynothing* to Ted Kerr, because it was about AIDS and Ted is also about AIDS.

"This is not a book about AIDS," he said.

"Interesting," I said.

Several months later, I put all of my drafts in a drawer, stopped trying to get any of them published, and moved on with my life.

Tonight, I'm staring at this filing cabinet with a familiar dread. I remember feeling this sensation in my flesh—forty pounds and eight years ago—at the New York Public Library, sitting in front of a box from David B. Feinberg's archive. David is a nightmare. He died on the day of my bar mitzvah, we never met, and I love him.

In the '80s and early '90s, David was at the vanguard of AIDS humor writing. But while most humor is designed to make you laugh, David's was designed to cause pain. There's a sort of egalitarian sadism to David's nonfiction—he's already suffering, so why shouldn't you? He begins his final book, *Queer and Loathing: Rants and Raves of a Raging AIDS Clone*, "Let me take this opportunity to inform you from the start that I have complete and total contempt for you, my dear reader," and goes on to attempt, in encyclopedic detail, to transfer his misery onto you. And onto me. When I spent time with his work, I got the needling suspicion that he anticipated me, and wanted me to suffer with him. Out of love. I, too, am Jewish, so I understood. But understanding didn't make me feel better.

I remember sitting in front of that archival box in the library—a coffin of his living thoughts—feeling paralyzed with terror. I felt death creeping up my arms. I wanted to leave.

Okay, here's the deal. In *thirtynothing*, I took stories and images from my childhood and juxtaposed them with stories and images from the work and lives of gay artists who died of AIDS while I was growing up. I wanted to find these men—to commune with their ghosts, hoping they would help me understand my place in the world, my place in my body, and my place in history. It was an extremely flawed endeavor. Because I was using myself (white, cis, male, HIV-negative, thirty-ish at the time) as an organizing principle, I was placing at the center of an AIDS narrative the kind of person who is nearly always at the center of AIDS narratives, and whose dominance perpetuates systems of subjugation that amplify the harm of HIV/AIDS in the first place: racism, misogyny, transphobia, HIV stigma, et cetera.

So I attempted to create a space of healing, but I really fucked it up.

A few days ago, I was catching up with Avram Finkelstein over FaceTime. We're both in a high-risk group for coronavirus death (I have chronic fatigue syndrome, which includes a host of nasty, ongoing respiratory problems, and Avram, among other things, has been recovering from a stroke), and we're both finding it difficult to ask people for help. I tell him, "Avram, if some young queer person wants to bring you groceries, that will be a story they tell their friends for the rest of their life. *During the pandemic, I brought food to one of the guys who created SILENCE=DEATH!*" He thinks people will feel similarly about me, but I am extremely skeptical. Then again, why do we need to be icons to deserve groceries? Why do we want to advocate for everyone's existence but our own? Who taught us to do that?

In 1997, when I was fifteen, a friend's mom drove us to New York City to see *Rent*; the original cast recording had just come out, and we were all obsessed. It confirmed my suspicion that, somewhere in the world, queer people were being themselves. On our off time, we decided to go to "the Village," so we could "be like in *Rent*." We didn't know where in the Village to go, so we just wandered. It didn't feel like *Rent*. It felt a lot like Bethesda, an upscale Maryland suburb near where we lived. I wondered why I didn't instantly come across a group of fun gay people. Everything felt empty. Abandoned. We had dinner at Jekyll & Hyde, a cheesy theme restaurant where the waiters sing and dance in costume. To clarify: I was obsessed with a show about AIDS, yet my brain never made the now-obvious connection that the very topic of the play might explain why the streets weren't swarming with my people.

Here are some things I took for granted as a teenager in the '90s:
- Gay men have AIDS.
- Gay men die young, of AIDS.
- This is completely normal, eternal, and does not warrant discussion or inquiry.
- I am SOMEHOW NOT going to get AIDS.
- Sensual contact is unbearably emotional, so I should never kiss a boy unless I am certain we are in love, and certain he will never hurt me.

- Gay men are frivolous, unserious, apolitical, and aesthetically garish.
- Gay men like dance music, which is bad.
- Gay men like fashion, which is fascist.
- Gay men like meaningless sex, which is why they all die young, and also how I will survive, because I will wait until I'm in love.
- I am special and feel things deeply.
- It is okay for my life to revolve around internet boyfriends, because language is pure and has no body, so a love formed through pure language is pure love.

On a summer night in 1997, hours after I came out to my parents, once we had all finally stopped sobbing and screaming, my dad came into my room and woke me up. "Who is Jason?" he said. I had no idea what he was talking about. He repeated the question: "WHO IS JASON?" It was four a.m., and a man had just called our house on the phone, claiming to be my boyfriend, Jason, and then hung up. I didn't have a boyfriend and didn't know any gay guys named Jason. The screaming and sobbing started up again. I swore I had no idea who this was, or why someone would prank call us on the same night I came out. Understandably, they didn't believe me. I tried to fall back to sleep, thinking: *Who is Jason? Who is Jason?* I still do not know.

In 1999, I had two internet boyfriends—a boy my age in California, who knew me as Dan, and to whom I had mailed physical photographs of my actual face, and a man in New Jersey, who knew me as Danny (a name I never use in real life), and to whom I had emailed photos I'd found on the internet of an Aryan raver boy with a visor and sweeTARTS bracelets. The man was in his thirties, and we'd met in an "m4m18" chat room on AOL. Our cybersex was literary. I had zero understanding of how gay sex worked, and he was entranced by my absurd approximation of ego-death bottomry, complete with graphic descriptions of my asshole slowly ripping open from the force of his huge cock and my gushing blood lubing his dick and swirling with his inevitable load. He asked me if I took dicks bareback in real life. "Exclusively," I said. (I would bottom for the first time eleven years later and only ever with condoms. Both times.)

Eventually, after months of hot, reliable cyber, I received a barrage of instant messages, the brrrrrng! brrrrng! brrrrrng! triggering a boner. "WHO ARE YOU!?!?!" he wrote. He had found "Danny's" photographs on a porn site. I immediately whipped up a fantasy:

"This is ... so hard for me to talk about. I have an ex-boyfriend. He's 40. He forced me to take those photos ... After all that, it's ... so hard for me to feel close to anyone ... But I feel close to you."

The man didn't believe me. He told me I was going to get AIDS and die. I knew he was wrong because I made smart decisions. I wasn't like other gay boys, whom I figured probably *would* get AIDS and die.

I wouldn't kiss a boy for another four years. And another one two years after that. I had sex for the first time one year after that. And I didn't have penetrative sex again until I was twenty-eight.

Smart decisions. Healthy decisions.

Ted was right that *thirtynothing* wasn't about AIDS. It was about loneliness. It was about anticipating community and finding none. The solution to *thirtynothing*'s problems wasn't to change its format; the solution was to change my life.

And so I tried to decenter myself from my own longing. In 2012, I started developing a bunch of projects that became the Helix Queer Performance Network—I organized performance festivals, workshops, public conversations, art interventions—all intergenerational and all relegating white cis gay men to the extreme minority, giving everyone else more room to breathe. In organizing, I was able to use the fruits of my privilege to divert resources from major institutions into the hands of marginalized artists. I fucked up a lot. But I also set the stage for some transformative work. And I gained many meaningful friendships. I stopped feeling so alone.

It nearly killed me.

I built Helix on fumes. I pushed through episodes of health collapse; I spent money I didn't have on cabs to shuttle my barely functioning body between events and meetings. I thought that if I built something beautiful, people would see its value, throw money at it, and give me the capacity to hire a staff, step back, and pass along the reins to the people who deserved to author a broad conversation about queerness in NYC for themselves.

That didn't happen.

Instead, I found myself totally depleted, without the resources to appoint a successor. I had been squeaking by on grants and help from family, so my financial position at Helix was neither sustainable nor duplicable. I didn't trust that anyone who had the independent wealth necessary to accept my small stipends would be an appropriate candidate to do that job. And we didn't have the money to hire someone who was. As I write this, Helix's future is in flux. All I know is that I can't do it any longer. And if all of those resources go away, that's my fault. Because I thought I could do it all myself.

I was sick when it started, and it started because I was sick. In early 2009, I came down with a strange pneumonia that wouldn't go away. Finally, the mucusy stuff ended, but I was still completely incapacitated. When my doctor diagnosed me with chronic fatigue syndrome, I asked if there was a treatment; he laughed and said, "I hope you're rich and like watching TV."

In the following months, I felt a strange and offensive sort of déjà vu. I was a young gay artist in New York City, on the cusp of a promising theater career, stopped in my tracks by a mysterious and incurable illness, trapped in bed, relying on friends, discovering which friends weren't really friends, feeling like my life was over just as it had finally begun. *YOU DON'T HAVE AIDS IN THE '80s, DAN,* I kept screaming at myself. *YOUR DISEASE ISN'T FATAL. DON'T BE FUCKED UP.* But I still felt like I was living some twisted nightmare in the crater of a worse nightmare.

Before I'd even gotten sick, New York City in the early 2000s already felt like a fag graveyard. I didn't know why I felt so alienated from nearly every gay person I met; I didn't understand why our spaces felt so dark and unwelcoming. The United States had just invaded Iraq, and I had no idea where to find queers as angry as I was. I was so naïve; I didn't understand that I'd walked into the epilogue to two decades of mass death.

By the time I was condemned to bed with chronic fatigue syndrome at age twenty-seven, I'd already (thankfully) gotten to spend a few years letting Penny Arcade scream at me about everything wrong with my generation, everything we didn't know, everything we hadn't experienced. So the darkness had more form than when I first arrived. I could see in the dark. But only a little. Only enough to finally realize how much was still hidden from me.

Earlier, I referred to David Feinberg's writing as sadistic. As a fan of his writing, I think we both know what that makes me.

In the *thirtynothing* performance, I mention that David accused everyone in ACT UP of having failed. Often, older audience members would approach me after the show and say, "Oh, I was there that night. It was horrible." Eventually, I found footage of the speech at the New York Public Library. David looks like he's already dead.

"I'm going to be nice for, like, five minutes, and then I'm going to switch to real nasty."

He's sitting in front of the crowd, reading from papers. You can hear the audience shuffling anxiously.

"These are all the ACT UP *T-shirts I've bought over the past few years. I'm donating them back to* ACT UP."

He tosses a garbage bag of shirts onto the floor.

"This is probably the last time I'm going to be here." He takes a photo of the audience with a disposable camera. *"Joe Keenan's gay episode of* Frasier *is on tomorrow. Okay, that's it. This is called 'ACT UP NEW YORK'S FAILURES SINCE THE DEATH OF ROBERT RAFSKY.' Can everybody hear me?"*

They can.

He launches into a diatribe about how ACT UP New York has become too politically correct, losing its focus on actually saving, he says, *"our friends' lives."*

He screams: *"I AM A TOTALLY SELF-ABSORBED, NARCIS-SISTIC PIG. I DON'T CARE ABOUT LATEX DENTAL DAMS IN EL SALVADOR. I DON'T CARE ABOUT AIDS IN AFRICA, ASIA, EUROPE, AUSTRALIA, ANTARCTICA, OR SOUTH AMERICA.*

"I AM A CORPSE," he says. And that's what I see: a withering, decaying corpse, shouting at the top of his lungs.

"I am no longer fighting with ACT UP," he says, finally. *"If* ACT UP *continues in this fashion, it may as well be plowed over into the same mass grave that is already overflowing with the rotting corpses of our friends who have. Died. Of.* AIDS. *And if anyone applauds, they are just applauding their own stupidity. Thank you. I have to go now."*

He pauses.

"I have to go. I don't want to talk to anybody."

He starts gathering his things. *"I've had it."*

There's an exhausted silence while he gets up, tottering to his feet like some kind of homicidal marionette. As he hobbles out of the room, he says, oozing sarcasm: "*Thank you for your attention.*"

I hear Avram's soft voice in the audience calling out, "Thank *you*, David." And another repeats, "Thank you."

It's a horror movie.

What's most terrifying is how clearly the disease had corroded not just his body but his moral center. This was a guy who had been committed to activism for years, not just to save his own life but to save the lives of everyone infected with the virus. He had been arrested in demonstrations that were focused only on women with HIV; that suggests to me that he wasn't a fundamentally self-centered person. Not totally, not irredeemably. The rapid approach of death did that to him. Death brought him to that place of desperation, cruelty, and selfishness.

When I saw that footage the first time, it made me bolt from the library like I was running from a monster. Walking is hard enough with chronic fatigue syndrome—I don't run unless I'm fleeing for my life. It was freezing, raining, and late. At night, when it rains in New York, the water and darkness wash off any sense of the contemporary. Dark, cold, rainy Manhattan could be any year. I was walking through everyone's New York, hearing David screaming in my head. I felt a dull pain throughout my body. On the subway, my jaw was clenched shut. When I got to my apartment, I walked in circles around my room, head down, fingers stretched out. I watched TV obsessively, miserably. I wanted to bathe in television, to scrub David out of my brain. I didn't talk to anyone. I didn't leave my apartment. I didn't write about the experience. I didn't write anything for a month. All I really remember is that feeling. My body, changed.

Earlier this year, I started a new trauma therapy, where I'm sup-posed to write for twenty minutes every day in the voice of the pet-tiest, meanest, most immature version of myself, and then destroy the paper I was writing on. The idea is that, if I release all of the thoughts and feelings I'm repressing, then my body will somehow become healthier. The first few months are supposed to be pretty rocky. Sure enough, the things I write terrify me. But the sensation in my body is familiar. Eventually, I realize I recognize the voice on the page. It's David. Or: David and I are both that voice. Or: David and I both have that voice deep inside ourselves. Or: we all have that voice deep inside ourselves. And:

What will we do with it?

After Trump was elected, I was doing a lot of laughing and crying at the same time, so I asked Facebook if there was a Yiddish word for this. I was just joking, but someone commented with the answer: "lakhn mit yashtshterkes." Literally: laughing with lizards. I was so overwhelmed that my ancestors had the necessary command over beauty and mystery to articulate my experience so accurately and so absurdly. And I was sad that I didn't have easy access to their wisdom. Like nearly all displaced peoples, we dream in a language we don't speak.

I send a draft of this piece to Avram and he tells me I'm being too self-deprecating. He also tells me he decided to accept a young queer person's offer to bring him food. He sends me a photo of the clouds outside his window.

When I don't want to hear from my ancestors, they scream at me, but I don't always understand the words. And when I do want to hear from them ... nothing.

Sometimes I lie in bed and think, "Why is this happening to me?"

Maybe this is another way of saying, "What is wrong with me?"

Maybe this is another way of saying, "What are you trying to tell me?"

Maybe this is another way of saying, "What am I made of?"

Maybe this is another way of saying, "Take me."

Maybe this is another way of saying, "Speak through me."

Maybe this is another way of saying, "Louder."

Maybe this is another way of saying, "LOUDER."

Maybe this is another way of saying, "*LOUDER!*"

Homeless Youth Are Still Dying of AIDS

SASSAFRAS LOWREY

When I was seventeen, I lived in a friend's house, a converted barn. It was 2002. I was the first homeless queer kid my suburban high school had ever (knowingly) had to "deal with" (as they phrased it). My first kiss happened in a borrowed bed, the woodstove that heated the house crackling outside the door. I was a seventeen-year-old baby lesbian who ran my high school's first gay-straight alliance. She was twenty-three, a sculptor and painter. She drove a van filled with art supplies—sometimes she lived in that van.

"Were there cuts on her hands?" one of my suburban dyke mentors asked me the next day when I bragged about the night I lost my virginity. She was panicked. She told me I was going to get sick, that I was going to die.

I had been charged and convicted for my gayness by my family and community before I'd even kissed anyone. I had been kicked out for being gay. I felt like I might as well finally have sex. For two weeks, I waited for my HIV test results to come back from the Planned Parenthood clinic. I was convinced I would test positive. I had not gotten any kind of sex education at my high school beyond sex equals penis into vagina equals pregnancy and should be saved for after marriage. The only thing we learned about HIV was that it could be spread by blood or bodily fluids of any kind, and that even kissing could be dangerous, especially if one or both people had braces. This was the level of understanding that existed in my semi-rural/semi-suburban high school.

The gay people I knew out there were terrified of HIV but almost as uninformed as our football-coach-turned-sex-ed/health-teacher. My first suburban lesbian mentors did not have a cultural or politicized understanding of HIV—they were just afraid. As we waited for my results, they tried to scare me, convinced me I was "dirty" and irresponsible for having sex with someone I'd just met.

I started hanging out downtown with other homeless kids, and I threw myself into understanding and becoming part of queer culture. I cut my hair off, I adopted a butch style of dress, and I begged the body piercer dyke who worked at an outdoor artist market to pierce my face without an ID, just with a letter from the courts indicating there was a restraining order against my mother. I was not legally emancipated, but I was as close to it as the homeless kids I knew could get because the courts didn't really care about us. I began spending all my time in Portland with queer activists who had just jumped into adulthood. I was being raised in queer culture by older queer generations (which in queer time often meant people just five to ten years older than me). Some of my new friends had been ACT UP and Queer Nation organizers—they were activists and artists, they weren't interested in being quiet or blending in, they showed me a possibility of queer adulthood and survival on our own terms.

When I went back to Planned Parenthood two weeks later, everything had changed because my community had changed and I was hanging out downtown with radical queers. I tested negative for HIV and left with my backpack full of dental dams no one I knew ever used. I began having lots of sex and hanging out with older leather dykes who preached harm reduction and gave me the kind of sex education I needed. They took me and my friends to sex stores and showed me where to buy boxes of black latex tattoo gloves. They made sure that all of us knew about what AIDS had taken from our community. They made sure we had facts, not boogeymen, and they made sure everyone got tested. As a homeless/couch surfing youth coming of age in the early 2000s, I didn't experience HIV as an abstract history lesson. Many of the youth I shared meals with at the drop-in center were HIV-positive and receiving health care at the homeless youth clinic downtown where we all went when we got sick or started transitioning.

A week after my eighteenth birthday, I followed a queer conference hookup to hys hometown of Jacksonville, Florida. In the Deep South, threats of violence and overt discrimination from politicians and the KKK against queer folks were explicit and everywhere. It felt very far away from the Pacific Northwest, where even in the conservative county where I grew up I had been able to escape to the "big city" of Portland. In Jacksonville, every young transgender girl I met was HIV-positive, and most of the cisgender gay boys were as well. Everyone was homeless, couch surfing, or living in gender-segregated foster care group homes. No one had bio family supporting them.

I remember one night sneaking into a "boys'" dorm where two girls who named themselves after Disney princesses shared a room. The state had put them together for their own protection after one had been stabbed by a boy in another group home. There were no city or state regulations that allowed for them to be placed in group homes that were gender affirming. Their doctors sent them away with HIV medication but never explained anything about their condition or prognosis.

These girls used hormones they bought from older trans women at the bar where you could get in either with a fake ID or at eighteen if the doorperson wrote a big X on your hand. Everyone lived for the moment. No one expected to grow old. My hookup romance ended after four months, and I moved back to Portland. This was a time when the internet wasn't as accessible, and before wide use of cell phones in my circles, and so proximity was an important means of staying connected. I don't know what happened to my friends in Florida—whether they left town once they turned eighteen and were no longer property of the state, whether they lived or died.

A decade later and living in NYC, I worked as the director of one of the city's largest LGBTQ homeless youth drop-in and street outreach programs. When I started at the agency, the program I oversaw was primarily funded by federal HIV-prevention testing and "treatment adherence" money. I was responsible for the operation of a large federally funded contract that was designed to provide LGBTQ youth experiencing homelessness with resources— from organizing street outreach to connecting them with shelter, housing, medical care, and GED programs. I also could make sure they got a shower, a new pair of socks, a hot meal, and a snack to take back onto the streets with them for the night.

At my agency (and every other agency in the city), an HIV-positive diagnosis for homeless queer youth meant access to safer and better shelter beds. If a youth tested HIV-positive, the counselors in my program could see them for an unlimited number of case management sessions until they went to the doctor, and after that they had to end sessions with the youth who had built trusting relationships with them. The assumption by the government contract was that if we could get HIV-positive youth housed before we had to close their cases, the government would pay the agency more money. This was funding for a drop-in center to work with "vulnerable populations." If a youth tested HIV-negative, they could have no further (government-funded) sessions with my team, regardless of how many years they had been on the streets, regardless of their "risk factors," regardless of whether they were in crisis and begging for help.

The youth I worked with were mostly between the ages of seventeen and twenty-four, and they knew the way the systems worked. The reality was that if you were HIV-positive, there were going to be more resources for you—more benefits and a quicker path off the streets and into better accommodations. I am not suggesting that homeless LGBTQ youth are intentionally seroconverting, though over the years I did meet and speak with youth who felt this was their only available path to resources. When you are freezing on the streets of NYC in February and have no possibilities for shelter that feel safe, what are your options?

This was 2010 to 2018, and HIV was everywhere. The longer I worked with homeless queer youth in NYC, the rarer it was to meet cis gay male youth or transgender young women who weren't HIV-positive. I was reminded of my own experience as a homeless youth in Portland a decade before in the early 2000s, how none of the kids in my suburban GSA was HIV-positive, but large numbers of the street kids who became my best friends downtown were.

A not-infrequent part of my job as a program director was sitting down with young homeless LGBTQ people who had just gotten off buses to NYC from other states, often in the South. These youth came to New York City without a plan, without connections—or rather, the plan was that they had heard there was a community in New York, that there were resources for them that didn't exist in their conservative cities and states. It was devastating to watch youth slowly, over the days and weeks, realize the limits to what contemporary LGBTQ community in New York City looked like and how few resources there really were. On a personal level, to be the face of an organization that could only provide limited resources and support, I felt like a failure. This wasn't what I envisioned when, as a homeless queer teen, I dreamed of growing up to be a program director. This overwhelming sense of failure led to my burnout, disillusionment, and, ultimately, departure from my job and my nonprofit career, in large part because I didn't believe that it was possible to actually do anything other than apply an inadequate Band-Aid to a community bleeding out. Essentially, I felt like I had become part of the problem, not a solution.

While there are significantly more resources in New York for LGBTQ youth experiencing homelessness, living with HIV, and seeking medical care than would be available to them in other parts of the country, there are not enough, and unfortunately, the majority of resources are reserved for the youth who are the sickest. Youth know that. They know that to get a private room in a shelter, or their own apartment, they need to be "sick enough." I was told that when your option is sleeping on the streets, on the train, in warehouse shelters where your belongings get stolen and you get beat up, getting sick doesn't sound so bad.

The youth I loved and worked with were sick in ways gay people blocks away in the gentrified West Village of NYC no longer had to experience—for these youth, lesions and wasting syndrome were still common. Just blocks away, HIV was now portrayed as an inconvenience, a disease that you prevented or treated. For the youth who lived on the streets, HIV still felt like a death sentence— the only benefit was it came with housing and food.

Today, LGBTQ youth still make up a disproportionate number of all homeless youth—the best numbers tell us that forty percent of all homeless youth identify as LGBTQ. LGBTQ youth of color, as well as transgender and nonbinary youth, are more highly represented among homeless youth populations. According to the CDC, youth make up twenty-one percent of new HIV diagnoses in the United States and are the least likely of any demographic to be connected with medical care. As someone in my mid-thirties who grew up amid homeless queer youth culture, and then spent the better part of a decade working with and on behalf of queer youth experiencing homelessness, I cannot be silent when I hear the pervasive narrative that young people do not know the impact of AIDS.

When we say that HIV is no longer a death sentence, we erase the reality of some of the most marginalized members of our community. Homeless LGBTQ youth are still dying of AIDS, and a lot of people simply do not care.

Leftover Lovers

EDRIC FIGUEROA

"We cannot even say these words aloud," my sex education teacher in high school said with his head low as he hastily wrote, *Gay* and *Abortion* on the whiteboard in front of me. Before I could even process the stigmatization occurring in front of me, he passed around an unwrapped York Peppermint Pattie and instructed everyone to touch it. When it got to the last student, he asked, "Would you eat that?"

At this point, I knew abstinence-only sex education was only going to teach me how to dissociate in order to avoid exploding with rage. It was 2003 in rural Georgia, where acceptance for me as a queer youth was still not a foreseeable reality. And my teacher's words were extra personal and absurd to me, since I was already wise to several queer family members, and I had friends who'd had abortions.

The public school system required each student to receive parental permission to attend just two periods of sex education from a gym coach, but the appalling impact of these two periods would stretch much further. The fear tactics were varied and unsubtle, from a large doll shaped like a sperm cell that coach made fly around the room to illustrate how easy it is to impregnate an egg cell to the overhead projector slides of genitals covered in syphilis, human papillomavirus, herpes, and other sexually transmitted diseases.

After the variety show, coach added a footnote on HIV. "HIV is a virus that causes a disease called AIDS that, like herpes, has no cure and can kill you." And there ended our "lesson." He closed this sermon with: "The only way to prevent unwanted pregnancy, STDs, and HIV is abstinence ..." Then, with a sinister smile, he added "Until marriage between a man and a woman ... and then, sex is *great!*"

The stigma of HIV surrounded me during adolescence. As a first-generation immigrant raised by Catholic Peruvian parents, the message that homosexuality is a sin was ingrained in my brain as profusely as "y'all" and "carajo" were glued into my vernacular.

The legacies of colonization and slavery were visible daily, from my high school mascot, the Chiefs; the school's name, Sequoyah; and the county I lived in, Cherokee, all named after Indigenous people long murdered and displaced, to the shadows cast from Confederate flags waving off big trucks in the school parking lot that reminded me of my brown skin and small stature. Still, with my back slouched, hair dyed, and an armor of black jeans and band T-shirts, I walked through those hallways determined to live.

My parents raised my siblings and me in a land with so many customs brand new to them. Perhaps holding on to Catholicism made them feel at ease; I suffered through church every Sunday and Wednesday for fifteen years, even though looks from catechism teachers made me want to die. My parents made me feel like rejecting the church was rejecting my culture, and coming out felt like the whitest, most *American*, act I could commit. Luckily, I wasn't alone.

My family has always been full of queers who didn't have the words to describe ourselves. Together, we got lost in the crowds at punk shows and the astrology sections in mall bookstores, dyed our hair, stole our parents' beer, and defied "normal." It felt better to stand boldly contrary to hegemony than to be shunned while trying to fit in. My kin made headlines in those years—some of us for starting the first gay-straight alliance in the county, others for protesting the war with Iraq, and others for robbing banks. We experienced structural oppression in the most profound ways and didn't know we were being eaten alive by meritocracy until it was too late.

After high school, my hardworking mother got me literally the shittiest job in the county. Cherokee County Animal Shelter would leave an impression on my life as lasting and poignant as the tinnitus from the roars and whines of the kennels. At five feet, five inches tall and 130 pounds, I was a baby-faced virgin homo thrown into the blue-collar world with a pooper-scooper and smile. It was here I would fall in love before falling into consciousness.

Six "lucky" inmates at the local jail self-enrolled in an unpaid seven-day-a-week workforce. Five of them mowed lawns and changed lightbulbs around the county, and one got the privilege of working alongside the shelter staff and a rotating cast of court-ordered misdemeanor and felony community service workers. Because my cousin was in jail, I had grown accustomed to conversations and kisses through bulletproof glass, and it was at that same jail where I met Aaron, my new unsalaried workmate.

Aaron was seven years, and ten years' worth of lovers, older than me. He had a kind, aloof, and forward spirit; when he found out I was gay and I'd never seen another man's penis, he flashed me immediately. I found him hilarious, stupid, and completely irresistible. I don't remember the exact moment we decided to be lovers, but it was only a matter of weeks before I was putting money on his books so he could call me every evening.

· Back in high school, I hung with classmates bold enough to be out, but still we craved an unwavering role model. The GSA chaperone, the school's closeted football coach, was the closest thing we had to a mentor. At our first meeting, he made us swear to never out him, for fear of losing his job. His heart may have been in a noble place, but he could not advocate for students outside of the weekly meetings we held in dimly lit high school trailers. As those four years went by, we were shoved into lockers and harassed by other students and/or teachers, and only a handful of queers left that school with diplomas. Structural oppression created impossible conditions for us to navigate as queer brown youth—in the end, we were just trying to survive.

Variations of "Don't sit with," "Don't touch," and "Don't get near *that kid* because you'll catch AIDS," were shared as often as "That's so gay" in my high school cafeteria. Abstinence-only education asserting that sex outside of heterosexual marriage was "dangerous" and "perverted" made queer youth the targets of these hateful jests. The false tropes about AIDS and gays kept students and teachers alike in self-defeating closets, teetering on seesaws of self-loathing and complacency. Maybe that's why I threw myself at the very first man who flashed me his dick.

Five days a week, I drove the shelter van and picked Aaron up and dropped him off through barbed-wire fences at the jail. I acted like my heart didn't break every time I saw him exit the van for a pat down. When he would call me on the phone, I would hide in the bathroom or lock my bedroom door and press 1 to accept the call so we could have those twenty-minute-max conversations in secret.

We both knew what was going to happen the second we were alone. I had no idea what I was doing; I felt like my only option was to trust him, and anything I could find on my limited broadband internet about gay sex. I walked into Walmart, grabbed the first bottle of lubricant I saw, hid it in my county-issued jacket, and walked right back out of the store because I could not risk anyone

I knew seeing me buy such a thing. The very first time I had sex, it was with liberated K-Y Jelly—the heating kind (ouch)—on a gray break room couch in a building that could not shake the smell of cat piss and bleach.

I had brought condoms, but before I could unwrap one, Aaron quickly stepped in to say, "Condoms leave evidence, and it feels so much better without them." I hesitated, but the excitement of the moment outweighed any fear of HIV. Sex was painful, a little bloody, and quick. I got through it with deep breaths, pushing the images of bacterial infections and incurable diseases out of my mind. He finished while still inside me, and told me that the pain, blood, and anxiousness were all normal for the first time. The mix of semen and K-Y Jelly burned my insides as they made their way out, and I wondered: *Did I just shorten my life? Was this pleasure worth the pain and worry?* One thing was certain: I had abandoned caution and could now throw myself carelessly into the depravity that had been promised to me by the church and public school system.

There were times when we heard a door unlock, or heard footsteps down the hall, and we both nearly died from nerves as we rushed into bathrooms or kennels to get dressed quickly. My anxiety hit a max I'd never experienced and I could no longer keep our relationship to myself. I took my cousin Kenneth into the bathroom during a family dinner, locked the door, and told him everything.

Kenneth stared in shock; he was a year younger than me, a fellow queer, and my best friend. "Wow ..." was all he could say. I told him that taking a dick was just about the worst pain I'd ever experienced in my life, but I didn't regret it, despite my terror about HIV, STDs, and of course, my fear of getting caught.

Kenneth's voice was full of hesitation yet supportive as he told me that I should be careful not just because of the potential legal consequences of my actions, but also because I had no way to be sure Aaron didn't have any STDs or HIV. Although we didn't go to the same high school, Kenneth's experience with sex education in another rural Georgia county had been almost identical to mine. We'd both internalized the lie that HIV guaranteed an arduous life, if not an early death, and that it would make us perpetually undesirable. I promised Kenneth that as soon as Aaron was free we would both get tested together.

Upon release from jail, Aaron would have no job, driver's license, or car, but he owned a house he'd purchased with his ex and a roommate he met while gambling at the horse racetracks. "I'd trade it all for your love" he would often say when discussing his past, quickly followed by "and sex two times a day ... and you know ... I'll still be drinking—but just beer ... Does that work for you?" Having only known him sober, I didn't know the full weight of what he was asking of me, and I exhaled a reluctant yes.

The first thing we did together as a free couple was clean his room. Cigarette butts and marijuana roaches covered his bedside table, and I found steel wool and glass pipes under the stained mattress he'd gotten for free from a neighbor. Aaron's most beloved poison, though, was Coors Light, the silver bullet of beers—he emptied eighteen cans that night, and they joined the aluminum graveyard in the bedroom and backyard, until once a month he collected the cans for recycling money.

The second thing Aaron and I planned for his fresh start was a long drive for HIV and STI testing. Like me, he had never had an HIV or STI test; unlike me, he started having sex at eleven years old. He made many half-witted attempts at reassurance with comments like, "I'm *clean*, we've got nothing to worry about," sardonically ending with "and if I have something, I got it from you."

The night before our appointment, I couldn't sleep. We drove to the county below us so we wouldn't be recognized, and I paid $200 for both of us to be tested at Any Lab Test Now. As the screener drew our fluids, her homophobia became evident in the way she inserted the needle brashly and spoke to us as if we were lepers. The worst part was weeks later, when she handed me the paperwork.

We didn't look at the results until we were in my car. All the blood rushed to my head and Aaron said, "What is it?"

I swallowed and stuttered, "It says ... it says ... I'm positive."

"What? That can't be," he replied, as he snatched the paper from my hand. "The fuck? This isn't even your paperwork," he retorted violently, as he threw it back to me.

It turned out to be the paperwork for someone newly diagnosed with HIV who *shared my last name*. As Aaron opened the car door and rushed back into the clinic, I quickly followed, and before Aaron could cuss out the screener, I made her aware of her mistake with the only composure I had left. She moved her eyes over the paperwork slowly, and then all she said was "Oh ... yeah, you don't want that one," as she handed me the correct paperwork. When our actual test results came back negative, Aaron and I left that lab scared shitless about HIV, and with zero information regarding safer sex practices.

A cycle of fight, fuck, cry, and feel hopeless would soon have us in its spiral. Every time Aaron and I tried to have a casual night of reconnecting with his friends over "just a few beers," things would escalate fast. Malicious words would spew from his mouth the second we had a conflict. He would go from telling me he loved and wanted to marry me to screaming "Fuck you!" and punching me in the face. There were nights I drank to try to keep up with him, blacked out, or yelled too, but anytime things got physical I knew I couldn't win. I knew I had to leave before one of us ended up dead, but even when my closest family members tried to stage an intervention, I chose Aaron. I felt like I was acting out of love for him, but I was shoving away care from people who genuinely wanted to support me.

Soon, our fights left the bedroom and I was running away from him in public parks, gas stations, and hotel rooms or apologizing to restaurant staff, my friends, and strangers for his behavior. The fights would always end with both of us crying ourselves to sleep or making love to feel close to one another again, and then the next day acting like nothing happened. Anytime I tried to leave, Aaron would threaten to kill himself and I would stay. I forgave him for all the fights, bruises, and public embarrassment. I could not, however, forgive him for the night he tried to force his way inside of me despite my tears and stern cry of "No!"

I knew that if I gave him complete control of my body there would be nothing left of me. I blocked his texts and calls, and am forever in debt to the friends who let me stay the night with them, drove by his house late at night with me, and listened to my endless rants and poetry about him. I'd managed to go five months without seeing him when I read about him in an online Cherokee County paper. The police found him in a ditch, alive but beaten up after what the paper described as a fight over "a personal vendetta." What the newspaper didn't print is that Aaron had been invited to a New Year's party, and when he arrived he was greeted by a baseball bat to the back of the head while his assailant screamed, "Faggot!"

"This is all my fault for leaving," I kept telling myself in a mania as I lost all restraint and drove over to his house. When I got to his front porch, neither of us said a word. He broke down as soon as he saw me and just sobbed in my arms. I held his swollen face in my hands—his stitches already tasted like cigarettes and alcohol as our lips pressed together for kisses we hoped could ease this horror.

I was still so angry about what he did to me, but I was even more upset that the world would never know the vile hate that motivated the bashing. We had an on-and-off affair for a couple of months, but then I definitively cut it off again because of old patterns reemerging.

Nine months went by, and I read about him online again. This time it was a vague obituary describing a ceremony I had not been invited to; instead of flowers, his family was requesting donations to Narcotics Anonymous.

Aaron's end was exactly as I had feared it would be if I left; he drank himself into a sorrow he could no longer bear, and he hung himself by his belt in the house that held so many of our secrets. None of his friends or family bothered to reach out and tell me. I held on to guilt about his death for a long time after his passing; I used it to justify displaced outbursts of rage and jealousy with new lovers. I moved to Atlanta to get away from Aaron's ghost and started volunteering, which eventually led to a job at the largest AIDS organization in the Southeast. It was there where I learned all the facts I'd never received about HIV, sex, STD prevention, and pleasure. I was introduced to harm reduction, to the history of AIDS activism and ACT UP, and I even started offering local communities the same HIV tests I had once sweated over, *for free.*

I learned that, in 1983, twenty years before my high school sex education class, a group of gay men with AIDS drafted a manifesto at the Fifth Annual Gay and Lesbian Health Conference in Denver, Colorado, which became known as the Denver Principles. These principles included the recommendation not to "scapegoat people with AIDS, blame us for the epidemic, or generalize about our lifestyles." I often think of who I would be today if these simple recommendations had been followed in my high school and my first testing experience. These suggestions, like the science to prevent and treat HIV/AIDS, are not novel ideas; they were just introduced in my life too late to prevent harm. And, unfortunately, these commonsense recommendations are still not observed in far too many classrooms, testing labs, and even in some community-based nonprofit programs.

Working in prevention deepened my analysis of HIV, the health disparities connected to it, and the limitations of nonprofit organizations. At the time, most of our funding came from CDC "evidence-based" intervention programs tested in major cities on specific "at-risk" populations to reduce new HIV transmissions. These programs, designed to be easily replicated across the nation, neglected to factor in the institutionalized oppression of the South, felt scripted, and fell flat across local communities. There was also never enough housing for clients and too many qualifiers for individuals to receive crucial supports like case management. Still, what we offered saved lives and was milestones ahead but only an hour-and-a-half drive away from what I learned in high school. The best part was the connections I made with other queers fighting for liberation.

While handing out condoms at MondoHomo, a queer music and arts festival, I met unapologetic queers who quickly called out the transphobic gender marker categories on the public health outreach forms required of me, and embodied the mantra "The personal is political." From poetry and punk bands to strippers and voguing, I witnessed queerness, gender, race, and art collide on the MondoHomo stage. I felt at home on those sweaty nights that ended over drinks and stories of resilience, triumph, and loss with other Southern queers. I formed lasting friendships that helped me connect the dots between the guilt still sitting in my gut and the structural determinants that created the conditions for stories like mine and Aaron's to unfold.

I chose to pursue a career focused on HIV and violence prevention, despite the institutional limitations. For me, this work is one way to honor the legacy of Aaron and the queers who came before me, and a way to advocate for those who fall through the cracks built into the foundations of nonprofits themselves. Although the nation now has the tools and science to end the domestic HIV epidemic, this will never happen without centering the stories and experiences of communities most impacted by HIV.

My experience is not unique. Abstinence-only sex education still exists across the United States, and to this day, lovers are beaten to death or back into closets, or driven to suicide because of internalized oppression and harmful prejudice that is normalized by the nation's pervasive refusal of truth and justice. Without deep systemic change, people like Aaron will remain collateral damage on the path to progress, and leftover lovers like me will be forever grieving and fighting in their memory.

Elders

MIRANDA RECHT

I.

I have heard that my godmother—gold-star lesbian; first responder to the human rights crises of the '60s and '70s; holder of my uncles' hands as they lay in their hospital beds, six months apart, dying of AIDS—does not like it when I use the word "queer." Especially when I use it to describe myself.

I can only imagine how I must appear to her, bringing a succession of boyfriends, and eventually a husband, through the living rooms of our family holidays, passing so well for straight that no one would even wonder. How it must rankle her to hear the word used to describe such an opposing and, dare I say, privileged condition, when she can still feel the bite of the slur as it seared its course through her young memory.

I wish—and not just for her sake—that I had another way to describe myself.

II.

In 2010, I am twenty-five years old and working at a needle exchange upstate. The building out of which the tenuously funded program operates is squat, creaking with age, on the right side of the tracks but just barely. From the windows, which are marbled with layers of grime and masking tape, one can just make out the overpass that bisects the city and parses the poverty line even finer.

I am one of a team of volunteers who admit clients, enter data, assemble safer injection kits, bag condoms, prepare grainy coffee and flimsy sandwiches, and offer an ear or a smile or a just-another-Tuesday attitude, as circumstance prescribes. Administering the agency's rapid HIV screening, which boasts results in less than an hour, is not among my duties. When the program director takes me aside one afternoon to ask whether I would be interested in obtaining my certification, I politely, summarily, refuse.

Where the popular imagination is concerned, AIDS has not been a terminal illness for more than a decade; though one need only set foot in our lobby to understand how, in many ways, diagnosis still represents the same social death as ever. And to me, AIDS will always mean the low-frequency sadness that dwells at the heart of family get-togethers, the snuffing of the light of an entire generation of artists, the fear that only ever shifts its object from one reviled community to the next.

I do not have what it takes to look into a person's eyes and initiate them into the legacy of this virus. Despite the good that it inarguably does one to know, I do not have the strength to tell it.

III.

Before "death sentence" became "livable condition":

My uncles were young, handsome, promiscuous gay artists living in New York City during the most lethal years of the plague. I was eight years old and it was autumn when they came back upstate to die. I remember them as powerful but insubstantial figures, all Virginia Slims and gaunt limbs and cheekbones. Presiding. Regal.

Between ages nine and ten, I bore witness to my Catholic grandparents' shame-disguised-as-love and to my mother ripping my brother from my uncle Larry's good-bye hug one Easter because "They still don't know, they still don't know," the words worried like a talisman during my parents' next big argument, as we cowered in the back seat of the car, infected by her fear.

Like so many other details of their sickness, their last days were shrouded from us. We were left only to imagine, told in the toxic lacunae of Catholicism that what was happening was "because of sex." It was not until we were much older that we heard about the opportunistic infection that took hold of my uncle Larry's compromised immune system and carried him off, in peals of agony, into the blacked-out night of American history: a strain of bacteria known only to affect smaller breeds of dog, and seldom fatally.

Of the months following the last of the funerals, I remember the refusal by the school administration to pray for the repose of my uncles' souls over the PA; the fear, given to me by an older boy on the bus and spread from class to class like contagion, that I had it, too; the sense of being othered, of being ashamed, of being queer.

I also remember my third grade teacher's concern, which she shared during a conference with my parents, that I had been traumatized. And I recall the heavy feeling in my stomach, uncertain what the word meant but sensing betrayal in it all the same, when my mother flung it at me like a curse one night after dinner.

But how can I be tromitized? I wondered in green, felt-tipped marker on the page of my third grade diary. *I barely even knew them.*

IV.

Then I am thirty-one and volunteering at a needle program in the heart of a rotting West Coast city, engaged once or twice a week in outreach.

On designated afternoons a small team takes to the surrounding neighborhood with totes of harm reduction supplies and brown-bagged lunches, calling, "Sharps! Condoms! For free!" as we make our way across heavily trodden and seldom repaired pavements, stopping to engage with familiar or curious faces or to pluck a stray syringe from the curbside debris.

Among the volunteers are some who have been here already, on the other side of the outreach initiative, and who now use banter and rapport as powerful tools in convincing their acquaintances to stop by the clinic during testing hours. I also meet a woman who has been involved in syringe exchange since her son died in the late '80s, who for years went around the district with boxes of sharps tucked into a baby carriage, managing to elude the unjust law of the time and place. As I listen to her talk of the old days while we are packing up one afternoon, I wonder what the movement will look like after those who suffered its first, unimaginable losses have finally retired from the trenches, especially now, in 2015, when PrEP is supposed to have made HIV/AIDS into as avoidable a condition as it is a livable one.

V.

For a few Christmases before my uncle Jimmy died, and then for a few Christmases after, my brother, my cousin, and I went to see him acting the part of an elf in a film stretched across the vaulted dome of our city's planetarium. Before moving to New York to follow his dream of becoming a Broadway actor, he had belonged to a local theater troupe, and this role had been his first foray into stardom.

Early in his illness, we sat with a smuggled box of Jujubes and giggled between ourselves at how fat he looked up there in his green costume, how scant his resemblance to the man of skin and bone who had just recently moved back upstate to live with our grandparents. The truth had not yet been given us to understand.

The year of his death, I was able to recognize some of the other elves on the planetarium's ceiling, though the contrast between their candy-cane-painted faces as they smiled benignly down at their childish audience and those belonging to my uncles' grieving friends as they sat in a circle on the floor of the theater where the wake was held—my brother, my cousin, and myself included—and reenacted outrageous scenes from my uncle's brief life was almost impossible to reconcile. That he had been loved, and dearly, was the only obvious thing.

Seeing my uncle Jim stitched into time and tradition, year after year, yet growing no older, I remember coming to a sad sort of peace that I would now only ever know him through his creative work. There was weight in this idea that was entirely novel, resembling nothing else in my experience, calling me to art.

VI.

At thirty-three, recovering from sexual assault and visiting family in the South, I volunteer for one day at the only syringe exchange in the state. Its existence, I am told, is of questionable legality, yet here, at the far end of an empty commercial plaza, sharing its parking lot with vendors of a more illicit commerce, it stands.

The clinician's careworn expression as he greets me in the reception area is one that I recognize, intimately and instantly, as burnout. His fatigue seems a part of the gathering huddle of gray above the city and the drizzle now beginning to pock the storefront windows.

Despite the warnings of severe weather, six of us load the van with supplies and head out. The driver is eccentrically attired and highly decorated, sporting a formidable collection of Narcan buttons to tally the overdoses that she has reversed in her long years of service. With the rain thrumming strange rhythms onto the roof, she imparts some local lore about the neighborhood we are visiting, how its nickname, the Bluff, is said to be an imperfect acronym for: "Better leave, you fucking fool." At this, the volunteer in the passenger seat lets out a mirthless laugh. As the van bumps its way along the increasingly pitted terrain, juddering me into the arm of my seatmate, it occurs to me dimly that this is the closest I've been to a man since one attacked me in my bed last March.

The sky is rent by barbs of lightning when we pull up to the curb. In garbage bag rain slickers, we set up our table beneath a tattered awning and greet the clients, who are already there, waiting. We pass out condoms, needles, and food, offer to share our meager shelter. I load the arms of a teenaged couple with brown bags and watch them clamber, through rain now falling aslant, over a chain link fence bearing a No Trespassing sign.

VII.

In 1996, less than three years after my uncles' deaths, I will learn—
yet will somehow fail to assimilate—that AIDS is no longer a death
sentence. That's exactly how the disembodied voice of memory will
tell it: "AIDS is no longer a death sentence." Still, the news will fail to
create a schism. I will continue into middle school fearing infection
as one might The Inevitable. I'll also come to imagine ties stronger
than mere blood between my dead and my self but will wholly lack
the words to make sense of what was taken from me.

At fourteen, I will begin to wear oversized men's clothing and
layers of sports bras to safeguard my strange new woman's body
against the omnipresent threat of the male gaze. At the same time,
I will imagine acting out variations of the same slow-motion love
scene with any in a rotating cast of cruel or imaginary boys, all of
whom I will desire for their very unattainability. For years, I will
dwell in a state of incorrigible fantasy, the creative life my only
refuge from the minefields of home and the torments of school.
Eventually, drugs will come along, too.

When I do finally begin having sex, the act will only manage to
produce a hollowed-out sensation, almost as if something absurd
yet deeply violating were taking place but at the protective remove
of a disassociated state. Yet in my continued attraction to men, I
will continue to dissociate. It will not be until my early twenties,
when my then-boyfriend is drunk enough to bring up the idea
of a strap-on that the broken pieces will begin to fall into place.
Through this initiation into shared fantasy—in which I am able to
fuck a man as might another, while at the same time sealing my
own body off from the subliminally lingering threats of penetration
and contagion—I will first begin to understand that I do not actually hate sex after all.

But what to do with the newfound kink once the relationship to which it belongs has run its course? A few years later, equipped with only an imperfect language to describe what I have come to think of as my sexuality, my queerness, I will be set adrift in the world of adult dating. In the months that follow, I will be drawn to the anonymous and infinite possibilities offered by the Craigslist personals. On those forums, where one can imagine the heart's most complicated desires via black text on a white background, I will learn, along with countless, nameless others, to articulate who and how I want to fuck. What this possibility of connection and expression will give me in the decade before it is demolished is, even now, impossible to overstate.

XIII.

A young trans man in the receiving room at work—twenty-one years to my thirty-three—tells me about his pain, tells me about the meds he is on and the meds he wishes he could afford. Flushed, he goes on to speak of his family's stingy and inadequate shows of acceptance after he came out to them.

Although we've never really spoken before this, I want to relate to him as one who has known something of what he has suffered. To take on the role, perhaps, of an elder. But in my black-and-white kimono top and sensible pumps, deriving my whole sense of queerness from acts performed in secret, I fear that, at best, he will consider me too much of a closet case to be taken seriously.

I decide to tell him a piece of my truth anyway. I am so nervous that I begin perspiring through my top. There is nothing in his response to make me feel judged; I've just never gotten into this particular habit of revealing myself.

Soon, I stop seeing him around the workplace. The few times I am able to seek him out, he acts distant, as if we hadn't spent hours of the company's time sharing our secret hurt. There is only the one night that he finds me stocking shelves and folds me into a weary embrace—which itself feels like an unburdening—to remind me of our brief connection. When, after a long period of his absence, I remark to one of his friends that I haven't seen him recently, she looks anxious and evades further discussion.

I imagine—probably only imagine—his friends looking at me differently. Then one day, on the manager's desk I come upon a doctor's note excusing a coworker whose name I've never heard before on the grounds of nervous collapse. The dawning realization finds me piling the letter with stray advertising leaflets, turning off the light, and closing the door tightly behind me.

It is the end of a holiday break and we are driving through Livingston County on our way back to the dorms, my mother and I.

My first coming out goes something like this: the weed I smoked beforehand lends me the courage to tell her that I think of myself as a gay boy and always have, since the time of my uncles' deaths. Discretion, after all, is a foreign currency between us.

The silence that goes up around this subject, engulfing the miles of night-blackened back road between the car and the campus, goes on for years. It is only after I have moved to the rotting West Coast city and she remarks on the phone, almost conversationally, about how she's surprised I don't have AIDS yet, that I let myself believe I actually spoke my truth out loud to her on that night whose silence continues to sear like a slur.

IX.

The cruel man, exquisite in his deceit, my response to his Craigslist post.

For years, we will lock ourselves away in hotel rooms. For years, he will punish me by playing abusive games with my head. I will be his dirty little secret; he will be my dirty needle.

"I'll spread my legs wide open for you," he'll text before closing himself off from me completely.

In time, I will learn to use the interims of his scattered attention as occasions to self-destruct. Once more, I will turn to Craigslist, and it will dispense more men: men for me to use and reject in my turn, men to take money from in exchange for acts that don't even feel like sex anyway, men who want my strap-on; some of them are beautiful, but none are cruel enough to inspire the crusade of violence I instigate against myself, not in their own right.

Risk, the thing once feared, will become (has probably always been) the thing that turns me on above all else.

Across the barroom table from a hollow-eyed stranger who'd replied to my post to say that he wants my fist, I will learn about the infrequent outbreaks and the recurrent humiliation of disclosing his incurable STD, which will—and not entirely by accident—become my incurable STD, too.

X.

My queer artist sister, seven years my junior, meets me on the morning after the Pulse nightclub massacre. The brunch-time mood of the establishment, the chatter and the laughter and the clinking utensils, seems to surprise neither of us as we sit across from each other, red-eyed and tense, aware in memory both lived and inherited that the world does simply just go on, indifferent to our tragedies. It all only adds to the enormous weight of the day.

For hours after, we drive aimlessly and talk about the great web of lives belonging to the transgressors and the creators and the criminal-saints, slung across the generations, of which we are certain—if not outwardly assured—that our lives are a part. We speak of the same loneliness, the same in-group rejection, played out in different ways. And of the traumas that, despite our never having sat, stoic, at an AIDS ward bedside of one of our peers, nor ever having run, half-wild with grief, beside a stretcher carrying the body of a loved one from the scene of a massacre, belong to us as well.

In parting, we tell each other, "You are my community."

And somehow, in spite of everything, this feels like enough.

XI.

At a feminist coffeehouse tucked into a trendy enclave of my home-town, I meet my godmother for lunch. This year has not been kind to her: in the span of several months she lost both her partner of ten years and their beloved dog, Sophie. Nevertheless, she has managed to be here, patiently waiting for me at a corner table, her resilience in the face of unimaginable grief one with the history of gay women in the time of the plague.

No sooner do I sit down from our hug than she hands me the newly published book written by my uncle Jimmy's former doctor, an AIDS specialist of large but humble renown, which chronicles his three decades of patient care. As I flip through its pages, I notice that the book has been inscribed to her by its author. This gesture, this passing-on, seems to be her quiet way of acknowledging that she knows what this fight means to me: that it is my fight, too.

Family Business

KATE DOYLE GRIFFITHS

Only a few students signed up for the Anthropology of HIV and AIDS course at the Catholic university where I was teaching, but they were all queer, which seemed auspicious. I was new to teaching this class, and my students, all dewy-faced and what we now call AFAB, excitedly told me about the nun who sponsored the newish LGBT student club.

I wasn't worried about teaching the class, because I knew I would have a lot to say about HIV; I like to joke that it's the "family business." I started out as a labor researcher but ended up as a medical anthropologist, in part because I grew up in Houston's medical center with a mother who treated and researched pediatric HIV/ AIDS, as well as a science journalist matriarch of an aunt who won awards for first revealing the "AIDS orphan" crises in Africa and Romania. I can't say when I first heard of the disease; I learned about its transmission and treatment in real time, with the doctors and some of the first child patients, my own age, though none of them lived to be thirty-nine, as I have.

As an anthropologist, I conducted my doctoral fieldwork over three years in the South African province of KwaZulu-Natal, starting in 2008. At this time, at least a third of adults there were estimated to be HIV-positive; as a nationwide campaign by the Treatment Action Coalition (TAC) frequently pointed out, everyone was affected. While I lived in South Africa, "rollout" of free antiretrovirals began, starting with pregnant women and those giving birth, eventually expanding to universal rollout, which gave everyone access to these medications if their CD4 counts dropped below a certain number—first 300, then 500, and then 600. My fieldwork involved asking people about their experiences of being sick, of caring for others, of getting diagnosed—but also of getting married, becoming parents, looking for work, navigating relationships, and organizing their lives, work, love, and beliefs.

So I had plenty of knowledge and material for the class, and I started by introducing HIV/AIDS as a *syndemic*—making the point that an epidemic, AIDS especially, is always also social and intertwined with inequality, systematic neglect and abuse, racism, and a hellish complement of other, equally social diseases. Looking out at my queer students' curious faces, I realized that, for all my commitments to coming out at work, we were still, somehow, talking about "other" people. I thought to ask them when and where they had first heard of AIDS.

Suddenly, after a moment of silence, they were talking about themselves, too, and I was learning some new things:

"Um, well—I went to Catholic school ... A girl called me gay and I cried. She said I would die of AIDS, and nobody would tell me what that meant. So I read about it at the library? And I found out [performative brow wipe] that lesbians don't get AIDS [lovely impish smile, laughs]."

[Blushing] "Well, at my school, which was also Catholic, we did *Rent* as the school musical, and I was in the chorus, but the thing was ... they made the whole play about syphilis because talking about AIDS was too controversial. I actually only just saw *Rent*. But in high school I had looked it up on YouTube. I ... I don't understand

why it was okay to talk about [jokey deepening of voice] *homosexuality* ... but not AIDS, uh, HIV?"

"I used to stay home and watch talk shows, and that's how I
figured out I am trans. But it's also where I first learned about HIV.
To be honest with you, I really don't think I know very much about
it. That's why I took this class."

All of this startled me, but I wanted everyone to have a turn.
The fifth student was looking very uncomfortable and took a pass.
The sixth explained that they first learned about HIV in preparation
for a senior mission trip to Africa. Not Catholic. There was some
muted shock at this information.

I composed myself a little, thinking of the other ways I first
learned what HIV/AIDS really meant, seeing the term "anal sex"
published for the first time in the news (by my aunt), or ... or ... Well,
mostly it was nothing like this, and I think to ask something else.

"Do you know how HIV is transmitted?"

They don't, and I revert to the role of dorm matron/'90s peer sex
educator. We need a whole second day where I answer questions
delivered anonymously into a cardboard box. For six out, active
queer adults in their twenties. In 2019. If I'm honest, I'm totally
devastated by their ignorance of fundamental facts. They lack the
basic sex education that I think of as crucial for their lives as queer
adults, and I wasn't expecting this.

My mom once took me to sleepaway cancer camp for a session
while she worked as the doctor on-site, and I was the only kid there
without cancer. I stayed up at night in the bunks while cancer kids
poured their hearts and fears out to each other, and some of them
talked about knowing they would die soon, and how. Most of these
kids weren't really that sick, but a lot of them didn't have any hair
and were on restricted diets. I thought about not dying, a lot.

After that, I told my mom that I didn't want to play with sick kids again, but I still did sometimes, because I was with her at work, and other kids were there and they hated hospitals and the smells and the bent railings and waxed floors as much as I did.

The AIDS kids were different from the cancer kids. They didn't know what to expect. Some of them didn't know anything at all. Most of them didn't seem that sick, but some of them looked oddly old, with old skin on young bodies, sometimes suddenly. They all thought they might live.

They didn't live. None of them did.

A couple times I helped make bits of the AIDS Memorial Quilt; it always happened that a kid's favorite song was supposed to be "You Are My Sunshine," which my mom also sang to me, and these were also her kids. Later, I went to one of those displays of the quilt at the George R. Brown Convention Center, and there were a lot of sunshines. To be honest, I didn't know which were ours.

When I was a kid, sometimes I would pretend to be sick, so I could stay home from school and watch talk shows. And I remember one show in particular—I think it was *Geraldo*, but it might have been *Oprah*, back when she was tacky, or it could even have been an early *Jerry Springer*. I think I was eight or ten, and I don't really know if this show really happened, and I haven't researched it, but this is how I remember it: the show hosted a debate between a flaming, radical ACT UP queer from New York—he called himself flaming, radical, and queer—in a debate with a homophobic family values pastor, or someone like that.

The interview had two moments for me—one, when the hero called himself queer, in response to being referred to, sneeringly, as a homosexual. It was definitely my first time hearing that word—"queer." Whatever it was, I wanted to be it. He explained, "Yes, I have sex with men, that's how I contracted this disease, why would I be ashamed of it?" My quote might not be accurate, but I'm confident about "queer," "yes," "this disease," and asking why he would be ashamed.

The end of the memory, but certainly not the show, was when that nasty old fucker declared that "AIDS people"? "Victims"? I don't know how he put it, but he said something like people with AIDS should be quarantined on Manhattan Island, and, I swear, he said, "left to rot." He said, "Why not? You are all going to die anyway!" And the queer said, "WELL, SO ARE YOU."

I didn't just want to be like him right then; I knew I was. I repeated this to everyone, constantly; I really didn't want anyone else to miss this opportunity. Well, so are you!

When I first heard the word "bisexual," in fourth grade, it explained some things about how I'd always understood myself, but I kept it to myself, mostly. When my mom told me I might as well marry the cat as a boy and a girl, I considered marrying the cat. But AIDS made me queer, the way I just told you. Well, so are you! SO AM I!

It's a belabored point, but the freedom to know you will die, as a freedom to live right now, was then, and is still now, everything to me.

I came around. My mom once asked me, "If you can choose, why would you choose to make yourself a target?"

My future husband courted me in a gay bar and confessed his bisexuality, and then, when we were in love, we went to more bars.

One was a straight bar with an all-gay, all-closeted staff; they even played the cheesiest of the international gay playlist, like Cher, like "It's Raining Men," while men got sucked off in the bathroom by twinks who drove in from miles around and women came to tell me and my intended husband that at least we weren't queers, presumably a comment on the relative acceptability of our Black/white coupling in South Africa fifteen years past apartheid.

We were constantly refused service, threatened on the street by bigots, spit on, chased with words that needed no translation, and treated as human representations of the dirtiest, shallowest form of sexuality—much more than I had experienced, at home, with the girlfriend I left for him.

I had told my mom I was going to marry a man and have a baby, so I would need her help. We agreed the wedding would be small, with a keg we decorated with a photograph of Lenin and Trotsky, and an off-duty Catholic priest we hired to perform the ceremony. For good luck, you have to get the priest drunk, but he only drank expensive whiskey and we didn't have any.

Our friends and my future husband's brothers came to our little cabin on top of one of the thousand hills just outside Durban; one friend was too sick to drink and slept through the ceremony in the other room, on the bed, only waking up when people started to sing. I was there to study HIV/AIDS, but everyone told me she had tuberculosis, even though I could see she had no appetite and was suffering from wasting and a steady stream of upper respiratory infections.

Almost all my friends were straight, or mostly straight, and they all had HIV, or their lovers did, or they did and didn't know, or their children did, so they found out—maybe their parents and all of their siblings were already dead; maybe they were keeping them alive with soup and magic. KwaZulu-Natal was the epicenter, where one third of adults, those still alive, had HIV.

I made friends with a friend of my husband, in Durban. He didn't live and I wasn't expecting it. Percy. He had a brilliant mind; he was a person who loved a lot, who always had an astounding political take, a plan, a clever move in the moment. He always figured out a way to laugh us out of a crisis, like when the cops stop you and misunderstand you and represent a mortal danger.

When Percy died, I was obsessed for days by all the minds and bodies and the artfulness and plans AIDS took from us, and not at random. I needed him; we needed all of them. And people do need me, too, I think.

In South Africa, I was told that when and where it is really Africa, there are no AIDS orphans. It's hard to explain, but it is true. There is, or there should be, always somewhere to go and someone to be with. There are also orphan grants—it's a fact—paid to the auntie who takes you on. There are families to be made. Family doesn't always mean care, but in some places you are never alone.

The first word I learned in isiZulu was "stabane"—a gender-neutral term for gay, or maybe faggot—because someone called me that, for driving a stick shift well. It didn't exactly feel like an insult.

I saw a lot of AIDS kids, and people kept mistaking me for a doctor and asking for a diagnosis. I refused, even when I was sure and I knew. In post-apartheid South Africa, government denial of the connection between HIV and AIDS had resulted in the unnecessary deaths of at least 250,000 people who were prevented from accessing essential medication. But after universal rollout, I got to watch survivors live like Lazarus; ten years later, so many of the sick are well.

People aren't dying now in the same way, and they aren't so ashamed. People say "HIV" out loud, all the time. I knew it was supposed to work this way, but it's not any less the most amazing medical stunt of all time, even if I was expecting it.

That's true, but it's not the whole truth. I didn't come around, we didn't make things work, and people are still dying, so will you. There is always tomorrow.

I moved home, to a New York island, got divorced, and came out all over again, now someone's mom. Lesbians do get HIV; I even wrote an article about it for work.

I went to a few International AIDS Conferences and I wasn't expecting the evident glee of drug businesses with shiny tents organized around rapid testing and slow management of "chronic disease," but it explained some things, like why testing was always so important to them, and why it mattered who controlled access to antiretrovirals. Somebody must have said, "Life is a chronic disease," and then, "There is only one cure for it," and that's true, but it's not the only side. Who is managing in the meantime, and what it might mean if it was us instead of the corporations, managing all of it—that should have been the question.

Death is inevitable, but some kinds of suffering are preventable, manageable, and maybe curable if you want it, if we do. PrEP isn't a cure; it's a symptom of powerlessness. Former South African president Thabo Mbeki was wrong for preventing access to life-saving medications, but he wasn't wrong that accepting the fact that HIV causes AIDS and providing treatment means giving in to dependency on foreign corporations; he was just wrong that this is only an issue for Africa.

I don't mind playing with the sick kids now; that's us. I'm not on PrEP, though maybe I should be, but I'm afraid of that magic under the control of my enemies. I'm afraid of feeling powerless.

Now that I know more of the history, I wonder which brave queer made such an impact on me when I was a kid staying home from school to watch that talk show episode I haven't been able to locate again. I'm still afraid of dying, or of being the only one left alive, but AIDS made me queer, and living queer means, to me, the other side of fear.

Taking the Guilt and Shame Out of Barebacking as a Sex Worker

LAURA LEMOON

I've been employed in the sex industry, by choice and by force, for more than half my life. Although I entered the sex trade by force at eighteen, I eventually went on to become an escort several years later, working for myself off Backpage. When I was working for my pimp, I didn't have a say in how I worked, where I worked, who I worked with—nothing. As an escort, I was my own boss and got to call all the shots. Men would pay for the privilege of just going down on me for an hour, and I actually got to dictate the terms and lie back and enjoy, instead of zoning out and dissociating.

I'm a proud sex worker. But I also have bipolar disorder, which affects my life greatly. What I'm about to tell you is something I never talk about with anyone except my therapist. When I become manic, which usually happens when I stop taking my meds, I become extremely compulsive sexually. Every time I'm manic, I try to expose myself to STIs. I'm sure you're wondering why, and I wish I could provide an explanation. All I can say is that when I become manic, I feel invincible. And I become obsessed with finding as many ways to hurt myself as I can. I'll give tricks my address and hope they'll come and rape me. I've even walked down abandoned highways before in hopes that someone would pull over and kill me. A few years ago, I stopped taking my meds because I felt like my bipolar was cured and I ended up trying to pay tricks to rape and kill me on camera.

I become someone different when I'm off my meds, and that person is an entity almost completely outside myself, someone who revels in watching Laura hurting and suffering. This outside person loves to put me in harm's way, loves to watch me get STIs, loves to sit in the corner and wait for my death with drooling lips.

This is a deeply shameful part of who I am, something I don't ever talk about. I've worked in public health for more than a decade; I'm an out and proud sex worker and activist for people living with HIV. The times I have tried to talk about this with doctors because I've been so scared that I can't keep myself safe, I have been shamed back into the closet with rhetoric that says that contracting or transmitting an STI (even unknowingly) means I'm a bad person. What's ironic is that this rhetoric, presumably meant to shame everyone into condom use during the '80s and '90s to prevent HIV transmission, means that as a sex worker living with severe, treatment-resistant bipolar I disorder (the more acute of the two types of bipolar) I don't dare ask anyone for help because of the way my mental illness manifests.

The hardest thing about trying to be honest about what happens when I'm manic is that people think I'm just stupid and uneducated about what it means to live with HIV or any other STI. People assume I must be ignorant, lacking in some kind of rational facts or data, and that if I knew all the information, then I would surely set myself on the right path. Unfortunately, this isn't about facts or rationality at all. And looking at me like I'm a bad person because of how my mental illness manifests doesn't help me get treatment any more than shaming people for not using condoms encourages open and honest communication between patients and health care providers.

As a kid, I learned that to have sex without a condom meant you were a bad, immoral person. Safe sex was a matter of life and death, especially before 1996, when the only forms of AIDS medication were toxic and ineffective. I grew up with a mom who was a nurse who would tell me horror stories of the earliest days of AIDS. People with AIDS would come into the hospital already moments away from death, and she described the trauma of just trying to make patients as comfortable as possible for their deaths, because in the '80s, death was basically inevitable. My mom was one of the only nurses who would treat these patients before HIV was discovered, when no one was certain how AIDS was transmitted and nurses practically wore hazmat suits or refused to treat people with AIDS.

What I learned as a kid in elementary school health class, as well as from the world at large, was that safe sex was a moral issue. Which only served to reinforce the lie that HIV/AIDS is a moral issue. Which, to me, means that when I'm manic and having sex with a zillion guys back to back with no condoms because I'm delusionally obsessed with giving myself an STI, my bipolar disorder is now a moral issue. Even when I'm on my meds, not manic, and not actively trying to contract STIs, guilt and shame are constantly directed my way for exercising my right to consensual pleasure and my right to make a living on my own terms.

I remember going to the gynecologist a number of years ago, and for some reason my gynecologist asked me how many people I'd had sex with in the past three months. I wasn't there for anything STI related, and I can't remember how many partners I said exactly, but I think it was something like twenty. She turned around, looked at me, and repeated ... "*Twenty* sexual partners? In the past three months?"

"Yes," I said, more than slightly annoyed.

"And what do you use for protection?"

"I don't," I replied.

She proceeded to tell me how irresponsible I was being, how I was neglecting my health and well-being, and how I clearly didn't understand that I was leaving myself vulnerable to STIS. I wish I could say this interaction with a doctor was unique for me, but sadly, it's very much par for the course.

There are a few things in this interaction I take issue with: first, there are more ways to "protect" (I hate this word) myself than just condoms. I take PrEP; I have open conversations with my sexual partners about the fact that I don't use condoms so that they can decide for themselves if they still want to have sex with me. I get tested every three months, and, most importantly for me, I know that taking my bipolar medications is crucial for my overall health and well-being. I can't take care of my sexual health if I'm not taking care of my mental health; it's just that simple. When I'm on my bipolar meds, I may still decide not to use a condom with a partner, but at least I know I'm taking other precautions and making decisions from a place of balanced brain chemistry.

Health care professionals are visibly shocked when I try to ask for help with my mania and the way it manifests, and they reinforce the false message that HIV is a death sentence in 2020. Or that to contract genital herpes or syphilis is shameful.

For a while, I would just lie and say I used condoms, just so I didn't have to be treated like an idiot. In fifth grade, my health class teacher told us, "Condoms protect against AIDS. Always use condoms." What's remarkable is that conversations around safer sex, from school health class in 1995 to doctors I see in 2020, have not evolved past "Use condoms, no matter what. Period." No, not period. There is so much more to be said about safer sex than using barrier methods, and we need to get beyond using shame as a scare tactic to get people to use condoms, which are not the only defense against HIV transmission anymore.

The landscape of sex in 2020 is very different from what it was in 1981, when the CDC first mentioned what would later become known as AIDS in its *Morbidity and Mortality Weekly Report*. Now, medication can make HIV undetectable and untransmittable, PrEP can prevent HIV transmission without condoms, HIV/STI testing is widely available and often free, and general HIV education is widespread, particularly in communities of men who have sex with men.

As a queer, nonbinary sex worker, I mostly had sex with gay and bisexual men in my personal life, whereas most of my professional partners were straight men. I had much more difficulty navigating HIV and STI risk in my professional life than in my personal life because of the criminalization of sex work. This meant my ability to talk openly with a client before sex was limited in so many ways; it was a risk for me to even have condoms on me, or to ask the client to wear a condom—especially if I did this after I accepted money, which meant that condoms could be legally used as evidence against me.

An additional difficulty is that in spite of all the work that has been done in gay male communities to destigmatize HIV, almost no real work has been done among heterosexual men to normalize conversations about HIV and STIs. So if female-bodied people, such as myself, who date cishet men are diagnosed HIV-positive, our challenges are completely different from those of our gay male counterparts. Cishet men are complete idiots about HIV and STIs! So when I date straight men, there is usually an even stronger belief that I must be HIV-positive if I have done sex work, whereas I find that when I date men who have sex with men, there isn't as much whorephobia and fear and ignorance around HIV and STIs.

I recently had a man say, upon my disclosure that I used to be a sex worker, "So, do you have HIV?" I got angry because, first of all, why would it matter if I did have HIV? And second, how dare he assume that because I used to be a sex worker I have HIV?

As a kid, it was drilled into my head that only bad people have sex without a condom. But as an adult, I'm able to see and pinpoint the shame much more clearly. I realize this messaging really only serves to reinforce stigma against people living with HIV—that they are bad people who were irresponsible about their health and got what they deserved.

In 2018, while working for the county health department, I was training a coworker on the HIV rapid test when two dots appeared on my results window, indicating the presence of HIV antibodies. I remember thinking there was no way I could tell people I contracted HIV through barebacking with clients—the ultimate sex worker taboo. If you think sex workers would be understanding about this, you're dead wrong. They're the hardest people to talk to about my choice to bareback. I'm bringing shame to the sex worker name.

There has been a push in sex worker communities to make sure that those who are vocal about our work promote condom usage in all cases, to protect sex workers and sex work as a whole from bad public perception. Most out and public sex worker activists talk about sex work only in positive terms. This is a protective measure for a community often on the defense. Unfortunately, this image-conscious messaging has also been used to shame sex workers who might reinforce negative stereotypes about sex workers (intentionally or not). The presumption of much of the general public that sex workers are "dirty" or "STD-ridden" is certainly an awful and negative stereotype, but putting it on the backs of all sex workers to be living embodiments against those stereotypes is not a fair burden to bear.

Because I got my preliminary positive at work from a trainee, I was embarrassed by the result, so I pretended like I already knew my status. Internally, I felt like my spirit left my body in that moment when I saw the positive test result. Who did I get it from and to whom could I have transmitted it? I had no idea. The possibilities were endless. How was I going to tell a doctor that I was having "unprotected" sex with countless people I didn't know, and that there was no way to find them or get in contact with them. Talk about shame; I beat myself up endlessly.

Normally, if you received a preliminary positive test, you would get a confirmatory blood draw right then and there. However, since I didn't get my test at a clinic but at work, the process took longer. It took me about two weeks of sitting with the preliminary positive test before I even told anyone.

I got my initial positive test, and the whole time I was thinking, *Oh my God, I'm such a dirty whore. I'm such a stereotype of the HIV-positive prostitute. Who will ever love me? Who will ever want to have kids with me?* The issue I was struggling with the most was how will any cishet man ever accept my status when straight cis men still think you can get HIV from a toilet seat? It was the queer community and my queer friends who surrounded me with love and support during this time.

I'm so lucky that my best friend, who is HIV-positive, was so good to me and was such a great shoulder to lean on during this time. He never judged me for my sexual behavior, and he not only helped me find a knowledgeable doctor, but he also made the appointment for me and went with me to get my confirmatory test. The whole process took about a month, and it turned out that my original test was a false positive. I was actually HIV-negative.

When I was eight years old, I remember watching *Liquid Television* on MTV and a public service announcement began to play in which Pedro, an activist, person living with HIV, and member of *The Real World: San Francisco* cast started talking about how if you can't use condoms, you just shouldn't have sex at all. This cemented in my mind the gravity of living with HIV at a time when AIDS equaled death. And the message was that anything other than sex with a condom equaled death.

In their 1994 hit, TLC sang about a man "chasing waterfalls." The song referred to those "three letters" (HIV), meaning it was doom if you didn't play it safe sexually. Growing up, safe sex meant condoms. That was it. But that's not true anymore.

Unfortunately, there hasn't been enough public dialogue (outside of gay/queer male worlds and HIV-prevention circles targeting trans women) around shifting the definition of safer sex for our current times. Even among sex workers who are public about their work, which is primarily women who work as escorts or strippers, there has been little willingness to expand this conversation around definitions of safer sex beyond condoms, condoms, condoms. We are doing a huge disservice to the most marginalized and vulnerable among us, including drug-using sex workers, trans women, street workers, sex workers of color, and people who fit into many or all of these categories, for whom condoms may not always be realistic, and who are often already heavily associated with perversion, dirtiness, and deviance.

I'm not going to feel shame anymore for choosing not to use condoms as a sex worker, and I'm not going to be shamed by a dominant culture that says people who don't use condoms and people who contract or transmit STIs are "bad" people. The sex workers' rights movement has done, and continues to do, so many amazing things for sex worker safety and destigmatization of sex work, but we still have a lot of room to grow. Let's commit to working even harder against guilt and shame in our choices as sex workers, and let's hold medical and scientific worlds accountable for whorephobia. Sex workers are not vectors of disease. We deserve just as much pleasure and fun and as many options for good times in bed as anybody else. Isn't this what sex work should be about, anyway?

Those Who Left and Those Who Stayed

AHMED AWADALLA

In the days following the Melbourne AIDS conference in 2014, around thirty participants applied for asylum in Australia. They were largely from African countries, but media reports don't reveal much more, so we can only speculate about whether they were fleeing political persecution, homophobia and transphobia, or other forms of discrimination and violence. It is also unclear whether HIV status played a role in their decisions. I often think about those people—those who left and those who stayed.

I was bewildered from day one of the Melbourne conference. We were haunted by the news of the Malaysia Airlines Flight 17 plane crash on its way to Australia, and the tragic deaths of several conference delegates on board. The conference was huge, with nearly 12,000 participants—from fancy panels with star speakers in large auditoriums to intimate storytelling events in a small charity office. At one point, activists interrupted Bill Clinton's speech, demanding passage of the Robin Hood tax on financial transactions to fund the fight against AIDS. At a more relaxed youth pavilion, I spoke on a panel about access to sexual health information and services in the Middle East. We had a modest but engaged audience, and the encounters and stories I accumulated at the conference were limitless.

But for me the turbulence of being in Melbourne was also personal. On the day after the conference ended, I went to a health center in a trendy part of the city to get an HIV test. The counselor posed a question I am now all too familiar with because it's one I routinely ask my clients: What do you expect the test result will be?

I said I had taken some risks, so my test result might be positive, but I hoped it would be negative. He took a blood sample, placed it on the kit, and we chatted for a while. Minutes later, he looked at the kit, and his white face turned red. "I am sorry. It's positive." I still wonder how I remained calm at that moment. I remember trying to reassure him because he seemed more nervous than I was.

I had a dinner scheduled the same evening, right after my test appointment. I hadn't planned for a positive HIV diagnosis. I went to dinner, trying my best not to space out. The impact of my diagnosis only began to hit me the next day. I went for a walk around my hotel. I saw an elderly couple walking together, one of them in a wheelchair. I couldn't stop the tears from flowing. I knew HIV didn't mean a death sentence anymore. However, I felt that I was sentenced to a life without love.

A friend from Melbourne offered to host me for the next few days. I rescheduled my flight to wait for the confirmation of the test results. I considered staying in Australia. Leaving Egypt was already on my mind, but I couldn't get myself to do it. The thought of leaving unprepared, without seeing my family and friends or my hometown, broke my heart. I had to return to Cairo, at least one last time.

I don't have a distinct memory of when I first heard about HIV, but I remember a public service announcement on Egyptian TV that showed a hetero couple walking together, with bats flying around them to warn the viewer about sexual contact. The PSA was addressed to a young man on his way to travel outside Egypt, suggesting that the risk came from being abroad.

As a teenager growing up in a small town in Egypt, I found an escape from my queer alienation in books and American TV shows. I was a fan of medical dramas. The character of Dr Jeanie Boulet, played by Gloria Reuben in the early seasons of ER, was imprinted in my mind. I would watch the show with my mother—unbeknownst to her, we shared a crush on George Clooney, who played a colleague of Dr Boulet.

A strong-willed and empathetic Dr Boulet learns of her HIV status after her husband tests positive when he's admitted to the emergency room after sustaining an injury. She is involved in an affair with another doctor, and she struggles to inform him and her other colleagues about her HIV status, but eventually, they respond with love and acceptance. ER had such a strong impact on me that I decided I wanted to become a doctor. I changed my mind at the last minute because I dreaded the power doctors had over patients' lives. I opted to study to become a pharmacist instead, fantasizing I would discover a cure for HIV. Deep down, I wanted a quicker degree so I could leave my hometown faster.

Once I finished university, I moved to Cairo. I did so well in school that at twenty-one I got a job at the Ministry of Health in the Department for Pharmaceutical Control. I also had my first HIV test there, albeit in another department. That was the only available option at the time. I decided to get tested after I broke up with my first boyfriend, who had told me he wasn't "a fan of condoms." Although I was initially terrified of talking about my sexuality at a government office in a country where homosexuality is de facto outlawed, the counselor was remarkably comforting, and I was able to open up. A week later, I went back and received an HIV-negative test result. Excited, I took some posters about the AIDS hotline so

I could spread the word. I tried to hang a poster at the entrance to my department, but a senior colleague reprimanded me for posting such content without seeking authorization from the head chief. *Bullshit*, I thought. *If it wasn't an AIDS poster, he wouldn't behave this way.*

I grew frustrated with the mundaneness of my job. I also detested the idea of working for pharma companies. Politicized by the severe economic disparities of Cairo, I started gravitating toward civil society and activism. When I got a job in 2009 with an NGO promoting sexual health, I felt closer to the mission I dreamed of—bridging health and sexuality by using HIV as an access point to advocate for sorely needed programs and services in Egypt and creating a progressive discourse on sex matters.

I met Happy while I interpreted his testimony during a collaboration with activist Scott Long. We were investigating Egypt's "debauchery" prosecutions. "Debauchery" is the vague term originating in Egyptian prostitution law that is currently used to prosecute those who deviate from gender and sexual norms. Happy and his boyfriend were arbitrarily arrested on the street and sentenced to three years in prison. Happy's HIV-positive status was used as proof of his homosexuality, just as the government does in these kinds of cases with condoms, makeup, or nude photos. The contacts list on Happy's phone were used to arrest more people. Happy said that he and his boyfriend suffered all sorts of violence in prison, and they were not able to access HIV treatment. I last talked to him a few months ago, and he was desperately trying to leave Egypt.

For a while, things began to improve in Cairo. More NGOs were opening up, some working with the people most at risk for HIV, including sex workers, drug users, and men who have sex with men, following the programs of the Global Fund to Fight AIDS, Tuberculosis and Malaria. I became involved with a newly formed civil society coalition, the Forum to Fight Stigma and

Discrimination against People Living with HIV/AIDS, which conducted unprecedented research on stigma in Egypt and laid out plans to engage media, religious leaders, and health care staff. This coincided with the momentum leading up to the 2011 Egyptian revolution. Hopes were high for a more supportive environment for our work. In this context, I met Magid. He was the first HIV-positive person to openly speak to the media without covering his face, an unprecedented move in Egypt. After this, the Ministry of Health decided to suspend coalition activities. They were afraid that people living openly with HIV, like Magid, were getting too vocal and threatening the image of the ministry by exposing the shortfalls of the national AIDS program.

The tension between the government and civil society groups was characteristic of the post-revolutionary period. In an atmosphere of state-sponsored xenophobia, NGO offices were raided and several activists were arrested on charges of operating with foreign countries and agencies. Overnight, I got an email that the refugee aid organization I was part of in Cairo was banned, depriving vulnerable groups of a necessary support structure.

Around that time, Magid left Egypt for the United States. "Egypt is no longer safe," he told me. His media visibility had gotten him in trouble. He complained of how people living with HIV were "being treated like animals" when accessing treatment. He was fed up with the lack of adequate equipment and interrupted medicine supplies. He told me he felt more respected accessing therapy in the United States. And he urged me to join him to build a community in the diaspora.

Magid left before things got even worse. In 2013, the crackdown widened to include mass arrests of queers. Traps were set up on dating apps; private gatherings and public bathhouses were raided. As I got more involved in activism, I felt less comfortable getting an HIV test in Egypt. I was worried that I would not be able to maintain my confidentiality. Access to treatment was only possible through the government, and I was anxious about how this information could be used against me. I managed to get tested whenever I traveled outside Egypt for a conference or meeting. Like in Melbourne in 2014, when I tested positive.

When I returned to Cairo from Melbourne, leaving Egypt seemed like an impending fate. My heart was breaking at the thought of leaving without knowing if a return was possible. The slightest of things would make me cry, like eating my favorite street food. A few months later, I received an invitation to a convention in Berlin. I had never been to Berlin and hadn't considered living there. It was a gamble, but I also felt that my life in Cairo was a gamble, and it certainly didn't help my situation that I didn't know how fast the virus was multiplying in my body.

I arrived in Berlin on a cloudy and wet day in November. A few days later, I filed my asylum application. I waited for six long months for the interview.

I had the perfect refugee claim, but I was terrified of the interview that would shape my life. A German friend encouraged me to lie and say that I only found out about my HIV status in Germany, that this would make me more convincing. After a long investigation of my life history, the interviewer posed the question, "Why can't you go back to Egypt?"

I described my experiences of violence, my vulnerabilities, and my fears, while he typed on a computer, not looking at me, no expression on his face. I asked him to add one more piece of information, that I was HIV-positive. "It's irrelevant," he told me, noting that my request for asylum was for political, not humanitarian, reasons. As long as Egypt provided treatment, HIV status was not grounds for asylum.

Soon after I arrived in Berlin, I met with a social worker in Schöneberg, the gay village of Berlin, to seek support. He was a middle-aged Scandinavian man who tried to reassure me by saying, "I understand you perfectly. I had to leave my country, too." He explained the services his HIV organization provided, and then suddenly paused. "The important thing is that you don't kill yourself. We don't want to work for nothing," he said. "Well, I haven't considered that up to this point," I told him. "I left everything behind so I could survive."

I would later come to realize that this blunt, self-centered style of communication was not uncommon in Germany. When I described my feeling of loss after my diagnosis, another counselor responded, "Somehow, sometime, you come to terms with it" and went on to talk about his own journey with HIV. I couldn't relate to what he was saying. When I asked about how to cope with isolation, he suggested I create a Grindr profile.

I got a recommendation for my first doctor—"a gay man like us," certified the counselor. His private practice looked cozy, like someone's apartment. There was a line of people waiting to speak to the receptionist. When it was my turn, she asked for my address. I spoke in a low voice, conscious of the people behind me in line. When she found out that I didn't know my postal number, she screamed, "Here in Germany, you must know your postal code!"

I wanted to disappear, but the doctor seemed jovial in contrast. He asked a lot of questions about when and how I got my HIV infection and whether this occurred in Egypt or in Germany. I went back a week later, anxious to find out how much my viral load and CD4 had changed since Melbourne.

"Your values are critical. You should start treatment immediately," he said.

I lived in a refugee camp back then. I shared a room with another asylum seeker, from Afghanistan. His asylum claim had been rejected in Sweden, so he was trying his chances with Germany. He was the only person I knew in Berlin who could understand this part of my life in the refugee camp: checking in and out upon departure and return, lining up at mealtime, our doors getting abruptly opened by security for random checks. Still, I had to hide my medicines from him, which wasn't easy, since we didn't have private lockers. Feeling uninvolved in my therapy, I asked my doctor for a copy of my results. My values were not critical; my viral load and CD4 were fair. I didn't understand why my doctor rushed me to begin therapy.

Later, my doctor started addressing me in German. I was taking classes already yet far from ready for such a conversation, I would explain politely. He would switch briefly to English before returning to German. The tipping point was when he found out that I had started working at an organization to support migrants and refugees affected by HIV. He commented, "You should support the good ones; too many bad ones out there." I never went back to his office.

Berlin is a gay man's city, famous for its openness. There is a big network of doctor's offices that cater to the gay community. I just needed to find the right doctor, I thought. I struggled to find a sense of safety. At the next doctor's office, the receptionist would text me on dating apps and smirk annoyingly whenever we interacted. I ignored him at first, and then stated a clear no. When he persisted, and I learned from friends that this was a pattern, I brought it to the doctor's attention.

"No, it's a personal issue that should be settled between yourselves," he said indignantly. All of my contact information, including address and phone number, were available to this receptionist. The doctor didn't see his harassment as a breach in conduct or feel a responsibility to address it.

His defensive attitude shouldn't have shocked me. I was scratching at one of the best-kept secrets in Berlin's medical community. In September 2019, a thorough investigation was published in

German media detailing reports of sexual assault by a prominent Berlin HIV specialist, going on for more than twenty years. Most of the survivors were queer men, many of them with a migration history or without medical insurance, and he preyed upon their vulnerability. Ten days after the scandal broke, the German court decided to remove the article from the internet, saying it was too biased against the doctor. I heard many stories of sexual harassment at the hands of that doctor, and at the height of the #MeToo movement I wrote about it. Using the power of his lawyers, and the draconian German defamation laws, the doctor was effectively intimidating anyone who broke the story. But none of this would be possible without a culture of victim blaming and feigned innocence.

I was struggling with my medication. I felt unwell, dizzy, and drained. Most doctors didn't seem to hear me or downplayed my complaints. I spent years not being able to tell if my symptoms were because of the treatment or just because I was uprooted from Egypt. Going to the doctor's office grew burdensome. After switching doctors several times, I found an office where the doctor, was a Black woman, and I was excited. Everyone in the office was a person of color, including staff and patients.

The doctor started our appointment in German, so I told her that I preferred English. My German was acceptable at this point, but I wanted to communicate smoothly. "How long have you been in Germany?" she asked. When I told her I'd lived there for almost five years, she raised her eyebrows and exclaimed, "And you still don't speak German?"

I wanted to remind her that she spoke accented German, but I remained silent. I could sense her awkwardness around my queerness. I left the practice in a rage. Five years of going to these appointments and doctors still wanted to give me a German class.

Of course, my experiences with racism and bias in the medical system were not limited to HIV specialists. When my skin started acting out, I got a referral from the gay network for a skin doctor. He prescribed a medicine known for its side effects, depression among them. The doctor shared that one of the 9/11 terrorists was on the same medication when he committed that crime. I was speechless. When I confronted him about this in an email, he found my suggestion of his bias "shameless" and blamed me for not comprehending.

In a vulnerable lab moment, I got teary eyes as my blood flowed into the tubes. The lab technician asked what was wrong. I had just had an unpleasant encounter with a doctor I was seeing for the first time. The German nurse had a theory about why I was unsatisfied. "It's capitalism," he said. "Doctors don't have enough time for patients." I agreed with him, but this didn't explain why I felt unseen and unheard in these encounters. And why my priorities were overlooked. It didn't explain why capitalism and competition did not improve the quality of care. It didn't explain how capitalism emptied people's souls.

One time during lab work, I shrieked when the nurse pricked my skin with the needle. "You are sensitive," she said. "It's good to be sensitive." She distracted me by talking about her decision to leave Portugal after the economic crisis. Her voice broke when she told me her son decided to stay. "He likes the sun," she explained.

It took years to find a doctor's office where I felt seen, and I was finally able to change my medication. Before I came to Berlin, my friends encouraged me—they said that Germany had one of the best health care systems in the world, that Germany had reckoned with its dark past, that everything would be better for me there. In telling my story, I want to disrupt an all-too-common narrative, one in which moving from the Global South to the North promises access to treatment, freedom from stigma, and availability of comprehensive care. A narrative where Germany welcomes refugees with open arms.

In my work with migrants and refugees affected by HIV in Berlin, I've learned about crass discrimination experienced by my clients. I am in a privileged position compared to a lot of other refugees. That's also why I don't simply recount a series of micro-aggressions. In *Plantation Memories: Episodes of Everyday Racism*, Grada Kilomba, a writer, psychologist, and artist based in Berlin, describes racism as not only the restaging of a colonial past but also as traumatic reality; "everyday racism is not a single violent event, but rather an accumulation of events that reproduce the trauma of a collective colonial history." A receptionist yelling at you to memorize your postal code is a reminder that you don't belong here, that these systems were not made for you. A doctor speaking of good migrants versus bad migrants propagates the same mentality that allows certain migrants to access HIV treatment while excluding others. Despite the rhetoric around universal access to health care in Germany, illegalized migrants can't access HIV treatment, which leads to preventable deaths.

These experiences recast the shadow of a system that demonizes migrants, treats us with suspicion, accuses us of exploiting the welfare and health care available to us. A system that draws borders, forces people into inhumane refugee camps, deports the "bad ones." A system that forces asylum seekers to undergo mandatory HIV testing, regardless of priorities and needs, and pressures us to begin therapy, lest we pose a risk to the innocent populace. A doctor comparing me to 9/11 terrorists offers a snippet of a Europe that is entrenched in anti-Muslim racism and at the same time funds dictators to prevent us from showing up on European shores. The general moral detachment of a health care system is a symptom of privatized health, where empathy equals wasted time and money. A system that if we dare to criticize, we are considered ungrateful, told that we should go back home. The irony of asking where my

HIV comes from lies in a Europe forgetful of how its colonial drive furthered epidemics around the world.

Perhaps someone like Dr Jeanie Boulet doesn't exist, except in American TV shows. Perhaps my mind was colonized when I thought that healing from my wounds could come through a pharmaceutical pill. Or that leaving to the Global North would mean safety. I've learned that survival is not healing. That safety does not equal serenity.

I think about those who left and those who stayed, and I hope we all find love, healing, and power, wherever we are.

Red Shadows

LESTER EUGENE MAYERS
EDITED BY MARIEL STEIN

My mother (whom I call QUEEN) contracted HIV in 1989 and carried me in her womb while positive—I was born HIV-negative on November 29, 1994, in Brooklyn, NY, after Thanksgiving and right before winter. In January of 1998, two months after my third birthday, QUEEN passed to the afterlife due to complications of AIDS. At the time, I didn't know the reason or cause of her death, or where my father went, nor did I feel comfortable asking.

Like the ever-running river that is the pathology of silence, anything too painful is neither revealed nor spoken of in a Black household. The shame, stigma, and ignorance surrounding HIV and AIDS left me in the red shadows.

Growing up, curious children and nosy adults would inquire about my parents, or rather, their absence. The absence of parents becomes a part of a child's identity, and not knowing what happened to the people who brought you into this world becomes just as essential as knowing how to spell your name.

I proudly labeled QUEEN a cancer warrior who had lost the war, because I didn't know any better and wasn't one for silence. That is, until one day in September of 2005, when a cousin (whom I had known in childhood to display fierce and vile behavior) straight-up asked me, "Yo Les, do you know how yo mother died?"

I remember my glands becoming swollen like I had ingested something I was allergic to, and, like the first snowflake of winter, I responded softly "No."

She chuckled, and said, "She died of AIDS."

Ignorance ran through my mind, propelling anger and confusion to rise immediately. I was mad as hell, mad that my cousin would toss information so carelessly—no shame in her delivery. She went into the bathroom, plugged in her flat iron, and began doing her hair, without ever asking how that information affected me at age ten.

That night, I remember going to sleep in fear, in ignorance; I had so many questions and no one to answer them. At the time, even with all the HIV and AIDS information posted in schools, public transportation advertisements, and commercials, it never addressed children and those emotionally affected by losing their loved ones due to the complications of HIV and AIDS.

I spent so many years wondering—

How did she get it? Who did she get it from?

And—

Am I infected?

I spent so many nights angry, having mental debates with myself—within myself—about how her health history fit into my identity. Worrying: What if she developed a condition late in life, either mentally or physically, that I could be prone to? Constantly asking myself: What if her trust issues were passed down to me? What if her feelings of betrayal were born into me? What if the price for love (that she paid) is so high that I could never afford it?

We have a saying in Brooklyn (& I'm sure it extends around the world): "Curiosity killed the cat."

A year later, my spirit was killed.

Let me explain. You see, not long after I received this information about QUEEN I ran away from home, due to a combination of
unlivable experiences, and never went back. However, after I ran
away from home, I remember helping one of my aunts look for
some "important paperwork." Like most old-school Black women,
she hid her important paperwork under her mattress, in the bottoms of closets, and in the Bible. As if it were divine intervention by
QUEEN herself, I picked up the brown-and-gold Bible on my aunt's
TV stand and flipped through to a section that held folded, stained
papers. These were medical papers that not only had my mother's
name but her HIV testing number, dated 1989, with positive results.

I quickly stuffed the papers back into the Bible and walked away.
I went into the bathroom and cried. I was tired. Tired of being lied
to, misled, and given information without any possibility of pro-
cessing it. So, I buried it.

The next five to six years of my young life were marked by shame
and paranoia, with me excessively forcing myself to go to the clinic
to get tested multiple times a month, scared, waiting for the day I
would test positive. At some point, I decided I would not relive my
mother's death. I would not make the mistake of trusting someone,
only to be deceived or burned so badly I could never recover. I
understood that my youth was not about immortality but about the
ability to make choices. I made the choice to no longer justify having unprotected sex, made this decision to honor my own reflection
and for my future child's protection. With the understanding that
life is life, I made sure to walk with this ideology, no matter how
deep in love I was. No matter how good it felt to have it raw and
real with a one-night stand, I made sure latex was always at hand.
I made sure that whomever I lay with at least knew my last name.
And yet, even while using condoms, there was always a pause for
thought—inner screams of *What if?!*

As a teenager, I remember watching a clip of *Oprah* one day, and I saw a young beautiful Black girl named Hydeia, who was born with HIV and diagnosed with AIDS at age five. I began to feel guilty. I thought—*Why me? Why was I one of the lucky ones?*

In my teenage mind I summed it up as having a second chance at life, even before being born. For a little while, as a working artist, every piece I created in dance, poetry, scriptwriting, and acting became a repository for honoring that second chance of being born physically healthy. Simultaneously, each piece mourned my guilt for being born at all. I never wrote for me, I never danced for me, I never acted for me; my artistic gifts existed only to tell someone else's story. Every time I hit the stage, no matter what I was doing or where I was, I always brought people to tears. While I was happy that they were feeling something, I always felt empty and alone. I always created with the notion that my second chance at living was not about me but more about being a vessel to hold a mirror up so that others could see their pain and begin healing. It wasn't until college, when I began writing and interviewing for publications and revealing some of my life story, that people reached out to me with similar backstories. Folks thanked me for having enough courage to share my own experience, poetically and without shame. I bear some of the stigma: starting out as an innocent child, making up stories just to fit in, and finding out the truth and denying all because I was embarrassed.

When a child experiences shame, that child can never experience unconditional love because the place where love lives in the body is already occupied. It took me running Toni Braxton's first album, over and over until the CD skipped, for me to find a path to immediate peace. It took me writing from sunup to sundown, to find my way in and out of confusion around all the questions I had about my identity. Questions such as: Which parent do I get my attitude from? Do I share the same love language as my mother?

Did my father share the same insecurities as a child about being dark-skinned?

The process of forgiving my QUEEN for leaving me so early in life came slowly, toward the end of my teen years. Learning to cope with this loss through my engagement with art also helped me to forgive myself for my early years of ignorance when I first discovered her health history. So, this is me—telling and reliving my history for every child, adult, and soul who shares a story similar to mine and my QUEEN's. Loving you unconditionally.

The Long Ladder of Shame

C.L. SEVERSON

Viruses are weird little buggers, but the way humans react to them is even weirder. One group, retroviruses, to which HIV belongs, has been trapped in our genome across evolutionary history. We share many of these with other vertebrates, and they accumulate over millions of years, creating a genetic mythology, a tapestry of infections in our DNA. See, we are the whole world to our viral settlers.

The word "immunity" comes from the Latin "immunis," which means "exempted from public service or charge." I can tell you, as a brown person living with HIV/AIDS in America, that this is the true immunity lost by contracting HIV; we become involuntary public educators persecuted by the people who fear us.

Immunity is cultural; there are distinct differences in the way various groups of people integrate pathogens into their collective biome. This shapes the natural immunity among the races. However, the singular truth is that if you have unmanaged HIV, across all cultures, you are disqualified from love. The "infected ones" are all carrying the weight of the trauma of HIV, but the viral load is not distributed evenly.

As a trans Chicana sex worker who is chronically homeless, I can assure you that I am qualified to speak on the socioeconomic layer that keeps people like me emotionally and socially quarantined, a major side effect of America's obsession with pathogenic medicine. It is my opinion that "quarantine culture" terrorizes communities of color.

At this very moment, a TV is blaring over my head about the novel coronavirus and people quarantined on ships for having been to China and contracting this airborne pathogen in Wuhan. There is a sentiment of dehumanization toward the Chinese for their government and even dietary practices. The Sinophobia is so thinly veiled it occurs to me that pathogens are used to embolden the fears and bigotry that already exist inside us. A virus is not a cause of terror but a magnification of it.

As a result, in racist America, the highest rates of new HIV infections are concentrated violently in the poor, colorful South, where I have spent most of my life. Latino communities are plagued by machismo and sexual shame instilled by the Catholic church and homophobic rhetoric. Many have no idea how to navigate the white man's health care system. Many are anxious about STD testing. Many lack the documents necessary to access routine health screenings. Sexual health is often not even a topic of conversation. Indeed, most brown men in the South would rather not know their status than find out bad news.

I was, and still am, dependent on ignorant men to feed myself, and this social structure of poverty ensures that people like me are going to get HIV, and then be left alone to deal with it. Sex work is the confluence of many intersecting rivers of oppression. In this fleshly industry, nondisclosure has always been necessary. Nobody will pay to have sex with someone with HIV—why buy something broken? However, with PrEP, not a single client even bothers to ask my HIV status, and barebacking is often required. This puts me at risk for many more illnesses and psychological trauma.

This sex work culture of nondisclosure makes it habitual not to disclose in personal relationships as well, and heaven help you if you catch feelings. Retroactive disclosure (telling someone that you have HIV after having sex) is a vulnerable and humiliating experience. Sometimes the stress from this causes me to dissociate for many hours, alerting my now ex-lover to not only my serostatus but also my very embarrassing mental health problems. I am constantly relearning to be afraid of myself.

Last year, when I disclosed my status to a man I had been dating after our relationship had become serious, he drafted a lawsuit against me. Failing to disclose is a crime in many states. He labeled me a serial rapist in the suit: "Not providing information that would affect sexual consent is a form of rape." Further, he used my criminal blood as leverage to extort me into indentured servitude for months. I paid off some of his medical bills, cleaned his house, took him to work, and picked up his dry cleaning, all while providing daily sexual services. When I attempted to hang myself in the living room, he decided I might be too unstable to extort further. I cannot describe to you the extent to which this ordeal damaged my self-esteem.

I notice that the responses to this retroactive disclosure social experiment vary based on income and, thereby, race. It's the difference between the Mexican man's "Eres sucia, puta?!" (You are dirty, whore?!) and the rich, and often white, man's "I'm relieved you have HIV, honestly. It's actually safer to be with an undetectable prostitute!" The difference in these outlooks is access to resources.

Disparity in education results in more of my long-term relationships being with white men, often former clients. Wealthier white men are able to have either long-term or open relationships with trans women without devastating social repercussion because they have the resources to more adequately hide us or the job security in a more liberal white-collar environment to present publicly with a passing trans girl. These men, in their financial dominance, routinely hijack my health and require that I maintain an undetectable viral presence in my blood, a kind of conditional romance. If reaching an undetectable viral load is directly correlated with whether I have access to housing and psychological support, and vice versa, then white men control my immune system.

As a late-blooming trans person, stigma also stunted my gender journey. I figured presenting as a gay man would put me in a more HIV-tolerant culture. I realize now that this was delusional. There is a sort of fear campaign used on young gay men, particularly in the South, that says being gay is a health risk to body and spirit. This campaign advises on how to avoid HIV, not how to live with it and among it. I believe this polarizes people into being either hyper-careful or hyper-careless, especially when no one offers the requisite compassion education to match the sex education.

Last year, I started hormone therapy to show myself compassion and to prove to myself that I can be soft. The people who are attracted to me are now changing. In many ways, it is in fact harder to disclose to straight-identified men, since they are less informed. For now, the gender alignment is worth the emotional labor. One man became hysterical after we kissed: "Am I going to die?" I soothed his fear, but who will soothe mine?

I have begun to put myself first, though I have no vision of my future. I am still living in a shelter and trying to overcome my suicidal tendencies, managing my roller-coaster health while going through a second puberty, an ironic tug-of-war inside me: I want to be healthy, and I want to die. Or maybe I just want to look well enough that people will still fuck me. Either way, I have every incentive to stay poor. When I am below the poverty line, I don't have to pay for the expensive medical care as different administrations of power often threaten. I don't exist; I merely preexist.

Truthfully, I am resentful to be dependent on a culture that is obsessed with profit but not healing and wholeness. A culture where a doctor can see that pathogens make you lose weight but not that sadness does, too. A culture that sees the key to healing depression as isolated neurotransmitters, rather than emotional connection. The loss of traditional healing systems and familiarity with natural medicine makes us susceptible to and dependent on colonial institutions for medical authority. Their methods of cellular warfare ignore innate healing mechanisms that remain forever a mystery to even seasoned physicians. What are these people staring at in their microscopes? At what magnification will they finally see that the double-helix structure of our collective DNA is but a long ladder of shame?

PrEP Will Not Save Us

The Ghosts of AIDS and Suicide

KODY MUNCASTER

When I was about twelve years old, I promised myself that if the bullies were right about me being gay, I would kill myself. When I came out at fifteen, my mother screamed at me that I was going to get AIDS and give it to her through a towel. This was in 2010, when we lived on the outskirts of a small city in Atlantic Canada. I did not know anything about HIV at the time. My mother's homophobic screaming stuck with me throughout my sexual encounters, the ghosts of queer ancestors who died from AIDS haunting me, warning of an uncertain future.

I escaped my violent house and ended up in foster care with a family that I love. I was diagnosed with post-traumatic stress disorder when I was sixteen. I resist the idea that my reaction to queer trauma is a disorder. I am haunted by memories, nightmares, and flashbacks of my father's extreme physical violence toward me. But that is not all that I am haunted by.

After foster care, I went to university. During university, I got tested for HIV more times than anyone I know. Each time I had sex, I was paranoid that I would fall victim to this plague. I did not know anything about HIV other than that I should fear it. The sexual health nurse at my university shamed me for using Grindr and going to bathhouses. She said that these places were cesspools for STIS.

I stumbled across information about preexposure prophylaxis (PrEP) online in 2016. It cost more than $1,000 per month in Canada at the time. I never thought I would be able to afford it, until I learned that my university health insurance covered it. I brought a ton of information to the university sexual health clinic, prepared to get slut-shamed. I convinced a doctor to prescribe it to me. I remember holding that blue pill, feeling like I had just found gold. Finally, I could fuck without fear.

I was working on my second degree in 2017 when my first boyfriend, Logan Cummings, killed himself. We had broken up years before. It felt like everyone in our small queer community attended the funeral. I dropped out of social work school and moved to another small city, this time in Central Canada, for a new job. I began working at an HIV/AIDS nonprofit in a position specifically focused on gay men. I had an outreach profile on Grindr and Squirt where people could message me questions like whether it is true that people with undetectable HIV viral loads cannot transmit HIV. It is indeed true for people who are privileged enough to be able to achieve an undetectable viral load. The consequence of this is that it can create a hierarchy of (un)detectability among people living with HIV that separates the "good" (read: wealthy, insured, privileged, housed) from the "bad" (everyone else).

A nurse practitioner sent me an email one day, asking if I would be interested in opening a PrEP clinic with her. I never thought that my management would approve it, but they did. It was an incredible experience. I designed all the forms for the clinic, the policies, and a manual for running it. We advertised through Grindr, Squirt, and the bathhouse. Immediately, we had a great deal of interest, despite being in a small city in Central Canada. However, most of our clients were white, cis, well-resourced gay men. Most of the clients were neither systemically at risk for HIV nor having that much sex beyond oral or doing that much barebacking.

The nurse practitioner was employed by a pharmacy—eventually, the pharmacy hired me, too. My job was to form partnerships with AIDS organizations and gay nonprofits to create more PrEP clinics. But there was part of me that struggled with the work. Was it wrong to help a company make money off gay men's fears? Would PrEP decrease the pharmaceutical industry's interest in searching for a cure? Putting everyone who is "at risk" for HIV on PrEP could make a lot more money than only having people living with HIV on treatment. When I came to the AIDS sector, I mistakenly thought that it would be like the fierce activism of ACT UP or AIDS ACTION NOW!, but anger was muted and we usually limited our discussions of a cure to our annual general meeting, when we would light a candle in hope for a cure.

I was asked to do a presentation about the history of Pride for the AIDS nonprofit where I worked. Many of my coworkers were experiencing racism from clients and other staff, and we wanted to start a conversation about it, so I discussed privilege and racism in the LGBT community and in the agency. My boss reprimanded me, saying that only an outside facilitator should be discussing those issues with us, and that in my next presentation I should include more "positive" information about gay marriage and rainbow crosswalks.

Public health campaigns imply that PrEP will end AIDS, but I realized this would never happen when I saw a news article about a gay men's research organization apologizing to Indigenous communities for failing to do adequate outreach with them around PrEP, even though PrEP is free for Indigenous people in Canada who have a status card. PrEP, while biomedically effective, is often inaccessible to the people who could actually benefit from it. PrEP is covered by provincial programs like welfare and disability in the province where I worked, yet most of my clients were affluent white gay men. HIV continues to disproportionately impact street-involved people, racialized communities, people who experience systemic violence in sex work, trans people, and other communities that are multiply marginalized and not adequately served by AIDS organizations.

Fighting for a cure is far from a priority in the corporate approach to AIDS. Having more people on long-term medication regimes, either preventative or treatment, will generate more profit than a cure or a vaccine. Even if a cure or a vaccine were to be developed, structural oppression would be likely to impact access (as we see with treatment and PrEP), and thus the end of AIDS is far away.

Suicide has now surpassed HIV as a leading cause of death of gay men in Canada. After Logan died, I began working at a suicide helpline before I moved to Central Canada. We were instructed to send the police on "wellness checks" to people who were struggling, a violent approach that I now deeply regret. Once Logan died, it felt like everyone around me was killing themselves. I would see a hookup's Facebook turned into a memorial page. I would get the call from a friend in distress because an acquaintance of mine, someone they went on a few dates with, just died. I became paranoid about who would be next. When someone mentioned not hearing from a person in my friend group in a while, I would check Facebook to see if they were online recently, and if not, I would panic, assuming they had killed themselves.

I was mentored through an AIDS grief program by a HIV-positive activist in his sixties. He helped me process the multiple losses I experienced from suicide and from leaving my abusive "family," using bereavement tools that he developed to cope with multiple losses from AIDS. His warm, grandfatherly presence helped me process an incredible amount of trauma. He would use stories from his life and things he had learned from his own counselors to help me.

At a meeting with my boss and representatives from a gay men's organization, I mentioned the statistic about gay male suicide and suggested they work on suicide prevention programs. Everyone in the meeting shut me down. They said that we were funded to work on HIV prevention, not suicide prevention. I was shocked.

When I was in high school, several suicides by white gay boys began to circulate widely in the media, so my school's gay-straight alliance showed us videos of the It Gets Better campaign. What they did not explain was that it does not get better for everyone, especially multiply marginalized people. The campaign encouraged us to fit into a respectable, homonormative cutout. As if the possibility of someday getting married, having kids, and making money could convince us not to kill ourselves. I've spent my whole life trying to talk queer people out of killing themselves. Every time I hear of a queer person dying, my mind immediately goes to suicide. I am always scared of hearing who will be next.

As queer people, we experience the trauma of societal homophobia compounded by the internalized homophobia that we direct toward ourselves. The unprocessed, generational trauma of AIDS is rarely discussed in connection to HIV-negative, younger queer people's mental health. While there are many differences between the AIDS and the suicide crises (for example, death tolls) it is clear that we are in a time when queer people are dying in large numbers as a result of social systems that see us as disposable.

One of the things we also miss by not discussing the trauma of AIDS is the resilience that resulted from it. We must consult the ghosts of the AIDS crisis, and those who have survived, so that we can remember the tools they used to combat AIDS, such as direct action, political funerals, die-ins, and strategies for grieving. We must resist the neoliberal approach that attempts to manage queer dissent by containing resistance in AIDS nonprofits and suicide helplines. The same approach that tells us to ignore our mental health struggles in hopes of a better, assimilated future. This organized forgetting attempts to erase AIDS resistance strategies from memory, but when we think of suicide prevention and HIV prevention as intertwined, we enhance the possibilities of success with both.

Disclosure

ROBERT BIRCH

Like many gay men, I've practiced sexual negotiation skills with varying degrees of diligence and catastrophe my whole adult life. Despite decades of teaching interdisciplinary communication skills, I've discovered that the erotic context often dictates how connections unfold. Throughout my twenties and into my early thirties, as a poz fag, I forged most of these furtive contacts in spaces of nonnegotiable silence. Now that I am older and living with more resources, this art of disclosure—the simultaneous coming out from and exposure to sexual, spiritual, legal, cultural, and class oppressions—can offer a return to dignity, and still unsettle any sense of belonging.

1996

We meet in a coin-operated jizz house in downtown Vancouver. Hungry for every inch of each other, we hail a cab, making out all the way to his dimly lit Gastown apartment. I jump naked into his bed as he sets the mood, lining up his fuck utensils. He turns on a lava lamp that projects platelet-like red blobs floating on the ceiling. I'm thinking some collective conscience has just lubed up my ethics. For the first time, I share my HIV status with a sexual partner. He drops his beautiful ass to the bed and sits there, does nothing, says nothing. A full ten minutes pass. He never moves, never says a word. With only a tad of my integrity intact, I dress and leave. Immediately, it occurs to me that this is my own initiation into the viral divide. I've been positive for less than five months.

On the day of my HIV diagnosis, I happen to be leading a guerrilla performance ritual called Happy Virus Day. A team of close friends and lovers spills onto the streets of Victoria, British Columbia. Our grassroots theater company, generation studio, stops traffic on Government Street. As the actors spiral through a spontaneous viral dance, I don fishnet stockings over my face and hoist a film camera over my shoulder. With microphone in hand, I interview passersby, "We're raising awareness about AIDS in our community. Do you know anyone with HIV? No? Hi, I'm Robert, you do now."

This monthlong series of workshops and performances explores the relationship between internalized structural homophobia and the contraction of HIV. We call it *Latex Café*. Participants write Dear Virus letters in an attempt to create some psychic distance from their own and loved ones' diagnoses, to construct a relationship, however naïve, that offers some semblance of personal and cultural agency.

My letter begins: "Dear Virus, We now live together. I am not you. I am *not* HIV-positive. As you need bodies as hosts, here's the rule to this house: you are the guest. I also name you, teacher. In exchange, let me live."

Fourteen weeks later, generation studio holds several workshops at the XI International AIDS Conference in Vancouver, including a three-day event called Blood Brothers, bridging the viral divide entrenched between gay poz and neg men. The overall theme of the conference is One World, One Hope. Organizers break the news of potentially lifesaving medications. Monday morning, I unplug the phone. For the next three days I sink into a dumpster-dived chair recently reupholstered by my first HIV-positive partner. My back defies the world while I sit in silence, attempting to hold panic attacks in their corner.

1998

Mark and I have been together for a year now. We never once discuss being in a relationship. We're two poz, cis, white men couch surfing, living on disability. Grateful to be alive, and to have found each other, like many poz folks, we find that HIV fills our days. On the West Coast of Canada, we receive the highest quality care in the world. Between us, however, years of doctor visits and alternative health care appointments, HIV research participation, LGBTQ and AIDS protests, as well as numerous volunteer shifts at local AIDS service organizations, means we live a life of surface tension; we arrive at our tipping point. We realize we have normalized the shock. We plan our escape from what we refer to as the "AIDS machine."

The scene has rapidly and necessarily shifted. New populations need support; the state barely acknowledges the rising co-epidemics of injection drug use, hep C, and HIV. The city feels less stable.

"Get the fuck out of the way!" a cop screams at us, as we're caught in the middle of a drug bust while taking groceries out of the back of our truck. Mark and I move to Salt Spring Island and within months join a tiny community-run HIV support group that soon becomes the Southern Gulf Islands AIDS Society, Canada's smallest AIDS service organization.

2004

Mark is diagnosed with AIDS-related cancer. We're determined to do this our way. He wears deer vertebrae around his neck during each spinal tap. We place salt water under his hospital bed to draw out toxins. We bless the chemo bags. I learn to ask for help. With his permission, I disclose our health statuses to our island community of 10,000. I write regular articles in the local community newspaper about our healing journey. I write about courage and the need for advocacy when immersed in the medical system, about the loneliness of sitting in the dark with another dinner left untouched. For the next two years, when many gay male friends turn away because it is too painful, I write about healing from the past and our profound gratitude to live in a community where the lesbians, single moms, old-time farmers, and many other friends drop off food daily and provide financial support to fly Mark to medical appointments in Vancouver. People express their deep appreciation for these articles. Sharing these stories inspires others to reach out as well, to not feel so alone as they, too, learn how to navigate family health crises.

2010

Jasper is twenty-nine and relatively new to the Radical Faeries, eyes full of stardust. We meet in the old wooden hippie sauna. I offer to scrub him down with exfoliating gloves. We're soon panting for air. We move out into the sunshine to dry off and calm down. A bearded Portlander closer to my age shows up and joins us in a playful Jasper sandwich. I caress him from behind as the other man kisses his gorgeous mouth. We frottage in what feels like a blissful moment of erotic liberation.

2011

Six months later, and Jasper must have heard me talk about my HIV status in a heart circle yesterday. He stands up in the middle of our circle of seventy-five other sissy-brothers and announces that last summer someone tried to infect him with HIV. "Not here! Not in this spiritual community!" he declares.

I sit directly across from him. He's clearly talking about me. A well-known, respected elder enters the circle to pick up the rant: "It's only a fucking condom!"

Shaking, I frantically try to recall if the tip of my cock brushed Jasper's asshole. I step inside the circle. I hug the elder as he places the threadbare story-soaked shawl over my shoulders. I say my name before choking out an apology. Then I hear my terrified voice cry out, "I need help!" Sobbing takes over. The one community space that welcomes me home over and over again as a gay man begins to evaporate.

Afterwards, Mark and my closest friends come over to walk alongside me. Their efforts soothe my heart, but my mind rails, *I am taking the hit for our community*. What compels me to hold myself accountable, when in years of sitting in circles I have yet to hear anyone else take a similar risk? I realize the burden of disclosure has mostly fallen on the shoulders of those of us living with HIV.

I grew up with the pervading belief that "AIDS has infected us all" and as such wrestle daily with the burden of accountability. I continue to define myself with the virus, whereas Jasper seems to define himself against it. If we cannot acknowledge this biocultural rift, how will we ever undo inherited patterns of vicarious trauma and its impact on our lives? How is it that these precious, fragile moments of community-making can still implode over how directly we have experienced HIV? My hope is that someday Jasper and I can sit across from one another, in another heart circle, and tell the parts of our stories that acknowledge us all as survivors of this generational trauma.

2012

I've been the gay men's health coordinator for a regional AIDS service organization for three months. It's Pride season. I head north to open an event to raise the rainbow flag at Nanaimo City Hall. On my way home I check Grindr and meet an emerging tattoo artist in his early thirties. Despite being wary of younger men, I quickly discover our bodies fit very well together. This time, my raw cock nuzzles into his sandy-haired ass before I rapidly pull out. Shame immobilizes me. He cuddles into my arms, "Hmm, Daddy."

I arrive home terrified I'm going to lose my job and put the agency at risk. I confess to my roommate what happened. I'm reminded to set aside fear and focus on caring for the guy I met. I phone him and apologize for not immediately disclosing my status. I explain I have been undetectable for years and, as if to reassure him with science, tell him studies suggest the risk is minimal. I recommend that if he's still worried, he could get PEP, post-exposure prophylaxis, our version of the morning-after pill. I point him toward what I am told are the right directions. He spends the next thirty-six hours in a panic, knocking on pharmacy and doctors' doors, facing homophobic sex-shaming from every counter. He never gets the meds.

His test comes back negative weeks later. He tells me he's in love with me. We have sex again. It's some of the most pleasurable sex of my life, a sensation of bodies belonging together. I just can't do it. I can't see him anymore. The shock, the risk; exhaustion overwhelms any desire to continue.

2013

Jay drops another hookup to join me in the conference hotel room. Short, muscular, always ready for sex, he undresses as I ask him if he would first be willing to write up his own disclosure statement. He grabs my pen and journal. In thirty years of this daily morning practice no one has ever written in one of my journals. It feels intimate. I'm sharing this private space I've created for my own legal protection. Canada's repressive HIV criminalization laws haunt me, and drive many poz people underground.

Jay writes: "To whom it may concern, I know Robert Birch is HIV-positive. I might be negative. He tells me he's been on medication for fifteen years. We take full legal and moral responsibility for fucking each other raw." He grins at me as he signs. His grin grows larger as he tosses me onto the bed. Later, he jokes about another hookup from last week, a bottom who labels every used condom with the date and name of each trick's initials before filing them away in the freezer.

The last shame attack is vague. I arrive numb. I'm in Northern California to meet my dear friend and mentor. Ed's a giant of a man who showed up to volunteer on the first AIDS ward in San Francisco at the beginning of the epidemic. As an international HIV counselor and trainer, he reminds people of the necessity of modeling the interactions we want to be part of and the primary need to reassure people in crisis—in the end, we all deserve amnesty.

We're high up in the Sierra mountains when Ed walks me to an enormous tree in the middle of a dry riverbed. He explains that each winter the waters rise high enough for fallen trees to tumble downriver to bash into this one large tree. In the center of this tree an enormous wound bleeds golden sap. Kirk, Ed's younger partner, has dubbed this the Lesion Tree. As the story goes, Ed and a few off-shift nurses brought some of the earliest AIDS patients here on camping trips each summer. Being out in nature inspired one young man to take off his shirt. His chest was covered in KS lesions, and he exposed those wounds to the sun for the first and likely last time. He died the next fall. The following summer, at his request, his ashes were brought to the Lesion Tree. Over the years, several young gay men who died alone of AIDS, and with no other resting place, had their ashes laid here.

It's my turn to take off my clothes. I settle into the base of the tree. Ed sits at the edge of the river, leaning heavily on a stick—his aching joints need rest. I reach out and touch the golden, viscous sap with my fingers. I place some of it on my forehead, my heart, and my asshole. I close my eyes and feel the heat of the river rocks on my exposed body. I think of those men, those times. I ask them for help, and forgiveness. I also offer myself to the tree. I imagine my ashes being placed here one day, too. The storm can't hold. Waves of nausea ride in on memories of dozens of interrupted and missed connections, failed disclosures, years of rejection and self-betrayal. Long-held feelings flood through my body. Shame's floodgates open. Compassion surges through me. I begin to wail, first for myself, then more deeply for the men buried here, and finally, for us all.

When the grief subsides, I stand, dress, and join Ed on a fallen tree along the shoreline. Graciously, Ed says watching me was like witnessing the spirits of those men rise out of the tree as if they were released from an indifferent world. He gently directs my attention to what grows behind the Lesion Tree. There, a stand of younger trees ready themselves for the waters of winters to come.

Half-Breed Blues

CHARLES CONN

1.

It was supposed to be a Sunday in 2019 like any other.

By noon, it was already sweltering. Seven years back from living in the States, I was still not used to Panama's sticky weather and tropical heat. I hadn't grown used to the traffic either. Sunday, the one day the city's streets weren't gridlocked, was when I took my senior-aged mother out for her weekly shopping trip. This particular day, my forty-four-year-old cousin Santos came along for the ride. He and I were the same age but not exactly close, though he helped a lot with my mom, his aunt, especially when running errands.

The grocery store that day was devoid of shoppers. The fluorescent lights cast a green glow over the tidy displays of papayas and bananas and bins overflowing with potatoes, yuca, and ñame roots. I placed my mom's items in the grocery cart, when suddenly, Santos went speeding down the aisle with the cart held out in front of him like a six-year-old playing a practical joke. But then, in slow motion, his hands let go, his knees buckled, and he hit the ground.

His body twisted as he fell, and he landed with a soft thud on his back. He'd blacked out. I could hear my mother scream as I rushed over to check his heartbeat, adjusting his head to open his airway. Ready to perform CPR, I was relieved that mouth-to-mouth wouldn't be needed when I detected a faint movement of air, his diaphragm gently moving his rib cage up and down.

Something had been off about him for a couple of years, though we weren't sure what it was. His health had declined dramatically, resulting in considerable weight loss that the entire family of aunts, uncles, and cousins commented on. He failed miserably to suppress his chronically congested lungs, try as he might with each and every cough. Small, dark bumps had developed all over his body, which he scratched at until they scabbed over, doing his best to hide them underneath his uniform of T-shirts and jeans.

In about thirty seconds, he came to. With one of the staff, I helped prop him upright against a pillar, where he sat until the paramedics arrived.

They didn't take long to get there. After checking his vitals, they determined massively low blood sugar was to blame. They told him to eat a more balanced breakfast and suggested he get checked out by a doctor.

"I'm fine," he said and turned down our offer to take him to the hospital.

We all lived together in the same house, my cousin's bedroom right next to mine. At seven that night, after wrapping up my freelance writing work, I learned he hadn't eaten dinner and had gone to bed early, to rest up for his following day's shift at the kitchen he helped manage.

It didn't feel right and I became alarmed. Worried that it wasn't a simple fainting spell, I called my cousin's brother, who came over immediately. Santos could barely make it down the stairs, even with his brother's help, and lost consciousness as soon as he got in the car.

It was now late at night, so they rushed to the emergency room.

Not long after that, we learned that Santos had el virus and had been hiding it for who knows how long.

You could say my cousin's life was a mirror image of mine, our reflections contrasting like a photograph and its negative. We were the same age, and massively closeted when it came to our family. Not that it was hard to tell we were gay.

Neither of us had dated a woman, at least not since high school. We both spoke with a girlish je ne sais quoi that was notably absent from the speech of most Latino alpha males.

Although I'd come out to my mother and two brothers, I never felt comfortable being fully open around them. Being gay was something I did in the States. In Panama, I fell back into a code of silence.

When Santos and I reconnected as adults, I could see he was also in hiding. We each carried our secrets so naturally, and this kept us from being honest with one another. We had never found a way to breach that space.

Our paths in life diverged wildly. He was full Panamanian, not a half-breed like me. His mom, my aunt, died from cancer young. When she got sick, his father abandoned the family, leaving him, the eldest of seven brothers, to care for his siblings.

Compared to him, I was born with a silver spoon, a Canal Zone gringo, a child from the edge of the empire. My father, a Virginian, lived through the Great Depression. He joined the service in WWII, deploying to Panama to protect the canal, and then stayed on to indulge his penchant for hunting.

In the mid-'70s he married a Panamanian country girl, my mother, a woman who was decades younger than him but shared a similar childhood entrenched in poverty. I think that's why they could relate, as neither grew up wearing shoes, for example, or finished high school.

Both were hardworking people, though it was mostly my mother who raised us. She lacked the experience, or stomach, to deal with her obviously gay son coming of age in the '80s.

During early puberty, I discovered my mom's Vidal Sassoon conditioner. After a few days of using it, sneaking small dollops of it in the shower, I reported back to her with excitement, asking her to touch my arm to see how remarkably soft the conditioner had made my skin, but she pulled back reflexively.

On another occasion, sitting next to me in the back seat of the car, she brushed against my legs, which were forever sticking out of Ocean Pacific shorts, and—aghast—felt the stubble of recent shaving.

"That's only for girls," she reprimanded. "Don't do it again!"

What no one knew was that I'd grown up believing I'd ended up in the wrong body, and shaving my legs at the first sight of hair was a way to remain gender neutral. I had much reason to hide. When I was six or seven, my mother had beaten me severely for coming home with my fingernails painted. My playdate had assured me the light beige wouldn't be noticeable, that I wouldn't get in trouble, but she'd been wrong. Punishment taught me to conceal myself to survive.

It wasn't just me. Abuse ran rampant on the base. One neighbor, a girl who was slightly older, talked me into playing a "new game," one involving taking off our clothes. She ended up sixty-nining me, a first grader, while another little girl watched, unconvinced and afraid to take part. Somehow, the instigator's housekeeper found out and phoned my mom before I made it home. When I returned, she gave me a lashing I wish I could forget, leaving a deep wound of scarred emotions I grapple with to this day. I used to wonder if the beating had something to do with making me gay.

Whatever the cause—which, who cares?—I've always thought my attraction to guys was a function of being a girl trapped in a boy's body, a simple logic that I still adhere to. When "Karma Chameleon" came out and I first saw Boy George, I thought this gorgeous creature was the most beautiful woman I'd ever seen. When I later realized that "she" was a "he," I was surprised but also calmly relieved. If Boy George was a boy, that meant I could grow up to be a beautiful woman, too.

Along with being older, my father was also sick. As a kid, I didn't understand what he suffered from, but for as long as I remember he was hacking up phlegm and spitting it out, launching loogies from the open window of moving vehicles. My mother claimed the poor state of Dad's lungs was because he smoked when he was younger. The main factor, I later learned, was that he had worked with asbestos when it was still considered safe.

As time went on, his condition worsened, especially after he retired. By 1992, at seventy-seven years of age, he passed away. On his death certificate, heart failure was listed, along with lung disease and mesothelioma.

On his deathbed, he told me that he didn't have any money for me to go to college, but he encouraged me to try anyway. Early on, he'd recognized the reader in me, and signed me up for a monthly mail-order book club, a treasure trove that offered me a way to dream, to escape, a gift for which I'll be forever grateful. The year after he died, I got accepted to the one and only university to which I'd applied, a school in Los Angeles that claimed to meet any student's demonstrated financial need. Not only did they open their doors to me, but I could afford to walk through them.

2.

It was the summer of 1993, and I was seventeen. I'd not yet declared "I'm gay" to the world, yet there I was, the only guy at the table in a fancy restaurant in Berkeley, all of us college freshmen, talking about our first times.

I was the guest of my friend Sybil, whom I'd met in a composition writing class. We attended the University of Southern California, both of us film students in that coveted department, but we were spending a long weekend in Northern California.

I'd jumped at the chance to go, to see as much of the States as possible. This was the fatherland I so wanted to experience, as if somehow that would offer me insight into the dad I'd barely known. It was a place I'd seen only on television, in Dad's hospital room— one in a series of hospital rooms—surrounded by my brothers, my mom, and a rotating cast comprising a family friend or two at a time. On a tiny screen suspended at an angle from the far side of the room, CNN displayed scenes of gay Pride, and I felt sickened that I might be one of these despicable, dildo-waving freaks dressed in spandex, the girls with armpits unshaved, shirtless, tits flapping in the wind in a motorcade of muscle bikes riding by.

In the Castro, I saw two guys holding hands on the street for the first time, and I could barely bring myself to look away from the hint of a life I desperately wanted but was unable to articulate. Sitting at that restaurant table in Berkeley later on, surrounded by the young women I'd just met, was one of the first times I'd intimated such things to anyone. Some of these women were openly gay, lesbians straight out of high school, so I felt comfortable, safe to share the story of my first crush. It just wasn't what they expected. It wasn't solely the tale, but my flippant delivery of it, that shocked them.

I was twelve and a regular at the neighborhood pool, located on the other side of the fence separating the United States from Panamanian territory. The lifeguard, who was maybe in his twenties, was a friend of the family and a member of Noriega's Fuerzas de Defensa.

Because he was friends with my father, my brothers and I got to sneak into the pool regularly. He was cool to us, a trustworthy person. My aunt even dated him for a spell. Tall, slim, and strapping, he soon became the object of my nascent sexual fantasies.

I didn't share every detail with my tablemates, like how it happened so suddenly and hurt so bad I went to a white-hot place of light in my mind, how afterwards I excreted a mucusy mix of semen and blood, how I felt used and grew angry, how I showered trying to feel clean, how I curled up in bed at six p.m., only to hear his voice again so soon, coming from the living room, where he sat at the dinner table sharing a meal with my dad ...

Still, when I finished my story, the women were slack-jawed and silent, until one of them finally spoke up: "My God. You were raped," she whispered.

3.

After the rape, along with my pain, I started burying other parts of myself—not just my homosexual desires but my self-worth. That Monday, my classmates in seventh-period history all seemed so childish, so innocent, so young. As they sat at their desks, snickering, passing notes, and fidgeting, I made my way to the front of the classroom to give a presentation, in a daze. Looking at them from the podium, I wondered if any could tell what had happened to me over the weekend.

Late afternoons, at home on the base, we had an established routine. After my dad arrived from work, we'd have dinner together at the table, then my brothers and I would sit with him to watch TV, a succession of shows on the one English-language channel run by the US Armed Forces. First, *Star Trek* at three, followed by *Oprah* at four, and then, after dinner with Dad, ABC *World News Tonight* with Peter Jennings.

It was on the ABC newscast that, as a child, I first heard reports of the new mystery illness affecting gay men. Pneumonia-like symptoms led to a wasting away, then skin lesions would mark the victims, and the outcome was certain death.

Conservative religious people on radio and TV and from the pulpit, commented, at first in hushed tones, and then later more vociferously, that the degenerate homosexuals were being punished by God, that He'd meted out some sort of cosmic justice, that the gays deserved it, that they had it coming.

Gay men were dying in droves across Reagan's America, in cities like San Francisco, New York, and Los Angeles. The media covered the crisis with sensationalist spin, as it affected people nobody seemed to care much about. The ailment became the "gay disease," the "gay plague."

It wasn't exclusively indifference finding expression. It was also straight-up hate. Like when Ryan White, a hemophiliac around my age, contracted HIV from a blood transfusion and was consequently rejected by his community and barred from attending school. Sure, he was shunned out of ignorance and fear, but if society could treat that sweet Indiana teenager that way, I reasoned, it would treat homosexuals, people like me, with even more disgust.

Around this time, one of the neighbors on the base had gotten a small pet monkey he kept on his porch in a cage. One afternoon, sharing beers with him as I played nearby, my father warned me to be careful.

"It's cute, but don't touch it," he admonished. "I don't want you to catch that thing that's going around." No one knew where the disease came from, and people feared it could be transmitted from contact with simians.

After the first cases began appearing in Panama, and the local news picked up the story, I started to fear there was a chance that I'd been exposed. My suspicion grew when I learned the disease was sexually transmitted, specifically from the type of sex forced onto me. Not only that, but one could remain asymptomatic for up to ten years after exposure to the virus.

A former altar boy at the Catholic church on the base, I used to pray fervently to be forgiven for jacking off, each time promising God that I'd never do it again. Suddenly, I was making a deal with my maker to let me live. *Please spare me,* I feverishly begged with all my might, night after night. In exchange, with visions of tending to patients in a hospital ward full of beds, I promised to dedicate myself to helping those with the disease in any way I could.

4.

The '90s got underway with a bang—literally—thanks to the US invasion of Panama, the first time in my life my fear of dying transformed from a frightening possibility that kept me up at night into something immediate and palpably real. This was Christmas of 1989.

My father had just retired, so we no longer enjoyed the protection of living on the base. Forced to move on to "the economy," we had packed up and into a humble ranch house my dad built with the help of friends on nearly four acres of farmland. Located in the far north of the capital, Villalobos was the boonies, a grassy landscape of hilly pastures through which a river gently snaked.

My brothers and I switched to a Panamanian school, but we lived so far away that there was little time for anything but to get there and back. Our school bus picked us up at five a.m. and dropped us back at four p.m., just in time for *Oprah*. It was a life of rural isolation.

On the morning US troops bombed downtown Panama, my brother shook me awake, yelling, "We're going to die!"

I didn't know how to feel, apart from scared. I wondered if the Marines would know to come out here to save us and immediately imagined a plan in which we painted "SOS" in bright white letters atop the roof in case a helicopter passed by. I wanted to think the troops knew of our little American family here in the boonies, that they cared about our safety and would defend us.

In the end, our isolation turned out to be our saving grace. All the action was far removed, in the middle of Panama City—all the looting and fires, the bombing of buildings, the shoot-outs.

Post-invasion, with life slowly returning to normal, my attention turned to high school. I had a meager social life and was eager for any bits of popular culture that would make its way down from the States: MTV and *Beverly Hills, 90210*; *Interview* and *Details* magazines; Madonna and Nirvana.

In 1990, *Red Hot + Blue*, a fundraising compilation album for AIDS services, was released, featuring covers of Cole Porter songs. One track, Neneh Cherry's hypnotic take on "I've Got You under My Skin," with its added, sinister layer of meaning, has stuck with me to this day.

The year my father died, 1992, Benetton published an ad featuring AIDS activist David Kirby on his deathbed, surrounded by his family, looking tragically, and beautifully, like Christ. It's agonizingly similar to Michelangelo's *Pietà*, Kirby in his father's embrace, looking peaceful, surrounded by relatives bearing witness to their loss.

In 1993, as a newly arrived student in Los Angeles, I saw the somber if depressing documentary *Silverlake Life*, sitting solo in a cubicle at the cinema department's well-stocked movie library.

The film humanized AIDS for me, showing how a couple's love for each other could transcend anything, even death. Illness was starkly portrayed, the slow wasting away of first one man, and then the other. Yet the couple, Mark Massi and Tom Joslin, kindled a sense of hope in me, hope that in facing the inevitability of dying we might find courage and dignity.

For my first HIV test, early freshman year, I was single. In high school, I'd dated girls for appearances, desperate to be straight, in the hope that doing so might fix me. Now, true to myself, I wanted a boyfriend more than anything. When it came to boys, though, I was stunted, stuck at twelve or thirteen, and emotionally very much a virgin.

I was happy to find out the campus clinic offered free HIV screenings, along with plenty of condoms, dental dams, lube, and information on safe sex. Going in, I felt calm, relieved even, because I'd finally get to clear up a huge fixation that was stressing me out.

It took a week to get the results. When I went back for the verdict, the fear I'd carried in me the six years since my rape welled up, knotting my throat. Gone was the sense of calm I had felt the week before. I could barely swallow, and all I could hear was my breathing, like I was completely in my head, floating.

I signed in at the clinic and waited for the attendant to return with my results, which were folded up and sealed in an envelope. After opening it, I could ask to see a counselor. Otherwise, I could sign a waiver and be on my way.

Once again I felt at ease, but I wondered if, after opening the envelope, I'd fall apart completely. I could hardly keep my fingers from shaking as they slid under the gummed seal, releasing the flap's edge to reveal my fate. But destiny spared me that day. Walking back to my dorm room, the breeze hit my skin, the sunlight my eyes, and I might have cried in thanks, but I was still too numb.

Six years into not having HIV meant four more years to go before I could finally set down the worry I'd been carrying with me for so long.

Soon after that, I found myself getting ready for a blind date arranged by a girlfriend, a fellow student who worked in porn. He was her makeup artist from the set, and she told me he drove a nice car, was cute, and was a total catch.

He picked me up in his Bimmer, a refurbished model, its seats redolent with Armor All, which sent me squeaking across their surface with every slight bump of the road. His face was stretched tight from plastic surgery, and with his cheesy leather jacket and biker boots, he looked like a Ken doll clawing back time. Over coffee at a WeHo café, as he chitchatted about what surgeries he thought would enhance my face, he slipped me a roofie.

As the drug kicked in, I started to feel like I was on acid, the dimensions of space around me taking on a menacing glow of neon imbued with my growing confusion, compounded by an inability to express myself, control my actions, and deal with what was going on around me. All I wanted was to be driven back to my dorm, but if there was one thing I could tell it was that there was no way that was going to happen.

Luckily for me, he turned down one of his friends who randomly showed up and suggested we do a threesome. He wasn't about to share, and soon, he was steering me to his apartment.

The next morning, I worked up the nerve to ask if he had used a condom, to which he replied with irritation, "Now's *not* the time to talk about safe sex." Then, dismissively, he said, "I only finger-fucked you. Don't worry."

I retreated into my head like when I was a kid. I wanted to scream at him, but I could barely speak, afraid it could cost me a ride home. I had no idea where I was or how to get back on my own.

On the drive back, I remained silent, nodding at the appropriate points in his stories or chuckling politely at his jokes. Scenes from the night before, or early in the morning, flashed in my mind's eye, and I remembered that I did fuck *him*. Bareback. "Come in me," I heard him say. And I did, angry that he'd drugged me, ejaculating into him, my sick hope that, if I had HIV, I would give it to him.

When he dropped me back on campus, I gave him a fake number and made sure to never see him again.

I met my first real love at the end of freshman year.

Like me, Kevin was a student, and together we explored Los Angeles's nightlife. We were ravers, fans of hard-core techno, the faster the better. The sound—frenzied, hypnotic, psychedelic—was sweeping in from Europe, but you had to go to illegal warehouse parties to enjoy it. My first such event, Insomniac, was held in an industrial park in South Central—row upon row of warehouses, no sign anything was happening, just the cold breeze blowing. But dancing away inside, I found everyone from skaters and Deadheads to hip-hoppers and cholos. I felt like I was home.

Our common denominator was the music pounding from speakers stacked on high. The chunky beats and penetrating, droning synthesizers went well, I discovered, with a hit of LSD. The experience was religious ecstasy, a revelation I wanted to re-create over and over.

Kevin and I did massive amounts of drugs in our steadfast pursuit of club kid status. At first, it was acid, as that was cheap, but we took what we could get—mescaline, MDMA, pot, mushrooms, 2C-B, crank.

Then I landed a stint as a club reviewer for a popular magazine, which meant free entry to most clubs and events. I had arrived.

Going out and partying became all-encompassing. Our outfits became wilder and more creative. Doing drugs and dancing became my life.

Kevin and I were monogamous and communicated openly and honestly about our sexual histories and previous partners. We used condoms from the start, supplying ourselves from the student health center, and we didn't stop until we got tested and knew for sure that we'd be safe without.

Then it became a matter of calculation, taking into account that antibodies could be detected starting six months from exposure. My date rape had occurred more than six months before our test, so we reasoned the results could be trusted.

This time, getting screened for HIV felt like a rite of passage, something gay couples do when they get serious. It still wasn't any easier than the first. I was scared again but reassured to have the support of a partner.

The meaningful intimacy with an honest-to-goodness boy-friend was exhilarating, and when our tests came back negative, I was overjoyed. My contentment, though, was not so much about being able to lose the condoms but more to do with the fact that, for our plan to work, Kevin and I would continue to be exclusive.

Our relationship lasted a couple of years, becoming tumultuous and toxic toward the end. By then, our lives revolved around meth. A year into being hooked, I called in sick to work and went for a checkup at the campus clinic. The doc, a kind woman, checked my lymph nodes for swelling, and I knew right away what she suspected. And it totally threw me.

Prior to leaving for the clinic, I'd lifted my shirt to admire my tummy in Kevin's full-length mirror, thinking how good I looked, how—finally—I'd slimmed down enough to where you could see my abs. Although I wasn't feeling well, my trim torso made me happy, because if I was skinny, I felt, everything in my life would magically click into place. So, shaken by the doc's actions—not her gentle words of caution—I brought my year on meth to a close.

Other drugs, though, were still free game.

Flash-forward to 1997. Jeff, my Texas cowboy, was nineteen then, and I had only recently graduated college. At twenty-three, I couldn't help but feel like a cradle robber.

We met outside a West Hollywood gay club that had closed for the night, its patrons emptied onto the streets. He and his friends stuck out from the regulars, who were glammed up and groomed. In contrast, his crowd wore baggy pants and tight, neon-colored shirts. One or two had backpacks, and all of them wore bright-colored bracelets. Clearly, they were ravers, so I was keen to connect.

Jeff and I traded numbers and soon were hitting up underground dance parties together, the sort I'd frequented with Kevin. I knew we'd hit it off when, a week into knowing each other, he had no problem driving me around at four in the morning on a Sunday, looking to score some weed. We were unsuccessful, but that mattered less to me than the fact that our priorities in life so clearly matched. Before long, we were officially dating.

As with Kevin, we spoke openly about our previous partners. He'd only had one serious boyfriend before me. Before him, I'd had two. I wasn't overly worried about getting tested this time, but I couldn't help feeling nervous going in for the results. On the way to the outreach center, I sensed Jeff was growing anxious, so I took his hand in mine. Despite our serious purpose, walking down the street, comforting him in open daylight, felt like heaven.

The HIV test I took with Jeff was newfangled, the results delivered quickly, in three hours' time. Our intake forms were litanies of substance abuse, each of us listing a long and varied history of drug use that wasn't about to stop. The nurse-cum-social-worker, a stern woman who wore severe judgment on her face, clearly looked down on the two of us.

We'd walked through Hollywood tripping on acid the week before. Jeff and I particularly enjoyed terrorizing the cookie-cutter Muscle Marys who dominated the strip with their bland fashion and desperation to resemble one another. With our rough-around-the-edges group of friends, we'd tumble in and out of the bars and clubs, dancing with abandon, sticking out like sore thumbs, with our street fashion, loud and baggy clothes, tattoos and piercings, and neon-dyed hair. Unwilling to fit in, we wore our freak badges with pride and partied constantly, taking GHB, smoking weed on the streets, and doing key bumps of Special K in any bathroom stall we could find. We detested West Hollywood's conformity and took every chance to flaunt that we didn't look and act like everyone else and that we were having a blast doing so.

When the nurse at the outreach center handed over the envelopes with our results, Jeff and I opened them after a brief pause. We were hesitant to rush into a possible life of wasting away, unable to afford the dubious drug cocktail the medical professionals promised would stave off death. But Fate again cast her die. Neither of us drew a short straw. We were both negative.

The smiles that broke across both our faces surprised the nurse, whose face had become pinched with concern. When she saw our reactions, her mouth and eyes softened, and she joined us, smiling.

"All good?" she asked. I think she was as relieved as we were, having avoided giving us a serious talk on the heels of bad news.

It had been nine years since my rape. I felt elated, light, and free. God seemed to have kept his end of the deal.

Since then, I've asked myself many times: *Have I kept my side of the bargain?*

I don't think so. But, in my heart, I'd like to believe that sharing this story is, at long last, a start.

5.

Because my cousin Santos started and then stopped treatment—the modern drugs that could take his viral load down to undetectable—he almost died. Soon after arriving at the nearest emergency room, he was transferred to a government-run hospital that had a special ward for HIV patients. As soon as he got there, he lost consciousness.

He had suffered a sudden heart attack and received defibrillation. After he was stabilized, next came an induced coma and intubation. Then kidney failure and dialysis, all while his body battled the pneumonia that filled his lungs with phlegm and fluid. After he had been unconscious for a month, hope that he'd pull through began to wane.

But, miraculously, pull through he did.

Of the people brought into the government hospital for urgent care that night, my cousin was the only one who survived. Now staying with his brother, he's a shadow of his former self, his larynx so damaged that he speaks in a whisper.

He's since regained a little weight but not much, and he can no longer stand upright for long periods of time. Amazingly, he got his old job back, with a change of departments, working admin in an air-conditioned office.

I think about how Santos's life changed so drastically over the course of six months; how it could have been me. Kevin, my first boyfriend, is HIV-positive now, as is Jeff's first love. Fortunately, they have access to the latest treatments, but I still feel a sense of survivor's guilt.

Why did our lives take the directions they did? Why, of those of us who made it through, did some come out less scathed than the rest? I don't have the answers, and speculation gets me nowhere.

I know that dealing with my rape instead of burying it reframed the way I thought about my trauma. I saw that perhaps my underlying fear of sex had pushed me toward monogamous relationships, which helped keep me from becoming infected.

I also figured out that the abuse I experienced as a child had been bubbling up in my behaviors as an adult, in particular when it came to addiction. Making that connection, which took me decades, was like a golden key. Among the better life choices I started making was a move back to Panama in 2012, to try out this being-a-writer thing. My only regret is not having done it sooner.

Jeff and I ended things more than ten years ago, and I haven't had a serious boyfriend since. It's easier this way. I've warmed up to the idea of dating again, but I'm not in a rush. Thoughts of sex still trigger me. My rape and fears of contracting HIV shaded my entire sex life, and as much as I wish it were otherwise, hooking up is not something I seek. Even if I had access to PrEP, my mental and emotional blocks are still there.

One of my lingering questions is why Santos gave up on himself and stopped treatment. I don't judge him, whatever his reasons were. I doubt I would have handled things better. In the end, his disease outed him, yet our family rallied with zero discrimination, putting our blood relations ahead of everything else. And that was wonderful to see.

Status Symbol

TONY CORREIA

St. Paul's Hospital in Vancouver is a study in contrasts. You access the building through a redbrick courtyard flanked by a gallery of alabaster saints. Entering the building through the automatic doors, you are greeted by portraits of Victorian nuns as you inhale the aroma of Starbucks coffee. The avocado walls are dotted with motion-sensored hand sanitizer dispensers and portable defibrillators.

Despite its Catholic beginnings, St. Paul's is the beating heart of Vancouver's gay community. Since the beginning of the AIDS crisis, it's where gay men have gone to get diagnosed and treated, and often to die. With the worst of the crisis apparently behind us, it's only natural the hospital is now slated to be converted into condominiums for oligarchs to launder their money.

The lab at St. Paul's is on the second floor—just follow the blue line on the wall up a short flight of stairs. You take a number from a box right outside the entrance to the small waiting area; it's easy to miss if you don't know it's there. The waiting area reminds me of a teacher's lounge from the '70s. The walls are lined with sturdy metal-framed chairs with harvest gold seats that have weathered the test of time. A water cooler with cone-shaped paper cups sits in the corner. The only thing that tells you this isn't the '70s is the absence of ashtrays.

I've been coming here every three months for the last fifteen years to get my blood work for my antiretroviral prescription. In British Columbia, HIV meds are free as part of a study managed by the BC Centre for Excellence in HIV/AIDS. You can't get the pills without a prescription, and you can't get the prescription without the blood work.

I'm not required to do my blood work at St. Paul's, but it's where I feel the safest from stigma. I was diagnosed with HIV in a physician's office that was approved by US Citizenship and Immigration while applying for a green card in San Francisco in the '90s. My HIV test was part of the immigration medical exam. A nurse read my results to me in the waiting room, unaware there was anything wrong with my blood work. A complete stranger was standing next to me when I learned my HIV test came back inconclusive. When I later tested positive, the doctor was more concerned with how I had contracted the virus than with my emotional well-being. Even with all its Catholic iconography, I've never felt judged at St. Paul's.

The intake process at St. Paul's lab exemplifies the best and worst of Canadian medicine. As recently as 2010, a medical secretary processed your lab requisition, while two or three phlebotomists summoned patients and drew blood. On a good day, you could be in and out in less than fifteen minutes. These days, the phlebotomists do everything, and the waiting room is often brimming with patients. The wait time can be as long as an hour. I'm sure some executive up the food chain got a bonus with the money saved by cutting staff.

There was a capacity crowd in the waiting area the last time I went to get my blood drawn. Five minutes, ten minutes, fifteen minutes ... The numbers in the queue refused to budge; it was like they were going backwards instead of forward. I would have left and come back another time, but I was going on vacation and couldn't risk running out of pills. It's moments like these when I remind myself to be grateful I don't have to pay for my meds. What is an hour compared to the rest of my life?

The waiting room is typically an impersonal place. When I recognize someone from the street or the bars, we acknowledge each other with a nod and say a pleasant hello, at most. I can count on both hands the number of conversations I've had in fifteen years of waiting for my number to be called. And yet, whether they are A-gays or C-gays, I feel a camaraderie with the others. We are all waiting together, and this inspires a sense of community I haven't experienced elsewhere since the height of the AIDS crisis. The lab has a way of leveling the playing field. It all comes down to blood.

I used to think antiretrovirals and PrEP would democratize sex between men, that we could finally erase the stigma of HIV from our lives. Yet when I read an online profile of someone who proclaims they are "clean" and on PrEP, I feel as though they want me to hurry up and die already. Even the barebacking sites, formerly a safe haven for serosorting between positive guys, are being encroached upon by HIV-negative men seeking the pleasure of unprotected sex, like a bachelorette party at a gay bar.

I open a book on my phone and try to lose track of time. The guy next to me recognizes the person looking for the number dispenser. Both guys are young and muscular, a blond and a brunet, thirty at most. They greet each other like guests at a wedding who haven't seen each other since high school. They pucker the air with kisses and surreptitiously squeeze each other's biceps for firmness, like melons at a produce stand.

It's the brunet's first time to the lab. He's from the States, and the whole process of getting his meds is foreign to him.

"First you get your blood work," the blond explains like a cheer-leader. "Then you get a prescription from your doctor, and then you pick the prescription up at the pharmacy on the first floor."

Orientation over, they take turns drolly reciting all the places they have recently traveled: New York, London, Paris, Palm Springs, San Francisco. Slam poetry for the gay jet set.

"I asked my boss for the week off between Christmas and New Year's to go to Miami," the blond says. "And she was all like, 'You've used up all your vacation time for the year.' So, I got in her face and was like, 'You know how I always work extra so you can take care of your kids? Well now I'm reclaiming my time.'"

"Payback is a bitch," says the brunet.

"Okurr?"

Who is this guy? And where does he work, in case I apply there by accident?

I've never been so relieved to have my number called.

The maple phlebotomy booths remind me of the confessionals at a Catholic church. The walls of each booth are decorated with soothing pictures of clown fish and otters clipped from nature magazines. There used to be a photo of a statue of Christ submerged in tropical waters, looking up at the sunshine coming through the surface. It's gone now, but even as a recovering Catholic, I always found it peaceful.

The first year after I tested positive, I had my blood drawn by a lesbian who wore thick black-rimmed glasses, clunky Doc Martens, and a pleasant smile. "This is a fine Merlot you have here," she'd say as she filled each of the five vials with my blood. It never got old. I think of her whenever I get my blood drawn. She was the only phlebotomist who ever looked me in the eyes.

I roll my sleeve down over the cotton ball taped to the inside of my elbow and gather my winter coat and hat. I see the blond seated in the booth next to mine. The phlebotomist is telling him that she can't find his requisition in the system.

"Do you know what tests you're having done?" the phlebotomist asks him.

"Whatever you need for PrEP," he says, like it's the secret password to get into an exclusive party.

The whole time I listened to him in the waiting room, I assumed he was HIV-positive. I didn't like him, but I empathized with him. Now his presence at the clinic makes me feel unwelcome. I walk out of the lab feeling like it's just one more place where I don't belong.

Undead Disco

Variations on a Theme

PATRICK MILIAN

The audacity of Robyn's "Dancing On My Own" lies in its brokenness. Not because it occupies a space of heartbroken jealousy and self-doubt with a voice fearless in its articulation of the overly familiar—though her now ubiquitous dance floor anthem does that too—but because its damaged sound is of a deconstructed disco: aural fragments that resist cohesion yet offer transcendence.

It begins with a persistently chugging synthesizer spelling out three chords. Although most chords include at least three notes—the first, third, and fifth scale degrees—Robyn's only include the first and fifth. That note in the middle is what differentiates a major chord from a minor one, what gives the chord its specific character and texture. Without it, we hear a hollow drone, loud but fragile, like an insect's buzzing exoskeleton. After the opening bars, a drum machine pulses with four kick drum hits and a snare on the backbeat—the necessary persistence and syncopation that our bodies recognize as fundamental to dancing but nothing more. The vocals are equally minimal, with Robyn singing the same melody four times in a row, leaving as much negative space between these repetitions as it takes to sing each one. Although the song builds over the course of four minutes, her vocals span barely more than an octave, and the drums are filled out with a hi-hat cymbal that doesn't even stretch over the full measure. Everything about the song is missing something, such that when the bridge reaches the final chorus with a protracted drum fill—not even a fill, just an extended stutter of sixteenth notes—deprivation becomes rewarding in and of itself. When she sings the song's iconic couplet, she's also summarizing her musical aesthetic: insufficiency transformed into catharsis. It gives a satisfaction more rewarding than the most extravagantly produced and orchestrated hit might offer.

As with many contemporary pop songs, we can draw a line directly back from "Dancing On My Own" to '70s disco. Everything—from that hi-hat and snare drumbeat to the chord progression to the melodic arc of the chorus—was heard on dance floors decades ago. The difference is that Robyn has flushed disco of so much as to leave us with the genre's constituent elements, just its ghost. Part of what's evacuated is the genre's roots in African American music—in gospel, blues, and Afro Cuban jazz—Robyn's whiteness partially erasing the work of Black men and women. Take Carol Douglas's 1974 "Doctor's Orders," for instance. It also begins with three chords, but these chords include not just the third scale degree but also often the seventh to create a hint of tension with an embedded tritone. The hi-hat taps the same sixteenth notes we hear in Robyn's song, but they come from human hands holding the drumsticks. Plus, the rhythmic opening and closing of the two cymbals give the rhythm shape and contour, as well as insistence and presence. And Douglas's vocal melody in the first verse is really just the same figure four times in a row, but it's fuller in range and augmented in length. There are swells of strings that buoy the listener from verse to chorus—a few spoken interludes to clarify the conceit of Douglas's doctor prescribing a certain lover to cure her loneliness—and some congas bringing rhythmic and timbral variety to the drum section, but at bottom, Robyn and Douglas's songs are kin. Loneliness is metamorphosed through music into ecstasy. Douglas sings about a love potion, but we know no potion will be coming. All that's coming is another chorus where she'll sing the same thing over again. This isn't loneliness transforming into its opposite but loneliness becoming so completely itself that we can't recognize it anymore.

Robyn is only one of the most remarkable practitioners of a certain kind of disco postmortem—the genre laid out on the operating table, cut into, cut apart. Carly Rae Jepsen's "Julien" employs a wahwah guitar and plenty of wind chimes to create an unabashedly campy disco sound. The song's bridge blares out a leading tone, creating the expectation that the final chorus will modulate up a whole step with all the melodrama of the Pointer Sisters, but that modulation never comes. Firmly bound to the same tonal center, "Julien" ends exactly where it began, affixing itself to disco's ankles like a shadow. Charli XCX, Troye Sivan, Lorde, and most artists affiliated with the PC Music collective follow a similarly flattened and precarious aesthetic. It bears emphasizing that when these overwhelmingly white artists discard modulations and scale degrees, they're undoing a lot of what Black women like Carol Douglas and Bonnie Pointer did, which was to incorporate the harmonic and rhythmic vocabularies of blues, jazz, gospel, and other Black musical forms into pop. In the '70s, dance music disguised its precarity—in part a racialized marginalization—in the excesses of glamour, gowns, and sex. But nowadays, a certain strain of music makes that vulnerability its signature: pop that doesn't deliver on its promises.

Obviously, I'm talking about gay music, music claimed by gay people and music that, sometimes retrospectively, narrates the gay experience. I'm also talking about AIDS. I'm reconfiguring one way the parallel queer histories of disco and AIDS have been told: Donna Summer, Gloria Gaynor, and the like soundtracked the hedonism of the '70s, an indulgence and joy that came to a disastrous halt in the '80s with the epidemic and the accompanying callousness on the part of mainstream Americans. Dance floors emptied out as the echoes of "Disco sucks!" from Disco Demolition Night at Comiskey Park went from subtly racist and homophobic to explicitly rageful. Reagan ignored the growing death toll, and Bush told the dying to just change their behavior.

In that story, disco goes silent, and nowhere was this loss so dramatically registered as in the very public death of the "Queen of Disco," Sylvester. I was born the year Sylvester died, so everything I've encountered about him seems like an artifact of a forgotten history in which a Black gay man not only appears on Dick Clark's *American Bandstand* in makeup and a kimono, but he drives the audience nearly rabid with a performance that's nothing short of transcendent. The first song he plays, "Dance (Disco Heat)," grooves for an unrelenting six minutes, as he and his backup singers raise their voices in a gospel of liberation. It's only matched by the second song, "You Make Me Feel (Mighty Real)," which somehow manages to push the tempo even faster. The fact that two of the greatest disco tracks both came from the same artist in 1978 is remarkable. That Sylvester put them on either side of the same single is almost unbelievable. But ten years after that television appearance, almost to the very day, he died of AIDS-related complications at the age of forty-one. In an interview with the *Los Angeles Times* a few months before his death, he explained how he had been hospitalized three times for what he thought was bronchitis before finding out he had AIDS. It's fitting that the virus would begin to show itself in his voice, where an androgynous falsetto that wove together the sounds of his Pentecostal upbringing with those of Afro Cuban rhythms would emerge. The excessive sounds of Black queer self-expression, of musical and sexual promiscuity, were choked out for the world to hear. AIDS took disco by the throat.

But in another story, disco doesn't go silent as much as it is drowned out. Sylvester embodies how a generation of Black gay men helped create the genre, but another generation gave it a second life. Starting in late-'70s Chicago, DJs like Frankie Knuckles and Farley Jackmaster Funk were spinning at the Warehouse, a members-only club frequented mostly by Black gay men. As disco waned in popularity among mainstream Americans, a new genre of music composed mostly of sampled dance music stripped of vocals, dismantled, and looped could be heard most nights at the Warehouse. Eventually, that sound was named after its birthplace and became, simply, house music. Although Sylvester found himself at the center of American pop music, Black gay men reeling from the AIDS crisis found themselves pushed to the margins and building a music without the studio space and session musicians the label system once afforded. Instead, they reconstituted the remnants of the '70s by picking through the bits and putting them back together. By looping a four-on-the-floor drumbeat along with an Afro Cuban clave pattern and squelching synth riffs from a misused Roland TB-303, DJs like Knuckles and Funk reimagined disco in a way that was darker and colder, harder but unrefined. House is the original deconstructed disco, stitched into the aural fabric of so much contemporary pop. Maybe AIDS killed disco, but the music made in response to and out of that loss is ingrained in the sounds that sustain me and the queers of my generation.

When I received my HIV-positive diagnosis in 2012, my doctors all assured me that the virus would not kill me, that I would have a long and uncomplicated life. The consequences of my sins could be managed and I could pass for a normal person. What I love about Robyn and musicians like her is that their house-and-disco-infused version of pop is unapologetically abnormal. It's danceable and ecstatic, but if it sounds like disco reanimated, it's a zombie: embodied, evacuated, hungry. There's music that sounds like disco come back from the dead, but then there's disco that's undead, a sound much more consonant with my experience of being positive.

No matter what songs you're choosing, however, the history of AIDS and the history of American popular music cannot be superimposed upon one another. To select music to narrate the epidemic is to enact a violence by highlighting the deaths of some and erasing the deaths of others. Although I want to acknowledge both their contributions and losses, I also hardly need to say that the ones most frequently erased are trans people and people of color. As a mixed-race cisgender man, I have always been struck by the image of the white gay man as splendidly degraded by AIDS as a ludicrous yet inescapable archetype for the epidemic.

I was twenty-three, and a year into a relationship with a white man in his late forties, when I was diagnosed HIV-positive. He and I had met during a stifling summer in Atlanta at a gay twelve step meeting. I'd been sober and in AA for a few years by that point, but I'd only recently moved to Georgia and intentionally sought out gay meetings to make friends and find dates. Most of the men I met were twice my age or older, and most had also been affected by HIV/AIDS, whether they were positive themselves or told stories about the friends and lovers they'd lost. These spaces were where I first encountered HIV/AIDS in a more direct capacity, but even then, it was something spoken about in the past tense—in someone's "rock bottom" during a share, or marked by the slow limp of someone's leg muscles atrophied by AZT. Like the drinking and the drugs, though, HIV/AIDS seemed like something that had happened, and living with the virus was part of "cleaning up the wreckage of the past," as the AA slogan puts it. I had already gotten sober, already done the work of the twelve steps. I didn't exactly consider myself immune to HIV, and I didn't think that relapse was out of the question for me, but I had imagined a parallelism between HIV and active addiction. They were in the past, not my present. Plus, I felt fine.

That wasn't how I put it to my partner, though. Instead, I lied and told him I had tested negative just a few months before meeting him. As confident as I was in my own status—a completely false confidence considering how I had actually never been tested in my life—I wasn't so confident in his. We had one conversation toward the beginning of our relationship to this effect, but he reassured me that he knew he was negative. Maybe because he belonged to the same generation of gay men I had come to associate with AIDS, maybe because he was only a few months sober and still liable to be dealing with the consequences of his drinking and using, or maybe, and most likely, because I had so straightforwardly lied to him, I assumed he was lying, too. I didn't trust him as far as unprotected sex went. The change didn't come with a conversation but with a blow job.

One afternoon in early September, I was moving into a new apartment and my partner was helping. On a twin-sized bed I'd bought at the flea market, in a bedroom where he'd just smashed a palmetto bug with my shoe, he went down on me and efficiently brought me to orgasm. For the first time, he swallowed my come. Coincidentally, my roommate came home immediately after. We quickly put our pants back on to finish unloading the car, and I never got the chance to reciprocate, but this was the instant our terms about sex changed. Swallowing my load was his way of saying he trusted me, and it was enough to get me to trust him in return.

Not long afterwards, he started getting sick. He'd experience chest pains, abdominal cramps, vertigo, and a sore throat that never went away. I, however, felt totally okay. The possibility that HIV might be part of what he was experiencing occurred to me once or twice, but the thought never had enough presence for me to actually do anything about it. For reasons both real and imagined, it didn't make sense that two sober and monogamous men, one of whom was completely asymptomatic, could also be positive. When he finally suggested that we both get tested, I complied. His symptoms had proven not to be acid reflux, strep throat, or allergies, so I imagined these tests would be just another possibility to check off. He thought I was naïve not to think that HIV/AIDS played a fundamental and concrete role in our health as gay men, and of course he was right. For me, HIV was something men of my partner's generation had survived, mourned, and memorialized. Though present, it was peripheral. His insistence that we get tested seemed like ascribing contours to something that was inherently indistinct. We, I believed, had passed through the haze of AIDS; we weren't supposed to come up against it.

But we both tested positive. And after another round of tests, I found out there were only 196 CD4 cells in each cubic millimeter of my blood. This means that I wasn't diagnosed with just HIV but with AIDS. The virus sharpened from a historical abstraction into a reality: blood tests, prescriptions, side effects, the health care system, telling my mom, and the tearful screaming between my partner and me.

His results showed a few hundred more CD4 cells than mine, and even though it's not like these cells count down from 1,000 to 0 at a steady rate, having more made him sure that I had contracted the virus first and passed it on to him. In light of my dishonesty at the beginning of our relationship, I was quick to believe the same. I took on that blame, compounding my own guilt and shame without questioning to what degree he might have been dishonest himself. I saw my body as more than unwell, as dangerous. Medical professionals tried to narrate my condition for me, but that narrative in which timelines are messy and consequences are delayed is flimsy compared to the massive self-hate and anger that amasses between two people, suddenly sick, locked in a domesticity gone toxic.

In the absence of a clear sequence of events with which we could ascribe blame and for what, we scrambled to create one ourselves. Still unwilling to admit that I had lied, or to interrogate his claims, I offered a story line that could at least simplify the terms of our relationship. In this plausible fiction, I became infected in 2011, before the virus would have shown up on a blood test, but still, I ignorantly and despicably gave it to a man I said I loved, a man who had managed to live through the crisis of the '80s and '90s, only to find himself betrayed by the young person, the ungrateful brat, he was taking care of emotionally and financially. It's an ugly story, one in which the villain not only takes on the disease and the disgrace of having given HIV to his sugar daddy, but he also takes on an entire generation's trauma and is singled out as the person-ification of an epidemic. Although I knew the pieces of the story were guessed at, if not wholly fabricated, the culpability I took on felt very factual. For him and for myself, I was the crystallization of infirmity, ignorance, and death.

Although the tension between us lessened, and the hate he felt for me dulled, it never really dissipated. Neither did my dishonesty, for that matter, since I never told him the truth about not knowing my status in the first place. Instead, it all changed shape such that we became mutually imbricated in an angry entanglement that lasted several more years. A formless shame had materialized in each one of us along with our diagnosis. For him, I gave shape to that shame. For me, the story I told, and that he would tell back to me, gave it shape. Internalizing someone else's pain by being complicit in a particular version of events was easier for me than dealing with my own humiliation and confronting my own lies. In a different sequence of events, he and I tell the truth completely, we heal and mourn without hurting one another, but in the events that actually unfolded we caused tremendous hurt to each other and ourselves as we slowly and destructively unmade the realities we had built. He would go off to get drunk in secret, and I would cheat on him. He would wake me up in the middle of the night to shout at me, and I would spend the next day hiding from him. We would each meet betrayal with betrayal and live in constant fear of losing the other.

We broke up after he found out I had been cheating on him. He took my journals and used them as blackmail: either I move out by the end of the week or he would tell my parents, my colleagues, my students about what he had found in them. Among the things he found were plenty of times when I put into writing that I had no idea whether I was positive when I told him I was negative. Sometimes I think of how this sequence of events gives the relationship a kind of symmetry: it begins in withholding and ends in disclosure, or it begins with me hurting him and ends with him hurting me. But, mostly, I think a song needs to admit its silences.

For me, HIV has come to define itself as a disease of unknowing, of absences and openings. A missing generation of gay men. Missing white blood cells. Missing information. Missing symptoms, in my case. And a long line of doctors assuring me that as long as I took my Atripla every night before bed, having HIV would be like not having HIV at all. I've been able to rewrite the narrative of self-loathing partially because this has become a disease of subtraction, of reaching toward zero, toward undetectability, of daily attending to my condition so that nothing doesn't become something, while still acknowledging and honoring that nothing.

The discourse of persistently working to keep a disease asymptomatic without ever eradicating it is familiar to me. I received my diagnosis nine days before I celebrated four years clean and sober. Even today, I attend meetings and work a program of recovery predicated on the addiction-as-illness model. This model is not the right fit for everyone, but for me it's always made sense. My drinking and using were symptoms. They could define what existed inside of me like an objectless modifier, one that described me as "less than" without a reason or story. Drugs sometimes fixed problems, but more frequently drugs expressed problems—like that free-floating sense of being wrong in my body. Long before my diagnosis, even before I had the vocabulary to call myself queer, I moved through the world with the feeling that everyone else managed to fit inside of it whereas I only scraped against it. I was unwanted, invisible, bad at everything and only seen when I was the biggest mess or most spectacular failure. Sobriety demands diligent attendance to these feelings that are left over and often amplified when I don't take drugs.

I continue to go to primarily queer AA meetings, and the stories told in those rooms—including my own now—often refer to HIV/AIDS at some point. Twelve step meetings are meant for more than telling war stories about drinking and using, but the repetition of these stories is a fundamental part of these gatherings. By telling and retelling stories, by adhering to unspoken conventions as much as to the rhythms and structures of them, we bring a legibility to our compulsions that resists being put into words. The addict, whether speaking or listening, can be folded into a chorus of voices, even if it's only mouthing the words. AIDS is part of what we sing together. It cements our collectivity, clarifies the terms of our interdependence.

One person's addiction may have never led to homelessness, but these meetings insist that facing homelessness is part of our story and therefore part of each story. In the case of my particular recovery communities, HIV/AIDS exists in the same paradoxical way: present in absence, absent in presence. This is not strictly a matter of empathy; empathy is enacted interpersonally and demands an individual's agency. In those rooms of queers sitting on our metal folding chairs, drinking gnarly coffee out of Styrofoam cups, reciting our aphorisms with all the conviction of people who know they're already living out a cliché, we claim a deep knowability to our shared stories and decipher them to one another. This is the other way I come to comprehend the generational trauma of the virus I find myself host to—return and refrain, catchy as a pop song.

Through these contexts—in my past relationship and in my recovery—my diagnosis becomes a double initiation into an ongoing rite that has preceded me by decades. In one, I personified epidemic. In the other, I represent survival. In one, I was singular. In the other, enmeshed. In both, the shape of trauma is traced in the lines of what's missing. At the center of my status, and of my favorite pop music, is an aporia. From the Greek meaning "without passage," an aporia is a rupture, a doubt, a contradiction, the missing note in a chord that would otherwise make it major or minor but instead turns hollowness into a sonic signature. By longing for something, you might explode and dissolve it into shards that jab into your body.

The poet D.A. Powell includes in his book *Tea* a list of ten disco songs that conflate sex and death through the complex metaphor of heaven. In order to pass into a realm of ultimate pleasure, you have to make the ultimate sacrifice. Desire and destruction are co-constituting. "Earth Can Be Just like Heaven" by the Weather Girls, "Heaven's Where My Heart Is" by Marsha Raven, and, of course, "Take Me to Heaven" by Sylvester are all based on the contradiction that the paradise of sex is also the pain of death, that to be completely in one's body you have to leave one's body. Suffering becomes salvation. Absence becomes presence. Disco is dangerous because, underneath everything, there's a fragile body threatening to shatter. And then it does.

For all its camp and cheese, disco gives shape to a feeling that is inherently paradoxical: the most sacred part of my humanity carries within it the hard seed of shame. The capacity to love another, even for a few minutes on the dance floor—a few more if you're lucky and get the extended mix—has the potential to destroy another. This works both ways. The longing to be loved is a risk and becomes a longing to die, to go to heaven. The fantasy dismantles itself, but it's through dismantling that the fantasy is reenacted and renewed. On the cover of her greatest hits album *Disco Queen*, Carol Douglas is depicted wearing a frothy pink gown while floating in a pink sky as fluffy white clouds drift by. She's been flattened out and ripped from somewhere else to be superimposed on this candy-colored fantasy. But she's made it to heaven.

The word "recovery" has always struck me as an inexact description for the state of being that comes after active addiction, after diagnosis. "Recovery" implies a sort of salvage, a recuperation and reconstitution to compensate for what was lost. But there's no compensation, just the accumulation of days, many marked by grief and a few by subtle joy. "Recovery" also feels imprecise because of its singularity, how an individual recovers, when in fact the effort is communal. The group—the meeting, the mass of bodies on the dance floor, or even the more dispersed collective of queer people all dancing on our own—is what goes through this process. And this group might be so spread out across space and time that its borders can hardly be delineated.

I have no interest in affixing "happily ever after" to this conclusion, in suggesting that the trauma of AIDS has been neatly metaphorized in four-minute songs, and that people are no longer dying. Many people are still dying, and the fact that I'm not—from AIDS or from active addiction—speaks to my privilege. The way disco haunts pop music is an aural analogy for an experience that refuses the semantic register. It offers a way of experiencing a shapelessness that resists direct experience. But there are others whose story doesn't yet have a container and who haven't yet obtained visibility, much less scrutability. For their song, keep listening.

Right now, I'm in love with someone new. He's two years younger than me, but he has his own history of dating older men. He's not an addict and he's negative. Because of the medicine I'm on, we're able to fit our bodies together in whatever ways we desire with no chance of me giving him HIV. It's funny that by fully confronting the risk of infection I'm able to, in essence, remove it altogether. Funnier still is how eliminating it has opened me up to all the other risks associated with intimacy, the messier ones of vulnerability and honesty, the ones that register as thornier and sometimes even more intractable than that of an incurable disease. We first connected over a shared love of the same kinds of pop music. For him, this music narrates a different set of experiences, both lived and inherited, and we carry those experiences with us into our relationship. We're learning to sit with friction and disconnection and to allow love to be expansive, textured, and ambiguous. We make room for rupture and contradiction, for openings and closings, for what look like passages into the future but turn out to be dead ends. We do this because love can take you to heaven. It can be a force for sublime destruction, but it can also be the gradual accrual of days in which more is gained than is lost.

Across the Gap between Us

LIAM OCTOBER O'BRIEN

"It was in my head that if only a fragment remained in the future, to fade in the sulfurous rain, it would say how much I loved him and how terrible was the calamity."

—Paul Monette, *Borrowed Time: An AIDS Memoir*

I was in the cemetery when I started reading *Love Alone*, Paul Monette's book of elegies for his lover, Roger Horwitz. It wasn't my plan to be morbid: the late-February day was bizarrely, blissfully warm, and my boyfriend, Stephen, and I had taken a blanket to lie among the gravestones of ancient Iowans and read.

He saw what I'd brought. "Wow," he said. "Why do you want to destroy yourself?"

"I've been meaning to read it for so long," I said and settled in, holding the book like a shield between my eyes and the sun.

Monette said of these poems that he wanted them "to allow no escape, like a hospital room, or indeed a mortal illness." This is his explanation of the form he uses, which hurtles forward without comma or stanza break, leaving the reader no rest, no ledge to catch hold of. The poems throw themselves at Rog's death, breaking again and again on its simultaneous impossibility and finality. In the cemetery, I read four poems. Then I was crying.

"I have to stop!" I told Stephen.

He reassured me, comforted me, gave me an extra book. Soon enough, the winter wind came back from its smoke break, and we went home.

I read all of *Love Alone* slowly, a few poems at a time, over the next several months. Whenever I return to it, as I did today, I notice the same physical reaction. My heartbeat speeds. My whole body tenses, from the stomach out. Breathing becomes harder. Eventually, as during a frightening movie, I shut my eyes.

"Would you like to see my place?" Sam asked and tapped his hand, anxious, on my knee. "No funny business."

"Sure," I said. I was in my early twenties, he in his fifties. I felt very new.

He drove me deep into the woods. Those ruts full of mud and the dimness between the trees. Eventually, came a clearing, and a field, then the house. Shingled, rambling, trellised for grapes and wisteria. I took off my shoes. We went up the spiral stairs to his kitchen, where he showed me a chair and offered iced Lipton. The room was done in red. Art nouveau posters and a hardy pale miniature of Michelangelo's *David* on a side table. That luminous rainy light, coming in through many windows.

"Oh," I said, "did you know a lot of surgeons use *David* as a model for trans guy cocks?"

"That's so interesting," he said, not blushing. He looked at the statue. "I guess it makes sense."

I finished the awful tea. I said, "Hey, I know you said no funny business, but if you'd like to, I would."

He said, "I would, too. But there's something you should know."

Hang on, I thought. *That's my line.*

"I'm positive," he said.

"Oh, that's fine." No thinking. As easy as if it were easy. He came and bent over my chair and kissed me. I was shivering.

In his bedroom, the windows were open. Rain on the screens and a light wind coming through. I shivered more once I took off my clothes. It smelled like new mowing. Sweet peas, dahlias. But all very wet and chill.

"Tell me what you like," he said.

"Just this."

I sucked his cock with my head resting on his stomach, no condom. We used one when he fucked me, but he didn't last. He said he was sorry, that happened a lot. I said, "Don't worry" and used my mouth on him again—that slight rubber taste on his skin. He couldn't come. He said it had been a while. We lay in the sheets, still cold, shivery. I held the back of his neck in my hand. He fucked me with his hand later, and I did come. And he drove me home.

I was born in Santa Fe, New Mexico, in 1990, the year Keith Haring and Ryan White both died of AIDS. It was the year the Americans with Disabilities Act became law. It was a year before the first Santa Fe AIDS Walk, before the red ribbon at the Tony Awards. It was several years before effective treatment for HIV, before the peak of AIDS-related diagnoses.

Within all this, I was a baby at a gay wedding performed within the Quaker meeting I was born into. I was a baby getting love and praise from gay men in the restaurants where my father worked. I was a baby too young to remember. Some people got sick, some didn't. I'll never be sure who I would have been close to, if I had grown up in Santa Fe, and if they had lived. But a lot of people died, and, for other reasons, we left.

Paul Monette writes in his memoir *Borrowed Time* that gay men put our history together from the scattered artifacts we can find.

"Fragments are all you get," he says. "You jigsaw the rest together with your heart." Coming of age in the years following the height of the AIDS epidemic, it's impossible not to feel resentful about having to rely so largely on fragments, instead of all the friends and lovers and mentors I should have known.

I've been thinking about the texts Monette wrote after he knew he was going to die soon. By all accounts, he worked obsessively: in one elegy, Elisabeth Nonas describes him "tethered to his IV, pushing the pole that had been Roger's from one room to another to write." Memoirs, novels, essays, poems.

I know, because he said so, that he thought of this writing as his own contribution to the collection of fragments. I know he hoped another generation would seek them out to inform our own sense of history and self. These are missives thrown across the gap between us.

In 1991, a year after I was born, Lou Sullivan died of AIDS. He was thirty-nine. "I took a certain pleasure," he wrote in his diaries, "in informing the gender clinic that even though their program told me I could not live as a Gay man, it looks like I'm going to die like one."

Lou was slight, with a funny oval face. He looked great with a parrot on his shoulder. An interviewer once asked him if he was happy in his choice to live as a gay man, despite the apparent "price" he was paying. "I couldn't think of any other way to live or spend my time," Lou said.

My friend Zach Ozma made gold medallions with Lou Sullivan's face on them, in the style of a Catholic saint medal. Saint Lou. The back reads "Our Father of Open Gates." I wear mine most of the time.

With Ellis Martin, Zach also co-edited a book of Lou's diaries, *We Both Laughed in Pleasure*, which came out in 2019. In a 1987 entry, shortly after his diagnosis, Lou worries about preparing his own diaries for publication, "as I fear it will never be done after I am dead. Stiff enough task for me, let alone one unfamiliar with a phenomenon such as myself." Now I can hold the pink book on my lap: a history, a future. A phenomenon such as myself.

There were at least two poz men I knew, growing up on a small island outside Seattle. One was a teacher at the high school, a mentor, a talented actor. I learned his status only recently. The other was Larry, who was profiled in the local paper in 2008. That means I knew about him at least by the end of high school, but I feel like I knew before. He drove the bus that runs from one end of the island to the other. The largest smile. And something about his face—a look of being aged in salt. Cured?

"Preserve your virginity, children," he says in the *Beachcomber* article. "If you challenge the line, use condoms and rubber dams." I would get on his bus and sit right up front, near him, wanting to talk. It was as if a force came out of him, friendly but completely stilling. I couldn't say a thing.

I still see him from time to time, take a ride on his bus. I think dirty thoughts about him, daydreams he'd maybe disapprove of.

Does anyone really use dental dams, Larry?

The writer Bryn Kelly died in January 2016. She was poz, and she killed herself: Would you call that a complication? Stephen and I had been her friends. That February, we went to the Cathedral of St. John the Divine for her memorial. It was too cold that night, and too dark to see the round bright blue of my favorite stained-glass window. The place was full of trans boys in suits—Bryn had a thing for us. She was always dating trans men and making fun of them. She had a long-running blog about it, and she never mentioned she was trans, too, so a lot of people got very upset. She thought that was hilarious.

But really, the cathedral was full, and it's a big place. And most of the people filling it were trans. I cannot describe how strange that felt. Layers of black cloth, white cloth, black cloth. Some in pink or gold.

We sang "What Wondrous Love Is This?" and "There Is a Balm in Gilead." Prayers, candles, censers, all the "smells and bells." Jack Waters read one of Bryn's stories aloud—"Other Balms, Other Gileads." Heather Ács read Bryn's "Tiger Blood Litany."

"YOU HAVE TIGER BLOOD AND ADONIS DNA," Bryn wrote. "YOU ARE EVOLVED BEYOND THE GRASP OF A MERE VIRUS THAT HAS CLAIMED THE LIVES OF 39 MILLION PEOPLE."

It's futuristic. Shades of the cyborg self, the one that clings on with titanium fingers. There were bursts of emotion as Heather read, coming in clusters, moving across the cathedral. By the time we sang "Come, Thou Fount of Every Blessing," I was crying too hard to hit a single note without cracking.

It's not possible for any gay death to happen outside HIV/AIDS. I don't think it is. Father Angelus, my grandfather's best friend, died in a hospital in New Jersey in 2016. He was eighty-two. I think it was his heart.

"Do you think Angie's gay?" my grandfather asked me and my boyfriend once.

"Gosh, I don't know," I said.

"I'd have to know him longer," Stephen said.

"I think he is." Da was driving, and his hands on the wheel were trembling, as they have for years. "I always used to wonder."

Angie retired from his parish in New York City several years ago. Da said he was too radical for the bishop. Before his retirement, he did HIV counseling at a Catholic center. He started a shelter for homeless men and an interfaith series of lectures on tolerance.

After he was sent to New Jersey, Angie told me he missed going to see live jazz.

"Some nights, I take New Jersey Transit in and go to Fat Cat or Birdland," he said. "I stay too late to get the train back, so I just sort of drowse in the hallway until they start running again."

We were at a family reunion. He was always invited. He showed up that day in turquoise corduroys, a pink polo with a red plaid shirt over it, and a single pink gemstone earring. A terrible outfit, but he was a beautiful man. Even at eighty? Because he was eighty?

I wonder what it is that I find beautiful in older men. The eyes get very tender. The bones are fine, and the skin is loose and soft. What do I want, when I desire them? Do I want to fuck my history, the men I would have loved, who died before that could happen? Or do I want to fuck my future, the men I could become? I want to hold on in both directions. I would have spent the night, gladly, with my grandfather's friend. I would have gone to the jazz clubs with him, holding him in the hallway until the trains began again.

One of the first things that I remember hearing about HIV/AIDS was a reassurance: you cannot get it from holding hands with someone, hugging or kissing them, drinking out of the same cup. I read this in a sex ed book my parents had bought, which I'd found a couple of years earlier than they'd intended to give it to me. In the book, an illustration shows a blond boy greeting his friends on the steps of a school. There's space around him, accenting him in the crowd: something is different about him. But everyone in the picture is smiling, friendly.

At eight years old, I thought the boy was cute. And I filed away the information that HIV is something people are very afraid of, to the point that they might not shake someone's hand. And I imagined drinking out of someone else's cup, which gave me a minor thrill, there on the threshold of eroticism.

This cheerful piece of anti-misinformation is a good example of how HIV/AIDS was presented to me as a child. I'm glad that's what I got, out of the available options. It was also frightening. There was a dissonance, I think, between two unspoken messages. One said, *You are safe.* The other said, *You are in danger.*

Years later, a young teenager, I watched the *Angels in America* mini-series with my parents. By then, I knew a little more. Still not a lot. I was moved, and angry, but in a vague directionless way that was more about the cruelty of the characters to each other than about government inaction or public indifference.

At fourteen, I was painfully turned on by some of the sex in *Angels.* I remember particularly the scene where Louis Ironson seduces Joe Pitt. Danger courses through that scene: the danger of infection, the danger of damnation. Louis gets through to Joe by talking about the senses and how they tell us what we want. He puts his hand down Joe's pants, then smells and tastes his fingers, saying, "Chlorine. Copper. Earth."

Sitting on the couch with my parents, I couldn't believe that I was experiencing such strong sensations invisibly, right next to them. I was plunged into something they were not: separate, with no words for why.

This scene is corny, looking back. But even now that I question Kushner's relatively conservative project about citizenship and nation, it can still turn my gears: the triumph of desire within fear.

What I haven't put into words until now is that I grew up with HIV/AIDS inevitably linked to my sexuality as it developed. A baby-faced trans teenager, I admired the good looks of older gay men in my life, while connecting certain physical particularities to their (unspoken) status. My image of partnership always included the possibility of caretaking and early loss. I grew up knowing people living with

AIDS long term, and with the common sentiment "It's not a death sentence anymore." The cocktail, the condoms, all the successes of years of struggle were part of my landscape. *Still* there was the fear. *Still* it was linked with love and desire, was inseparable from them. Even now, when I am "safe." I think it will always be there.

After the first night Stephen and I started kissing, we spent a week or so in bed. We were in college. I had a room in a green cooperative with the branches of trees lapping my windows on two sides. I was delirious with the new experience of taking my clothes off with another person. In bed with him, I literally trembled.

Then, in the middle of the idyll, the rash began on my left hand. It reddened, swelled, blistered. Overnight, it was on my face, spreading up from my cheeks to my temples, forehead, eyelids, the curve of my ear, hot and itching. Something like this had happened once, a few years before.

"It's herpes," I said. "It's congenital. It'll pass in a week or so. I'll go to Health Services on Monday."

It was Saturday. Stephen stayed with me. He was terrified; I was humiliated. We went out in the warm night, sat on a boulder by the dark dining hall. My face was swollen, pink and crusty, bubbling. It didn't look like mine.

"What if something's really wrong?" he asked, under the lamplight.

"It's fine," I told him. "I promise."

When I turned up at Health Services first thing on Monday, they took one look and called a van to take me to the emergency room. Stephen and our friend MJ piled in, holding me on either side. I remember waiting a long while. I remember the triage nurse saying, "Oh, boy." I remember being wheeled down the hall on a stretcher, Stephen walking beside me. I remember a CT scan that I didn't understand. A doctor in a room, questioning, superior and detached.

I saw Stephen angry for the first time, then. He punished that doctor, coming back and pushing for clarity, refusing to let the man escape. "What's going on?" he wanted to know. "What are you going to do to fix it?"

Nobody knew what was wrong. They admitted me and started to try out drugs. I remember the dull pain and itch of the IV in my arm. I remember barely being able to open my eyes, the lids so swollen. I remember Stephen standing by my bed, not sure if it was safe to touch me, holding on to my knee under the hospital blanket. Kissing me there. They wouldn't let him stay overnight, so he ran back to campus through a thunderstorm. He told me later that he knew then he was seriously in love with me: because he thought I might die, and he understood what that would do to him.

The only drug name I remember is the one that worked. It was Bactrim, and I didn't think of it again until reading Paul Monette's *Borrowed Time* this year. Among other things, it's an antibiotic used to treat pneumocystis pneumonia. Doctors put Roger Horwitz on it during his first episode. "I explained that the organism in the lung was bacterial and would respond nicely to Bactrim," Monette records. "The mere brand name would tip people off these days, but not then."

Bactrim doesn't mean AIDS-related pneumonia these days, or any specific illness. I would leave the hospital after five days, my face returned to me. We never found out what had happened. Nothing grew from the cultures the doctors took. Every few years, I will find a hot red patch on my hand or my ear, a couple of clear blisters, and my breath stops. But the blisters have no strength to spread and fade within a day.

In *Borrowed Time,* I read Monette's account of Rog's first hospitalization. The vertigo of uncertainty, helplessness. Then knowledge, thrusting two people into "the crack of silence," the terror, the future. I was *lucky, lucky* to be all right without ever knowing why:

to have the luxury of not fighting for a reason. Yet I look at myself and Stephen, young lovers, and know we imagined a horrifying possibility ahead. We had plenty of models for death in the face of love.

ACKNOWLEDGMENTS

Thank you to Brian Lam for taking on this project with such enthusiasm, intimacy, and depth of support—here's to our generational stories... And to Shirarose Wilensky for astute line edits as always, Jazmin Welch for the stunning cover and design, Kirk Maxson for the gorgeous cover art, and Darin Klein for making that connection. To Alyson Sinclair, Cynara Geissler, and Jaiden Dembo for publicity savvy—and to everyone else at Arsenal Pulp Press, it's an honor to work with you again.

Thank you to all the contributors for trusting me with this vision, and to everyone who sent me brilliant work that I couldn't include. And thank you to Reed Miller and Black and Pink for circulating the call for submissions in prison.

For tangibles and intangibles: Kevin Darling, Andy Slaght, Joey Carducci, Adrian Lambert, Tony Radovich, Jed Walsh, Sarah Schulman, Corinne Manning, Jennifer Natalya Fink, Eric Stanley, Jory Mickelson, Katia Noyes, Jesse Mann, Dana Garza, Yasmin Nair, Jessica Lawless, Alexander Chee, Lauren Goldstein, Jessa Crispin, Sara Jaffe, Carley Moore, Conner Habib, Cari Luna, Matthew Schnirman, Zoë Ruiz, John Criscitello, Karin Goldstein, Kristen Millares Young, Chavisa Woods, Steven Zeeland, Jason Sellards, Jessica Hoffmann, Lynn Melnick, Gabriel Hedemann, Karen Maeda Allman, everyone at Elliott Bay Book Company, Book Workers Union, Elissa Washuta, Hugh Ryan, Dean Spade, Calvin Spade, Amanda Annis, Zee Boudreaux, Sophia Shalmiyev, Keidy Merida, Ananda La Vita, Alyssa Harad, Sarah Neilson, Michael Silverblatt, Tim Smith-Stewart, Jack Curtis Dubowsky, Cara Hoffman, T Clutch Fleischmann, Andrew Spieldenner, Madeline ffitch, Daniel Allen Cox, David Naimon, Maggie Nelson,

Hedi El Kholti, Jackson Howard, Steven Thrasher, Tony Valenzuela, Pato Hebert, Vivek Shraya, Amber Dawn, Zoe Whittall, Peter Staley, Stesha Brandon, Rob Arnold, Michael Lowenthal, Christian Kiefer, Rebecca Friedman, everyone in ACT UP San Francisco in the early '90s, and anyone else I may have inadvertently forgotten.

Every anthology is a communal project. Let's do this together.

ABOUT THE CONTRIBUTORS

AHMED AWADALLA is a sex educator, psychosocial worker, writer, retired pharmacist, and recovering workaholic. Their work has focused on the intersections between health, sexuality, gender, and migration across Egypt and Germany. They are also engaged in antiracist activism, particularly from a queer refugee perspective. Their writing has been featured on Global Voices and other platforms, and can also be found on their blog, *Rebel with a Cause*.

MANUEL BETANCOURT is a film critic, a culture writer, and a lapsed academic interested in queer and Latin American cinema. He's the film and TV editor at Remezcla and a contributing editor at *Film Quarterly*. He's one of the co-writers of the Eisner Award–nominated graphic novel *The Cardboard Kingdom* (Knopf Books for Young Readers, 2018) and its sequel, *The Cardboard Kingdom: Roar of the Beast* (2021). He's the author of *Judy at Carnegie Hall* (Bloomsbury Academic Press, 2020), which focuses on Garland's famed concert and double album, as well as its enduring gay appeal. *mbetancourt.com*

Born as a white, cisgender faggot on the unceded territory of the Anishinaabe people, **ROBERT BIRCH** was raised by the shores of the Otonabee River, which in Ojibwa means "river that beats like a heart." In the past four decades, he has participated in more than 10,000 hours of educational, community, and ceremonial circles; co-directed one of Canada's most culturally diverse theater companies; and continues to explore the intersections of personal narrative, spontaneous ritual, and social activism. He co-facilitates week-long workshops on sex and intimacy (*faeriesexmagick.org*) and co-leads a community food security farming initiative on Coast Salish lands (Salt Spring Island, BC) alongside neighbors and his playmate-husband, Mark. *robertbirch.ca*

EJ COLEN is the author of *What Weaponry*, a novel in prose poems; poetry collections *Money for Sunsets* (Lambda Literary Award finalist in 2011) and *Waiting Up for the End of the World: Conspiracies*; flash fiction collection *Dear Mother Monster, Dear Daughter Mistake*; long poem/lyric essay hybrid *The Green Condition*; fiction collaboration *Your Sick*; and fiction collaboration

True Ash. Nonfiction editor at Tupelo Press, and freelance editor/manuscript consultant, she teaches at Western Washington University.

Canal Zone–born author and artist **CHARLES CONN** began his writing career at *URB* magazine, documenting the '90s rave scene in Los Angeles. His film articles have appeared in the *Austin Chronicle*. Calling Panama City home since 2012, Charles worked as the editor of various tourism and logistics print newspapers, afterwards serving as managing editor for digital media and marketing company Live and Invest Overseas. Charles tweets under *@chkzulu*, and his first book, *3-Minute Meditations for Busy Bodies*, is available on Amazon.

RYAN CONRAD is a queer activist, artist, and educator living in the Ottawa Valley. You can learn more about his work online at *faggotz.org*.

TONY CORREIA is the author of the memoir *Foodsluts at Doll & Penny's Café* and the young adult novels *Same Love*, *True to You*, and *Prom Kings*. He lives in Vancouver, BC.

DAN CULLINANE is a freelance writer whose worked has appeared in a number of anthologies and publications. He worked in LGBTQ publishing for many years before relocating to Northeast Tennessee to work for a wilderness therapy program.

RORY ELLIOTT is a Portland, Oregon–based student, a chapter member of the abolitionist organization Critical Resistance, a member of the *Abolitionist* newspaper editorial collective, and an organizer with the anti-policing campaign Care Not Cops PDX, who just finished community college. She is a dyke, a femme, a transsexual. With her partner, she is co-running the ACT UP Oral History Project fundraising campaign aimed at revitalizing the project's website to be able to host all of the 188 interviews with ACT UP NY activists. She is passionate about intergenerational queer connection and collaboration, obscure activist histories, and sending and receiving voice mails.

EDRIC FIGUEROA is a queer, first-generation Peruvian American born in New York and raised in Georgia who strives to build self-determination, embrace the intersections of identity, and address the structural determinants of health in his professional and personal endeavors. Through grassroots organizing and HIV prevention work in Atlanta, Edric grew resilient and connected to activists across the country. He spent six years in Seattle, supporting LGBTQ survivors of violence, families, and youth before returning home to Georgia in 2019. He stays loving, grateful, and accountable to his values through the support of a community that stretches across coasts and borders.

DAN FISHBACK is a playwright, performing songwriter, and host of the podcast *Sick Day with Dan Fishback*. His plays include *Rubble Rubble*, *The Material World*, *thirtynothing*, and *You Will Experience Silence*. Fishback has released several albums, both solo and with his band Cheese On Bread, which dropped *The One Who Wanted More* in 2018, along with a video for their song "Bad Friend," directed by Stephen Winter. As director of the Helix Queer Performance Network, Fishback created La MaMa Experimental Theatre's annual series La MaMa's Squirts: Generations of Queer Performance. He is a member of Jewish Voice for Peace.

RIGOBERTO GONZÁLEZ is the author of seventeen books of poetry and prose. His awards include the PEN/Voelcker Award for Poetry, the Lenore Marshall Poetry Prize, the Shelley Memorial Prize of the Poetry Society of America, a Lambda Literary Award, the Poetry Center Book Award, and Guggenheim, NEA, NYFA, and USA Rolón fellowships. He is director of the MFA program in creative writing at Rutgers–Newark, the State University of New Jersey.

KATE DOYLE GRIFFITHS is a writer, medical anthropologist, and teacher based in Brooklyn. They are a member of Red Bloom Communist Collective, a parent, a partner, a daughter, a lifelong cat lady, and, more recently, a pug dad.

NELS P. HIGHBERG is a professor of English and modern languages at the University of Hartford. His literary work has been nominated for a Pushcart Prize and appeared in journals such as *Concho River Review*, *Riding Light Review*, *Duende*, *After the Art*, and *Intima: A Journal of Narrative Medicine*. In 2020, he received an Artistic Excellence Award from the Connecticut Office of the Arts.

Originally from Denver, Colorado, **BRYAN M. HOLDMAN** engaged in storytelling from an early age—through theater, writing, and illustration. He holds a BS in radio/TV/film, and a certificate from the Creative Writing for the Media program at Northwestern University. After moving to Los Angeles, Bryan earned his MFA in screenwriting from UCLA. Ultimately, the Disney ABC Writing Program launched his career as a television writer on the sci-fi teen drama *Kyle XY*. Bryan's produced television credits also include *Everwood, The Vampire Diaries, Pretty Little Liars, Step Up: High Water,* and *Famous in Love.*

A survivor of childhood abuse, bad relationships, and testing positive for HIV in 1996, **TIMOTHY JONES** firmly believes that no matter what we have been through, what we are going through, what anyone has told us, we hold the power to not only change our lives but also to control them. Timothy's contact info in prison is Timothy Jones #107654, Tomoka C.I., 3950 Tiger Bay Rd., Daytona Beach, Florida 32124-1098.

THEODORE (TED) KERR is a Canadian-born, Brooklyn-based writer, curator, and organizer. He is a founding member of the What Would an HIV Doula Do? collective. With Alexandra Juhasz, he is the co-author of *We Are Having These Conversations Now: The Times of AIDS Cultural Production* (Duke University Press, 2021). You can learn more about him at *tedkerr.club.*

KEIKO LANE is an Okinawan American poet, essayist, memoirist, and psychotherapist writing about the intersections of queer culture, oppression resistance, liberation psychology, racial and gender justice, HIV criminalization, and reproductive justice. Her writing has appeared most recently in *Queering Sexual Violence, The Feminist Porn Book, The Remedy: Queer and Trans Voices on Health and Health Care,* the *Rumpus,* the *Feminist Wire,* and The Body: The HIV/AIDS Resource. "What Survival Means" is an excerpt from her memoir *Blood/Loss: Toward a Queer Poetics of Embodied Memory (a love story).* She is a long-term survivor of ACT UP and Queer Nation.

LAURA LEMOON is a queer, neurodivergent sex worker and sex trafficking survivor. Their writing, interviews, and activism work have been featured in the *Huffington Post,* AP News, NBC, *Rolling Stone,* the CBC, *BuzzFeed News,* and *Vice.* Laura has collaborated with the Centers for Disease Control, the US Department of Justice, local health departments, and the United Nations Office on Drugs and Crime as a peer adviser on issues related to HIV vulnerability among people in the sex industry. They live in Seattle with their rescue pup, Coco Bean.

CHARLES RYAN LONG is a Chicago-born/based multidisciplinary artist, activist, and Black liberationist. He explores issues of representation, legacy, and loss through papermaking, print, performance, and other mediums that lend themselves to the principles of the democratic multiple/communal resonance. His work seeks out the audience and hopes to stir within them a push toward the future where we center the needs of those with the least among us. Find out more at *charlesryanlong.com*.

SASSAFRAS LOWREY is a straight-edge punk who grew up to become the 2013 winner of the Lambda Literary Emerging Writer Award. Sassafras's books *Kicked Out, Lost Boi, A Little Queermas Carol*, and *Leather Ever After* have been honored by organizations ranging from the National Leather Association to the American Library Association. Sassafras's work has appeared in numerous anthologies and in publications including the *Rumpus, Catapult*, and *Narratively*, and Sassafras has taught at the Center for Fiction, LitReactor, and colleges and conferences across the country. Sassafras lives and writes in Portland, Oregon, with hir partner and their menagerie of dogs and cats. Learn more at *sassafraslowrey.com*.

LESTER EUGENE MAYERS is a Brooklyn native, graduate of the Department of Theatre Arts at SUNY New Paltz, and MFA candidate at the Jack Kerouac School of Disembodied Poetics. Gay-Black-feminine, and a feminist, Mayers tackles issues that have historically been ignored by the public. He has been published by the *Huffington Post*, Arsenal Pulp Press, Sojourner Truth Library, and I'm from Driftwood LGBTQ archive. His first book, *100 Poems for 100 Voices*, resulted in a sold-out poetry tour and a poetry album available on iTunes, Spotify, and Tidal. His second book of poetry, *African Booty Scratcha*, is available on Amazon.

ALEXANDER MCCLELLAND is a critical criminology assistant professor at Carleton University's Institute of Criminology and Criminal Justice. His work focuses on the intersections of life, law, and disease. He has developed collaborative and interdisciplinary writing, academic, activist, and artistic projects to address issues of criminalization, sexual autonomy, surveillance, drug liberation, and the construction of knowledge on HIV. Portions of McClelland's chapter first appeared in *Maisonneuve* magazine in his article "Unprepared," published in 2019. He thanks Selena Ross, Jesse Vogel, Ted Kerr, Estelle Davis, and Mikiki for their support in this writing.

BEREND MCKENZIE is an award-winning freelance playwright, writer, actor, and producer. His writing credits include *Bloodbath at St. Paul's*, *Fashion Police*, *Meet the Munts*, and *Jonesin'*, as well as his two full-length plays, *Get Off the Cross, Mary* and the critically acclaimed children's play NGGRFG.

PATRICK MILIAN lives and writes in Seattle. He teaches writing and literature at Green River College and is the author of the chapbook *Pornographies*. His poems and essays have appeared in the *Denver Quarterly*, *Fourteen Hills*, *Mid-American Review*, and POETRY. His book, *The Unquiet Country*, a collaborative project with the composer Emerson Eads, is forthcoming from Entre Ríos Books.

STEPHEN H. MOORE grew up on the traditional homelands of the Cherokee people in what is now Georgia. He is a graduate of Smith College. Today, he lives and writes on the traditional homelands of the Massachusetts people. His hobbies include gardening, bicycling, wood carving, making music, and growing legal cannabis. This is his first published story. He thanks the ancestors.

KODY MUNCASTER is a PhD student in the Department of Gender, Sexuality, and Women's Studies at Western University. They are a queer who has spent much of their career in social services, including co-founding an HIV PrEP clinic and working at a suicide helpline. Their interest in this work is a result of having lost several queer folks to suicide.

AARON NIELSEN's fiction has appeared in SCAB, *Mythym*, *Userlands: New Fiction Writers from the Blogging Underground* (edited by Dennis Cooper), *Instant City*, *Fresh Men 2: New Voices in Gay Fiction*, and *Mirage #4 Period(ical)* (edited by Dodie Bellamy and the late Kevin Killian). Aaron has been featured on KQED's podcast *The Writers' Block*, and he was the editor of the short-lived but critically acclaimed zine *Jouissance*. Additionally, Aaron has reviewed books for *Fanzine* and *Maximumrocknroll*. He holds a bachelor's in English literature and a master's of fine arts in creative writing, both awarded by San Francisco State University. He lives in San Francisco.

LIAM OCTOBER O'BRIEN grew up on a small island. His writing has appeared in *A&U Magazine*, the *Denver Quarterly*, the *Boiler*, *bæst*, the *Bennington Review*, and the *New Delta Review*. He received his MFA at the Iowa Writers' Workshop and is one of the founding editors of *Vetch: A Magazine of Trans Poetry & Poetics*. He lives in Brooklyn.

ALYSSA PARIAH is an Afro Puerto Rican trans woman from New Jersey. A founding member of the TransJustice community school program at the NYC Audre Lorde Project in 2009, she is self-trained to think strategically about how we harness the creative potential that we all bring to the work in the fight for justice in order to build a visionary future based on solidarity. Now a community leader based in Portland, Oregon, she is one of the activists in the social justice movement that very deliberately forges collaboration between people of color and transgender organizing and action. Alyssa regularly emcees rallies, keynotes conferences, and facilitates group discussions. Alyssa focuses on clarifying terms and concepts often mentioned in social justice discourse. She intentionally helps people better understand heady terminology.

MIRANDA RECHT lives and writes in an RV, somewhere. Her work on the AIDS crisis has appeared in *Saints+Sinners*, vol. 15 (Bold Strokes, 2018) and *Day without Art* (Pandemonium Press, 2019).

LIZ ROSENFELD (USA/DE) is a Berlin-based artist who works in film/video, performance, and experimental discursive writing practice. She explores the sustainability of emotional and political ecologies, cruising methodologies, and past/future histories in regards to the ways in which memory is queered. Departing from the personal, her writing is rooted in questions that contend with how queer ontologies are rooted in variant hypocritical desire(s). The essay included in this anthology is an excerpt from a longer piece that will be included in her first book of experimental essays and writings from her performance and film/video works.

ADRIAN RYAN developed a respectable readership as a longtime weekly columnist and senior contributing writer for the *Stranger* in Seattle. He has been featured in six books, including: *Ghosts of Seattle Past* (nominated for a Washington State Book Award, 2018); *Weed: The User's Guide* (David

Schmader, 2016); *Mommy's Little Girl: On Sex Motherhood, Porn & Cherry Pie* (Susie Bright, 2001); The Stranger *Guide to Seattle* (2001); and his own *Way Too Gay Seattle Survival Guide* (2009). He has been retweeted by every sister in the original cast of *Charmed*, and Natasha Lyonne once called him "the Elaine Stritch of the Lavender Pen." He somehow survived Seattle throughout the '90s. Hello!

HUGH RYAN's first book, *When Brooklyn Was Queer*, won a 2020 New York City Book Award, was a *New York Times* Editors' Choice in 2019, and was a finalist for a Randy Shilts Award and a Lambda Literary Award. His next book, *The Prison on Christopher Street*, explores NYC's Women's House of Detention and the queer case for prison abolition. He was honored with the 2019–20 Allan Bérubé Prize from the American Historical Association. He is a graduate of the Bennington Writing Seminars and is represented by Robert Guinsler. He can be found on Twitter *@hugh_ryan*.

C.L. SEVERSON is a transfemme poet and sex worker wandering around the country giving lectures on herbalism and astrology. She is the director of Queer Astrology Club (QAC) and loves providing free coursework on all things ancient and magical to queer people of color. Her current obsession is the contemplative art of tattooing.

ANDREW R. SPIELDENNER, PhD, is an associate professor in the Departments of Communication and Women, Gender, and Sexuality Studies at California State University San Marcos. Dr Spieldenner's writing is at the intersection of health and culture, particularly looking at HIV and the LGBTQ community. A longtime HIV activist, Dr Spieldenner serves as vice-chair of the US People Living with HIV Caucus and North American delegate to UNAIDS.

For twenty-seven years, **GAYSHA STARR** has captivated audiences with her quick wit, glamorous looks, and memorable performances. Competing in drag pageants and campaigns, she has been awarded with a wide range of titles, from the first Miss Neighbours (in 1993) to Community Leader of the Year in 2020. Gaysha sits on the board of directors for the Imperial Sovereign Court of Seattle, is the dean of the College of Former Emperors and Empresses, an ambassador of Pride ASIA Seattle, and a Washington Drag Ambassador for

Drag Out the Vote. A self-identified single transgender woman, she is the store manager of a luxury retailer in Bellevue, Washington. You can always send her a friend request on Facebook or follow her on Instagram *@gayshastarr*.

EMILY STERN is the author of *This Is What It Sounds Like*, a memoir about her childhood and her mother's death in 1993 from complications of HIV/AIDS, and the manuscript "The Shape of What Spilled," about her experience and ongoing recovery from a mild traumatic head injury. She founded Intersectional Consulting and uses original educational tools, including El Corazón Deck, designed to inspire intersectional critical thinking. Emily is full-time faculty at Santa Fe Community College and holds an MFA in creative nonfiction with a critical emphasis on women and AIDS in literature from Goddard College. Find more at *emilystern.com*

EDDIE WALKER was born and raised in Canton, Ohio. He attended Kent State University and graduated in 1998 with a BBA in computer information systems. After graduation, Eddie Walker moved to Seattle, WA. He continued his writing education by attending classes at Seattle's Hugo House and is working on his first memoir. For recreation, Eddie Walker enjoys fishing, gardening, and going to the gym. Eddie Walker lives in Seattle, with his partner and three Labradors: Judah Valentine (chocolate female), Paco Versace (black male), and Kayla Vanderbilt (yellow female).